Residential Treatment of Emotionally Disturbed Children

CHILD CARE SERIES
Sheldon R. Roen, Ph.D., Editor

Critical Incidents in Child Care
By Jerome Beker

Child Care Quarterly (Journal)

When Mother Is a Prefix
By Nelson Henry

The Mental Health Team in the Schools
By Margaret Morgan Lawrence, M.D.

Behavior Modification in Residential Treatment for Children:
Model of a Program
By Frank J. Pizzat, Ph.D.

Children of Mentally Ill Parents
By Elizabeth P. Rice, M.S., Miriam C. Ekdahl, M.S.S.,
and Leo Miller, Ph.D.

Residential Treatment of Emotionally Disturbed Children
Edited by George H. Weber, Ph.D.,
and Bernard J. Haberlein, M.A.

RESIDENTIAL TREATMENT OF EMOTIONALLY DISTURBED CHILDREN

Edited and Introduced by

George H. Weber
Deputy Chief
Center for Studies of Crime and Delinquency
National Institute of Mental Health
Rockville, Maryland

and

Bernard J. Haberlein
Director
National Children's Rehabilitation Center
Leesburg, Virginia

With a Preface by
Donald P. Kenefick, M.D.

Behavioral Publications   New York

1972

Library of Congress Catalog Card Number 78-189948
Standard Book Number 87705-067-8
Copyright ©1972 by Behavioral Publications

Dr. George H. Weber's contribution to this work was made
in his private capacity. No official support or endorsement
by the U.S. Department of Health, Education, and Welfare is
intended or should be inferred.

BEHAVIORAL PUBLICATIONS, 2852 Broadway—Morningside Heights,
New York, New York 10025

Printed in the United States of America

CONTENTS

PART IV.   TRAINING AND MANPOWER

PREFACE

The United States has always demonstrated some very paradoxical behavior toward children. On the one hand, we have no difficulty in eliciting expressions of concern for children, and we have been holding national conferences on this topic at frequent intervals. Nevertheless, some of the suggestions made in, let us say, the White House Conference of 1930 are still far from being implemented. A cursory examination of our institutions for children gives rather striking evidence that many European nations, far poorer than we, seem to be able to devote a good deal more effective energy to child care problems than we seem able to do. Another paradox is that many of the concepts in child care used by European nations will seem, at least to them, to have originated here. Indeed, we have been fortunate in having had numerous ingenious thinkers and a small number of first-rate, pioneering institutions. This has resulted in a rather good press abroad so that, for example, a visitor to certain child care institutions in Scandinavia is struck by their feeling of indebtedness to the United States for conceptual frameworks. Their able implementation of some of these notions on a scale rather greater than anything that really exists in the United States is gratifying but embarrassing.

The United States, then, has, here and there, islands of great sophistication in residential child care, but its child care system, as such, leaves a great deal to be desired. Lacking, probably luckily, any centralized bureaucratic apparatus, the United States cannot by executive fiat raise its standards, though the federal government has tried manfully to improve the situation by what must remain an indirect approach, namely, by rather ponderous funding mechanisms. The major stimulus for change, in our society, must come through multiple, individual and small group efforts. These efforts will be successful only if the groups concerned are operating on the basis of adequate knowledge of relevant conceptual systems, that is to say, from an effective education. In the long run, this kind of multiple effort probably achieves as effective a system as those more deliberately planned and designed—or at least we must hope so. Effective long-range planning for improved child care standards does not seem to be part of our immediate future.

This book of readings gives the necessary step toward the high level of sophistication that the child care worker increasingly needs. It gives a useful, authoritative, and relatively broad beginning for effective study. A professional or paraprofessional who has mastered the content of this volume and, hopefully, followed up himself some of the fascinating byways it opens up will be a good deal better prepared than most of us of an older generation were.

Donald P. Kenefick, M.D.
Dean, New York School of Psychiatry

INTRODUCTION

This selection of readings presents a series of articles on the practice of helping emotionally disturbed children in residential settings. The volume is addressed to those engaged in this type of work as well as those preparing for it. Center activities including their theoretical underpinnings are described. In addition, the salient issues in residential treatment are discussed in the articles and the Overviews that introduce them. The book's four sections are headed by topical captions. They, along with the Overviews that follow them, provide the structure for the book.

The tasks involved in editing an anthology include developing a framework for the book, specifying criteria for selecting the articles, building and screening bibliographies, reviewing, evaluating and selecting articles. In the process of accomplishing these tasks, journals have to be obtained, various lists have to be typed and retyped, and permissions to reprint articles have to be requested from authors and publishers. A number of people's diligence and skill helped us move the project through these activities. Thus we would like to express our appreciation to Mrs. Betty Compher, Mrs. Harriet Moss, Mrs. Helen Piltch, Mrs. Mary Reid, Mrs. Shirley Scholl, and Mrs. Kay Watson, who helped on one or more of these important tasks. To Miss Mary E. Weber we are indebted for editing the Overviews of the book and two articles in Part I, "Problems and Issues in Residential Treatment" and "Residential Programs: Their Components and Organizing Theories."

Part I
Concepts and Strategies

OVERVIEW

The influences determining the program and organization of a residential center are several, including the nature of the center-community relationships, characteristics of the patients and the treatment objectives that are sought for them, and the theory of treatment it employs. Also, the availability of funds and personnel are no small influences in this determination, as are the residuals from a center's historical development such as a particular theory of treatment and personnel left by a charismatic leader.

Such influences determine the style of a center's leadership and how it perceives the treatment task, develops its resources, deploys, communicates with, and rewards its staff. Typically, a center's organization may be viewed as that which appears in print — program descriptions, public relations releases, and organizational charts — and the spoken statements of a center's leadership. Along with these features of an organization are those that emerge informally in a center and channel action among the staff and the patients. Such informalities include the special friendships and affinities among the staff.

The articles in this section present material on the organization, activities, and problems of treatment centers. Weber and Haberlein ("Problems and Issues in Residential Treatment" and "Residential Programs: Their Components and Organizing Theories") describe the many considerations in organizing the providing residential treatment. Criteria for judging treatment centers are also set forth. Nordstrom ("Unique Challenges of Institutional Administration") presents various complexities of administering a

3

center for emotionally disturbed children. In so doing, he reflects the integral part that center administration plays in patients' total treatment.

1. Problems and Issues in Residential Treatment

George H. Weber and Bernard J. Haberlein

A PROBLEM PERSPECTIVE

The residential treatment of emotionally disturbed children has its storehouse of philosophies, objectives, methods, and procedures. These remain, however, largely unarticulated or, at best, vaguely defined. Staff with a keen sensitivity to vagueness of this sort is recognized for its intuition or clinical sense; whole institutions that reflect this intuitive understanding are described as having good psychological climates or atmospheres. Individual perceptions then remain in the private armentoriums of staff, and in lieu of concrete disciplinary definitions, they dictate action.

As practitioners, staff members are constantly rushed to deal with a myriad of problems that demand immediate attention. Consequently, they have little time for either a theoretical or research approach to their work. Even descriptive written reports of their work are a rarity. Rather, the staff focuses on the development and maintenance of viable center programs.

The specification of knowledge on residential treatment has also been ignored to a large extent by the theory-building and research community. Little research data are available on existing programs, and systematic new models of practice are not available for implementation and testing. The need for practical assistance with program planning and daily operations that might be provided to researched models is distinctly felt by the administrative personnel and the clinical, adjunctive, and child care staff. There is no accurate and concrete direction available to them when the activity of the center does not proceed smoothly.

Suppose the referrals of children with illnesses appropriate to center services fail to materialize. Do the director and staff decide to accept other types of referrals? Does the director talk with the referring agencies about his problem? Suppose a fight develops between two patients. Does the child care worker forcefully intercede, risking increased dissension and personal injury? Does he simply ask them to stop? Or might it be better to allow them to fight it out? Suppose the children start throwing paint at each other during school. Does the teacher politely request that they stop? If this fails, does he demand and perhaps shout? Suppose patients skip their treatment appointments. Does the therapist assume patient resistance? Does he interpret this as the staff discouraging or even stopping the children from coming? Under any circumstance, how do these individuals proceed?

If residential treatment were thoroughly defined and researched, a manual or handbook might be in order, dealing in precise fashion with the various alternatives of planning and problems of residential treatment. However, as such knowledge is not available, residential staff must depend instead on material that describes the various elements of a center program and their underlying concepts. Articles in this collection present such material. In preface to these articles, several issues will be given introductory attention to provide a more general context of understanding. Consideration will include some of the broad problems that face centers, the implications of change resulting from the adoption of new ideas and procedures for implementing and coping with such change, and, finally, research as a technique for improving the knowledge about residential treatment.

PROBLEMS OF DEFINITION AND DIAGNOSIS

There are serious uncertainties about identifying disturbed children. It is not an uncommon experience to have some youths identified as emotionally disturbed, while others having the same characteristics and behavior are identified as delinquent. For those who are diagnosed as disturbed, a more refined definition may be provided, but many are left with simply this gross label.

Several factors account for these discrepancies. Levels of skill among diagnosticians vary widely. The use of different conceptions of personality maladjustment and imprecise measures contributes to the diagnostic confusion. The influences of the immediate circumstances surrounding the problem behavior, such as the individual to whose attention the problem came and his role, the social class of the child, the various pathways leading to the public and private agencies, and the mandates that govern agency practice, receive various degrees of consideration in diagnostic decisions. Even if the initial identification is correct, it may later become invalid due to the fluid nature of children's personalities.

Such criteria as the following define admission to residential treatment: "the child's disturbance must be within the neurotic range, yet beyond that with which the home and community agencies can cope," "acting out, if it is part of the child's problems, must be of a neurotic character, as character disorders are not acceptable," and "the child must be able to adjust to group life in a residential center." Referral criteria such as these lead to confusion due to their excessive generality and ambiguity. As they do not specify a child's individual need, they do not recommend the particular type of treatment that might be helpful. They might imply boarding or group home care with psychotherapy and other supportive treatment instead of residential treatment.

Additionally, referrals reflect the great range in family and community tolerance of deviant behavior. This tolerance is dependent on the degree to which they will permit variation from their norms of appropriate behavior for children. Those allowing little flexibility and variation are likely to press for residential care of those children whose behavior, being unacceptable in the community and family, has labeled them as mentally ill. The propensity to commit these children to residential treatment depends on the education, socialization, and ideology of those in the decision-making positions.

Criteria couched in the language of psychiatric nosology attempt to be specific and avoid the confounding influences of community and family tolerance. However, problems still exist. Diagnostic categories such as schizoid personality, infantile personality, schizophrenia, anxiety neurosis, and character neurosis are again too gross to specifically indicate residential treatment. Consequently, other characteristics of the individuals carrying such diagnoses must still be considered, such as the extent of the child's disturbance, the level of his anxiety, the degree of his home and school conflicts, and the length of time they have been manifest. This once again introduces the distortions of individual perception, substituting that of the diagnostic personnel and their particular personality, training, and frame of reference for that of the community and family.

In daily practice, gross criteria for residential placement may be sharpened substantially at the point of admission. The admissions staff, with their intimate knowledge of the center's capability, will hone the general criteria to indicate more clearly whom a center can adequately serve. They will also be familiar with the population that the center has defined as acceptable, whether this be a variety of maladjusted patients or a limited range of illnesses. Criteria are apt to be sharpened further in an effort to maintain a therapeutic balance in the patient population. For instance, an excessive number of autistic children in a center serving a variety of illnesses would encourage the staff to seek children who are less seriously disturbed. On the other hand, if the center limited its practice to autistic children, the admissions staff would be encouraged to seek both those who speak intermittently and irrelevantly and those who are mute.

PROBLEMS OF DISPOSITION AND SERVICE

The family, school, and other social institutions are

usually urged to maintain disturbed youngsters within their frameworks on the community level. Some of these institutions have considerable tolerance and resources to work with disordered behavior. Unfortunately, many have little or none. When the incidence of misconduct or maladjustment rises either through a genuine increase in the problem or a definitional change, demands for additional services or different handling by community agencies develop.

When action is demanded on a particular type of problem behavior, the complex question "What action?" then faces the community. Thoughtful community members will seek a thorough understanding of the situation as a basis for a reasoned approach to the handling of the problem. They will be plagued by both the absence of evidence on the effectiveness of the different service alternatives and the definitional confusion. Some elements of the community, however, will reject the investigative approach, proposing instead ready solutions that lack insight into the full nature of the problem. A dramatic event such as a delinquent gang killing or a child suicide that precipitates or occurs during planning may give these immediate solutions precedence over the rational deliberations.

Under these circumstances, the decision made on the services and funding to be provided may be poor, but it does dictate what will be available. If this is inadequate, the task remains to work for improvement. In the meantime, action must be based on the existing situation and referrals made to the available services.

Decisions on community facilities have far-reaching implications for residential centers. A dearth of community-level services may encourage agencies to deluge a center with admission requests. Diagnoses may be slanted to admit children for residential treatment who would be more appropriately treated on the community level were the facilities available. On the other hand, a concentration of community services in proportion to those of residential treatment would result in children needing residential care being kept in the community. Finally, if both community and residential services were inadequate, children might be channeled to an inappropriate agency such as a school for delinquents.

PROBLEMS AT POINT OF ADMISSION AND INTAKE

In considering the applicants for admission, a center may draw some initial impressions from the diagnostic material submitted by the referral agencies. The staff must concurrently assess the quality of this diagnostic material and the appropriateness of the applicants themselves. On the basis of the referral information, they may decide that the child is obviously not a suitable patient for the center. Alternatively, they may decide to consider the applicant further and to seek interviews with parents and child, administer tests, and gather social history material. If diagnostic complexities of a prospective case create a questionable situation, a center might admit the child for further study. The child's continued treatment at the center would then depend on the staff's final evaluation after observation in the residential situation. While this procedure would give adequate basis for decision on perplexing cases, it would not be without problems. Additional diagnostic and administrative staff would be required for residential diagnostic service. Then too, the uncertain status in which the child would be placed while undergoing the further study could undermine an already tenuous security.

The willingness of the parents to involve themselves in the child's treatment should be evaluated at admission. They should be attuned to the necessity of counseling that focuses on helping the child solve his problems. If they have serious personal problems, they should be encouraged to seek help for themselves as well. Finding both amenable parents and suitable treatment facilities, the center must then plan an approach meshing the therapies of parents and child.

In addition to relating the parents to the children's treatment, a center must consider the parents' ability to help the children upon discharge from a center. This not only requires an evaluation of the parents and their abilities but also an estimation of the effectiveness of a center program on the child and of the services that the parents may receive.

Various other tasks face the center at admission and intake including establishing a working relationship with the child, presenting him pertinent information about the center, and discerning his specific interests. The basic aim of this is the facilitation of treatment by creating in the child a positive feeling toward the center. Testing, ranking, and hazing by those already in residence should be eliminated if possible. Though subtle and seemingly benign, such initiation rites are likely to bring out negative feelings in an already anxious, fearful, angry, or discouraged newcomer.

PROBLEMS OF CENTER GOAL SETTING

In some instances, centers aim for a near-ideal state of maturity in patients: interpersonal competence, personal happiness, and psychological adjustment. If associated with optimism, determination, and resources, striving for such an ideal state may enhance the patients' improvement beyond the point achieved with more ordinary goals. Pursued uncritically, though, they may become frantic and ineffective.

Usually, broad program goals are not set because of the inability to predict the course and outcome of children's treatment. This is due technically to the facts that the condition of the children is not thoroughly understood and the efficacy of treatment techniques is uncertain. Functionally, problems of recruiting, training, and supervising personnel make the maintenance of a high-quality treatment program difficult and often necessitate change in treatment plans. The parents and community too may mistake the positive language of overall program goals for promises of cures.

In view of these problems, rather than setting goals, centers often favor emphasis on activities of the program. Psychotherapy, group work, casework, special education, and other activities are highlighted. Failure to set overall program goals, however, distorts the structure and restricts the functioning of the organizations. Activities stand alone as ends in themselves rather than as means to program goals. Some staff will perform with enthusiasm and determination; others will uncritically pursue what they believe is helpful. Without the stimulation, direction, and criteria of achievement offered by center goals, their efforts can be little more than enthusiastically ritualistic. Such a routine program, if supported by the administration and protected from outside criticism, could unfortunately sustain itself over a long period of time.

PROBLEMS OF SPECIFYING CENTER MEANS

When a center's activities are systematically ordered to achieve its goals, they function appropriately as the center's means. However, questions arise on the selection, organization, interrelation, and emphasis of these activities. Since there is no firm research evidence indicating the relative effectiveness of the various activities and their usage, intense debate may result based on individual and center experiences and the theoretical rationale for particular activities.

After such basic activities as living, dining, education, recreation, casework, and psychotherapy have been chosen for the program, questions may arise over supplemental inclusions such as group work, group psychotherapy, family therapy, and sociodrama. Some may even argue that these are more significant than the more basic therapies because they focus directly on the critical sources of problematic family and peer relations rather than on the less tangible intrapsychic phenomena.

Even after the program has been formulated, controversy is likely to develop over the specific shaping of the included activities. This will range from the therapeutic benefit of living units with different architectural designs to the feeding arrangements with various cafeteria and living unit arrangements, from psychotherapy with different techniques to education with assorted curriculums, from recreation with emphasis on certain activities to group work holding different philosophies.

Beyond these facts, questions arise as to the manner in which these activities should be related to each other. For instance, in dealing with the interrelation of education and the program, should studies be carried on in the living unit? Should the living unit supervisor become involved with the child's schoolwork through assistance and reviewing of homework and conferences with the teacher? Should the caseworker assume some of these tasks? Could the information gleaned by the various professionals in their work with the children be shared to make their respective treatments more productive and enhance the child's education?

Associated with the issue of the posturing of various activities in relation to each other is the concern of emphasis. Some programs propose individual psychotherapy as the primary form of treatment with all other activities auxiliary, supportive, and subject to manipulation. Excluding such approaches as behavioral therapy, psychotherapy seeks to resolve unconscious conflicts, strengthen ego functioning, reduce the severity of superego sanctions, and so on through a process of specialized interviewing and related techniques. This type of program having considerable detail to explicate its strategy might imply substantial rigor in its organization and effectiveness in its efforts. In reality, however, neither the theory nor the technique is sufficiently systematic to indicate the particular combination, intensity, and duration of techniques to achieve specific effects with the varying problems and types of patients.

Milieu therapy, another approach, suggests that the forces of the environment should be the primary therapeutic force with psychotherapy and other individual services functioning as auxiliary. The child, rationale indicates, can be treated most effectively by involvement and exposure to the planned management of a center's psychosocial processes. The children's daily living experiences are indeed the treatment. Because milieu therapy is less well developed than individual treatment, its conceptual problems are greater. Various types of milieus have not been sufficiently developed to indicate how different kinds of children should be treated. Nor has an overall milieu been differentiated to indicate either how or which submilieus might be developed within an overall milieu to serve special subcategories of patients.

An even more basic problem in the attempt to specify the detailed character of the program lies in the lack of terms with which to articulate the center environment. The conceptions available to deal with the dwelling units, the program and its activities, the character of staff and peer relations, and the administrative structure of a center are mainly descriptive words borrowed from everyday English. Those terms that have greater usefulness relate to the center's social structure, its impact on patients and staff, the subculture of different activities and adaptations generalized to unusual situations. These are still merely words that have been adapted, though they do come more technically from the terminology of social and behavioral science. The language of the residential center, then, remains largely unrefined and unspecified; the staff lack a unique set of conceptualizations or frame of reference with which to work. The problem becomes increasingly difficult when the concerns expand from an individual situation to one involving individual and group or intragroup relations, for in this realm there is little even borrowed terminology.

PROBLEMS OF RELATING CENTER GOALS AND MEANS IN PRACTICE

The diagnostic and program-planning procedures conducted when the children are admitted to a center serve as practical efforts to relate a center's goals to its means in the consideration of the individual case. Abstract program goals such as the improvement of patient adjustment or mental health are reduced to more concrete statements through the consideration of particular individual needs. Helping a patient strengthen his ego, resolve his sexual problems, unravel his unwarranted guilt, overcome his school phobia reflects this.

The tasks of reducing highly abstract center goals to an individually operative level and inferring the patient's need from the diagnostic material must be a simultaneous process. This deductive-inductive manner of relating center goals and patient needs is complicated in two ways. The lack of knowledge of exactly what results can be achieved in which cases and with which treatment makes it very difficult for the staff to define specifically what approach should be taken and what expectations should be fostered with respect to the individual case. Coupled with the lack of knowledge about treatment effectiveness, no logical or systematic procedure has been developed to relate center goals and means to patient goals. Staff must rely mainly on gross indicators drawn from case history, tests, and other clinical data and on their past experience and intuition.

Also, relating goals and means in practice is clouded by the "human equation" of the individual examiners. Their insights, oversights, and distortions in studying cases vary considerably. These individual perspectives are multiplied in the conference situation. The dynamics of case conferences including the interplay of the presentation styles, conferencing techniques, and statuses of the various participants have a substantial impact on the eventual decision on the patient's condition and treatment plan.

Once planned, a patient's program remains to be implemented. The task of converting the deliberations and conclusions of the diagnostic and planning conference into treatment is profound, considering that this includes the subtleties of guiding the child's development, treating his illness, and managing his problematic behavior. The difficulties of the translation of these planning abstractions into daily action may result in misunderstanding and confusion for both child care staff and professionals. The direction to child care staff that a manipulative child should be supervised with consistent firmness may result in harshness; sensitive handling of a shy child recommended by a staff committee to a psychotherapist and caseworker may be confused with an overly passive approach; and confronting a child with his problems may be distorted to include assigning him blame as well.

Even after a program for a child has been developed and communicated throughout the staff, treatment plans may fail to materialize fully. A center may not have the actual resources to institute the plans. Staff assigned to carry out certain treatment responsibilities may lack the skills to do so. In other instances, they may have the ability but arbitrarily decide to drop a case or to handle it differently than prescribed. Staff turnover may disrupt or temporarily suspend a particular center activity which may never again achieve the original therapeutic value when resumed. The children's treatment may be lost in the shuffle of various other center problems.

Once a child has entered the program, lack of continuity among the various activities may hinder his treatment. Psychotherapy may encourage the young patient to vent his problems, while the cottage or school may discourage such expressions. Or psychotherapy may confront the child with his behavior and ask for a responsible reaction when the cottage or school is allowing permissiveness.

Such lack of coordination wreaks havoc with both the technical aspects of treatment and the interpersonal relations and morale of the staff. Staff failure to inform each other of problems and progress of children and to maintain a common approach not only confuses the children but produces open staff conflict. Once this becomes serious, the children are especially vulnerable to being caught in the turmoil. Hence, the purpose of removing the child from disruptive environment by placing him in a center is defeated. The resultant situation may repeat or even be worse than the child's previous experience.

Various other difficulties may arise among the staff in their relationships to each other. These include competing with one another for the attention and loyalty of the children, vying for power in the center's clinical and other decision-making processes, being jealous of each other's pay and working conditions, and overstriving for personal recognition from the administration and peer groups, both within and outside the center.

CENTER MANPOWER PROBLEMS

The exceptionally high degree of specialization in a center's work leads to a narrow range of practice and a segmented relationship between staff and children. The exception is the child care workers who are in close and continuous contact with the children. They get the children up in the morning and put them to bed at night, supervise their personal hygiene, plan for their leisure time, help them meet their schedules, enforce personal discipline, and discuss their problems with them. Difficulties arise constantly during these contacts, some of which these workers handle routinely, while others they refer to professionals.

In spite of their unique closeness to the children and the high-quality performance that is expected from them, formal training and significant promotions are rarely open to child care workers. Rather, they are merely exposed to inservice training and given some merit increases to their basic salaries. This block in the opportunity structure results from the nonprofessional classification of their position and the relative lack of effort to upgrade it. The hypothetical opportunity for them to enroll in academic work toward undergraduate and eventual graduate degrees is usually not feasible. Centers may not be located near institutions of higher learning. Even if they are, the child care workers, because of their age and family responsibilities, must continue to earn a living wage and therefore cannot take time to enroll in school. The demands of their work and families leave little energy for concentrated study that would be involved with even part-time education.

Many such people, however, continue to dedicate themselves to their work. Others, while remaining on the job, withdraw their commitment to the center's goals and abandon the prescribed techniques for working with the children. The quality of their work may vary from that of passive maintenance of a routine to sabotage of the program. A dramatic deviation would probably result in discharge, but if a substantial number of disenchanted workers slack on their jobs unobtrusively, they might well continue in the center undisturbed by the administration or clinical staff. A unique job accommodation may even occur between child care workers and professionals in the tacitly permitted use of disapproved supervisory methods to insure control of the children. Thus the professionals are assured that the children will not be unruly, and the child care workers are not bothered with employing complex treatment techniques.

PLANNED CHANGE TO IMPROVE PROGRAMS

Some Elements of Planning Change

In the residential field, there are a number of potentially useful ideas that are not utilized. Inadequate budgets and staffs, poor leadership, and overall organizational complacency or rigidity may contribute to the maintenance of existing plans. These problems, coupled with the complexity of engineering an idea into practice, suggest that careful planning must precede actual efforts to implement new procedures.

Before selecting an activity to be instituted and the tactics of its introduction, a number of steps should be taken. These include identifying and assessing the problem situation, the alternatives available for improvement and methods to implement them, and the possible problems that may be encountered in the change effort and plans to compensate for these. However, planning does not require that these steps be followed rigidly. The identification of potentially better practices does not necessarily await the completion of a full assessment of the problem situation. These may be recognized in the process of initiation and institutionalization of previously planned change. By viewing these steps as parts of a flexible process, planning becomes a continually interrelated comparison and integration of data gleaned from observations, discussions, various other sources, and the projection of new or refined activities into the ongoing program. Such program standards as are available can be used in this process. These are mainly based on the consensus of practitioners and thus reflect their insights and style of work. Since these tend to be very general and without research codification, the planners in a given locale might interject considerable individual belief and bias.

One way to help check this difficulty is to introduce outside consultation to help discussions and planning. This, of course, runs the risk of merely reinforcing the bias in existence or introducing another. Another check is to devise systematic evaluation measures, check lists, and interviewing and observational schedules that could collect specific data on the activities under examination. The complexities of using such an approach, however, suggest that it be used as a part of an ongoing research-evaluation program rather than a one-time planning evaluation.

Reviewing the Situation

Problems of a center that emerge in the process of its daily operations are normally identified by administrative and clinical personnel in the course of their work. Various changes are routinely made to deal with them. As a matter of ordinary activity, social workers and child care workers share information to strengthen the living unit program and to increase the productivity of casework; teachers shift their instructional techniques after sharing the insights of the principal and other teachers.

Yet there are unusual problems that cannot be handled in this routine manner. These may be either a unique situation or a severely extended or intensified state of a routine problem. Either could demand creative new action, but the latter is more likely to involve an extensive revamping of the faulty center in existence. In both cases corrective action would necessitate a review of the center situation to determine the nature and causes of the difficulty. A review procedure itself, however, is not without obstacles.

Whether a problem is defined as unique is partially a function of a staff's experience. Inexperienced staff members struck by the newness of situations may see an overabundance of unique problems, while more experienced personnel, dulled by their time at a center, may see most problems as repetitive, even routine. Uniqueness may be blunted out of their perception. Thus different staff perceptions of a problem's uniqueness must be evaluated as well as the problem itself.

The compounding of daily problems that have many roots, however, is the major concern of centers. The problem may begin its development in one area, enlarge in others, and become manifest in still another part of the center. Since the various staff members are unable to perceive the total situation, even if they are aware of an unsettled situation in their area, they could not predict the final outcome or degree of seriousness. Those at the climax point may not even be in a position to anticipate a problem.

The compounding of daily problems often runs a longer course and has more serious implications than a dramatic outburst. In many instances, daily problems are left to become chronic because the immediate impact is insufficiently compelling in comparison to those with seemingly more pressing demands. A dull, uninspiring school may continue because its behavior problems are relatively unsevere. Only after a pressing demand such as extensive complaints from parents or staff or an end-of-the-year evaluation of the educational program might the situation be given careful review. In the meantime, many patients may be seriously disillusioned in regard to education.

Frequency and intensity can serve as immediate indicators to cull the serious from the routine problems. But theoretical orientations and value judgments must still remain a critical influence in this determination. Baseline data are not available on centers to indicate the frequency of angry outbursts, fights, runaways, skipped psychotherapy and casework appointments, personnel absenteeism and lateness. Drawing from research procedures, probability sampling might be used in this absence to get a measure of the problem. However, without pretending to get a representative probability sample of center problems, the approximate incidence and intensity of a problem can be tapped by talking with a number of center informants considered to be reliable. This approach carries the danger of a built-in center bias, for those approached may well be selected by the degree to which they hold the same opinions as the center's inquirers. Demanding that all information, though, be obtained by a probability sample is to commit the staff to a procedure with which they are likely to be unfamiliar and which is grossly inappropriate to their circumstance.

Considerations in Selecting an Alternative

Alternatives to an unsatisfactory process may be quite easily identified; their evaluation, though, is a highly complex process. Almost no data on effectiveness is available, with the result that decisions must be made on construct or face validity. The myriad of contingencies and interrelationships involved in predicting the future make projections of viability for a particular center treacherously difficult. A critical assessment of patient needs and center resources can greatly increase the significance of the projection.

The lack of concrete data encourages the influence of therapeutic tastes and styles that are the current vogue. Thus pressure to modernize may distort the validity of an old method. A positive emphasis may be placed on the mere process of change, and it may occur simply for its own sake. The same lack of data may alternatively foster a strong conservatism or even reaction.

The process of selecting a particular change then requires a careful evaluation of all alternatives in terms of the specific center. This must include their internal and external logic to the ongoing program, their supplemental assumptions, and, as much as possible, their potential success.

If, for example, on-the-spot counseling for problematic children by child care workers was proposed in lieu of referral to social workers, this would first have to be considered in relation to the rest of the child care worker program. Items such as the role of the child care worker in relation to the child, relative importance to other activities, and influence on other patients would necessarily come into such an evaluation. A similar evaluation would be required for the social work program to project the external consistency of the change. The theoretical ideas underlying the proposed change must be reviewed for their congruence with the overall center ideology.

Assuming such consistencies existed, the evaluation must turn to the supplemental assumptions required for the functionality of the change. What abilities or additional training would on-the-spot counseling demand of the child care worker, for instance? With this change of task, what activities must the child care worker give up, and what activities will the social worker then acquire?

Finally, although no definite predictions are possible, an attempt must be made to project the success of the proposed alternative. This must consider improvement over the ongoing program, merit to the various components of the center, and effect in terms of the overall center goals as well as the preceding elements of the evaluation.

Implementation Considerations

A primary focus for change should be those issues of concern to the staff. Frequently, staff are reluctant to participate in change efforts, for they fear or resent an outside force intervening and acting upon them. For this reason, all staff members should be involved in activity to rectify their immediate problems through planning and implementing change with the administration and their co-workers.

Problem and conflict situations then become productive, for they produce the momentum for change in themselves. The process of recognizing disharmony and conflict openly makes the staff both comfortable in their efforts and utilizes their resourcefulness. The center then rechannels dissatisfaction to alertness; constant improvement may be projected with a staff continually thinking through ineffectual and problematic aspects of their work.

The informal structures within a center are as important as the formal ones. Strategy for change then must consider not only which departments and staff positions should be involved but also the values, attitudes, and informal statuses these departments and individuals hold. These variables may have particular relevance for timing and coordinating the introduction of changes. The sequence of progressive involvement of center staff requires special attention with far-reaching changes to obtain support from both formal and informal status structures.

The rapidity of the communication flow within an organization such as a residential center denies a close control on the introduction of new phenomena. Both accurate and distorted information are likely to precede the administration's effort to introduce its plans to the staff. Plans for change must include methods of coping with rumor and informational leaks as they occur. Even if the casual informing process is accurate, staff must still be informed by official sources to legitimize the change process, to clarify staff understanding of it, and to reassure them of the necessity of their role in it. Such communications should be positive yet candid, including discussion of individual participation and its relation to the overall program, potential problems and methods of handling them, and desired results. It is important that the new effort not be oversold to avoid subsequent dissatisfaction upon implementation.

Inservice training and appeals to intellect, humanitarianism, and personal pride in change efforts should be backed up by economic incentives. Particular consideration should be given to incentives proportional to the degree of complexity in the task to be performed. Budget pressures and reliance on various appeals to center staff discourage the utilization of economic incentives; however, this neglect places unrealistically heavy dependence on non-economic sources of motivation which is inconsistent with the economic realities of the community outside of the center.

Unanticipated Problems

Even the most carefully planned changes are bound to be troubled by unanticipated problems. A successful implementation is facilitated naturally by a detailed consideration of all problems that might occur. Some of these may be discovered by checking with other institutions that have attempted similar change programs. Various projections may also serve to identify these difficulties. This could involve a consideration of negative outcomes for all the expected positive effects. Though somewhat pessimistic, this may creatively challenge the means to be employed and encourage a realistic planned outcome. The opposite technique, assuming all planned achievements will surpass their expected levels, might also uncover some unique problems. For example, the demand on intake and aftercare services caused by earlier improvement and discharge of patients or the development of one section of the center far beyond the others might seriously disrupt the functional balance of the components that comprise the center. Another way to pinpoint problems is to consider the relevant outside agencies. Community agencies, board members, and funding sources may not support the change initially or later or may be replaced by those who do not. The administration, therefore, should plan on constant and close communication with these potential sources of intervention.

Since forecasting techniques are not well developed and those employing them may not be skillful, not all problems may be identified in time to avert or cope with them. In some cases their use may forestall spontaneous initiative or confuse and paralyze change activity. Development and implementation may often occur simultaneously and void the need for forecasting at all. In fact, in some situations, excessive concern with possible difficulties may be employed as a tactic to hinder change in favor of the existing situation. In this case, the planning for change becomes a ritual.

RESEARCH FOR KNOWLEDGE DEVELOPMENT

The Potentials of the Setting

Centers have considerable potential for research. Studies could focus on the children, especially on the dynamics and etiologies of their various disorders. The processes of the disorder's treatment and subsequent course could be investigated. The techniques of diagnosis and treatment and the degree of their effectiveness could be considered. The unique social organization of the center itself and its contribution as a treatment mechanism might be analyzed.

In spite of its attractiveness, research cannot be initiated on immediate notice. Many factors besides the identification of a research topic must first be identified and provided for. The place of research in the daily operations of the center and its overall plans must be clearly delineated. This includes the role and relationship of research staff in relation to the treatment staff and to the patients themselves. To insure viability among these groups, channels for continuous communication on topics of mutual interest, for clarification of difficulties, and for collaboration of effort must be provided. Availability of data must also be insured.

Analyzing Center Data

Data collected routinely during intake and residence and occasionally as a follow-up may afford an opportunity for the immediate initiation of research in the form of retrospective analysis. A systematic ordering and statistical analysis of this data could significantly increase the information available on specific children and on the impact of the particular residential treatment. Important relationships, for example, could be revealed when significant experience during developmental phases, social and economic backgrounds, school and recreational activities, and peer group associations are correlated with intake diagnoses, important center experiences, release diagnoses, and aftercare experiences. Both quality and definition must be thoroughly appraised, of course, preceding such action; the specific manner of collection, recording and storage, the representativeness, the exact meaning of categories of information are the types of things with which such an appraisal must be concerned.

These retrospective analyses could also indicate many things for subsequent research. The problems and usefulness of various categories of information and the techniques of collecting and analyzing the data should become apparent. Variables that were highly correlated would indicate further research, as would both consistent and inconsistent relationships between the research findings and various related theories or common-sense or common-usage ideas.

With the readiness of a center and the researchers to cooperate in controlled studies, the center could then proceed to prospective research projects. The data to be collected and its manner of collection and consideration could then be guided by a conceptual and methodological schema forged in part from the retrospective studies. The specific definition of the problem to be studied and the properties and indicators of this problem would further direct the data collection effort.

Clinical Case Studies

All children receive intensive psychological and related examinations at admission and usually at least once again before release. In addition, they are under constant observation in all their activities for the duration of their stay in the center. These are the sources of data for the clinical case studies, essentially forms of exploratory research that seek to stimulate insights or hypotheses that uncover empirical regularities and their causes. Although the clinician may not pinpoint them as such, his techniques involve organizing the raw data into descriptive patterns or themes and then inferring a more refined or higher-order classification from these. The descriptive patterns and higher-order classification of them should provide a workable summary of the wealth of elements in the original raw data and include at least a first approximation of the basic elements necessary for a hypothetical explanation of that phenomenon under study.

The case study method encourages care and rigor. Yet it is a sufficiently unstructured procedure to discover new information and insights and provide opportunities for imagination and speculation. In contrast with rigorous experimental design, procedural changes can be made in the case study approach as research is in process. Thus additional cases may be added to a sample, and data collection may be broadened in the testing of a tentative hypothesis. Moreover, intensive study of the unrepresentative, particularly atypical cases may reveal much about themselves and their particular category of pathologies as well as being indirectly instructive for more common cases.

The creative character of case studies suggests that those cases that have apparent research usefulness be studied. Thus, a series of uniformly gathered cases on children having mixed neurotic character disorders might result in new classifications for such disorders along with new information about the etiology of their problems.

Studies of the Center as a System

The study of a center as a system goes beyond the analysis of the usual center data such as the characteristics of the patients, patient flow as reflected in intake, length of stay, and discharge statistics, or descriptions of center activities and staff credentials. Rather, system studies seek to understand the full ramifications of a center's purpose and its operations.

Such studies might begin with an examination of a center's formally stated program, its goals, and means to achieve them. A review of each staff member's conception of the center's aims and activities would probably be a further technique to understand the character of the center. Observation of a program in operation would then evidence the relationship of program statements, staff conceptions, and actual practice.

In the interest of learning more about center

organization and its effects, various structural components of a center and their relationships to children's treatment could be investigated. The administrative style of leadership, the staff's division of work, specialization, and departmentalization could be explained. The hierarchical arrangement of positions and lines of supervision and communication would undoubtedly be considered as well as the effect of these organizational components on the rules of children's treatment and on the freedom to deviate from these rules. Although a majority of center decisions are determined by organizational rules and procedures, important decisions do not usually evolve from such a routine alone, especially when the informal organization of the children becomes a participant. This spontaneously formed, yet at times highly integrated form of organization may have considerable impact on the staff decision making.

Further, the interplay of various aspects of a center and its children's organizations may appreciably modify various prescribed staff roles and the organization of the center itself. In an instance of pressure from an aggressive faction of patients, for example, child care workers may give up a substantial part of their authority, shift the communication patterns, and change the style of their work. With only a minimum of compliance to child care direction, such factions in the children's organization could manage many facets of the program, especially those involving the less powerful patients. In the extreme, a powerful clique operating with strong antistaff and antitreatment norms might destroy the effectiveness of the program.

Developing and Testing New Models of Treatment

Developing experimental research in centers raises ethical and methodological problems. The ethical issues may arise when an experimental design requires that a given treatment be offered to some children and withheld from others. Practitioners dedicated to providing a broad range of services tend to reject treatment strategies that limit the range of services that may be offered to their patients. This may be rectified partially by providing a specified degree of freedom in the administration of the service and procedural safeguards to cope with demonstrable damaging effects and partially by the fact that no particular treatment has any consistent research evidence supporting its effectiveness.

The following discussion considers only several of the many methodological problems involved in creating an experimental treatment model. Perhaps the item to develop is a typology of emotionally disturbed children that identifies those personality aspects having the greatest potential for treatment. The terminology and details of such a diagnostic model could categorize and classify a person's particular intrapsychic makeup and its reflection in his characteristic behavior in various kinds of situations. This typology must include the staff as well as the children to facilitate matching of staff and children whose personality types would produce therapeutic relationships.

A set of measures — tests, interviews, and observational check lists — should be developed to establish the existence of the conceptualized conditions and the aptitude of each staff member for coping with these conditions. These measures should be narrowed to test for the presence and the degree of only those conditions particularized in the typology. In this fashion, a complicated and circuitous logic would be avoided in the interpretation of the test interview and observational data. It is also important that the measures include a consideration of the staff-child relationships so that these may be planned and developed according to a firm set of criteria.

Various center and aftercare treatment models could be developed in which the components of treatment are specified in detail and related to each other to provide systematic and comprehensive approaches to treatment. Such models should be based specifically on a typology of disturbed children, and more generally on personality theory, program theory and experience, and the available and obtainable resources. The children's living units, institutional routines, styles of administration, peer influence, types of staff, various education programs, social work, psychotherapy, and aftercare supervision would all have to be examined for their potential contribution to the development of treatment models. The various manipulations of the program components in consonance with the treatment needs indicated by the diagnostic schema would produce a variety of distinct program models. If each were effected in different centers and followed by exacting studies, valuable comparative data would become available, not only on the effectiveness of the treatment but on the overall process of development and maintenance of programs.

Since the ongoing programs of centers are not likely to match the requirements of newly developed models, a technology for the implementation of the changes required for the new models would be necessary. This would have to focus on development of the methods for determining what elements of an existing program need to be changed and how such changes can be made effectively. The complete spectrum of residence and aftercare services of the center and its organization would come under review. The staff's degree of technical preparation, their training potential and receptiveness to the new or revised program must be evaluated.

After models and approaches for change have been developed, centers could actually begin changing their programs to bring them into alignment with the models. Research should be initiated at this point to study the process of effecting center changes and determining the center's readiness to test the effectiveness of the models. Once these programs including aftercare are functioning, the study of their process and impact could be initiated in part through before and after measures. Quality controls should also be set at specified points during the course of the experimental program to determine the extent to which the programs actually deliver what they promise and to provide information on which to base appropriate adjustments.

Group Living Studies

The formation, structures, operations, and culture of patient groups should be studied. Of concern in this area are both the highly organized and the transitory aspects of group life and the impact of these on treatment. How and why various groups come into being, absorb new members, influence the treatment process, change, and perhaps eventually dissolve should be investigated.

Topics for consideration in the organized group structure are varied. It is not clear, for example, to what degree and in what combination variables such as race, home-community factors, age, and personality determine the acceptability of a newcomer to a particular group. The impact of the different patient roles within the group, including that of leadership, and of the ideologies of the center and the outside community on the patient could also be researched.

Understanding the collective behavior phenomena of transitory groups ranging in size from a few patients to small crowds appears to be especially important in the further development of treatment procedures. The process of unrest expanding from a few individuals to large groups might be studied to understand the conditions of the individual and the milieu that prepare and sensitize the patients to enter the ready rapport of tension, dissatisfaction, and action. Potential causes to be investigated might include the types of lapses and inadequacies in the program, the various kinds of interstaff conflicts and their aggravation of the patients, the turmoils and abuse of the patients' informal organization and intrapsychic conflict. The alternative ways in which social unrest resolves itself or progresses into other forms of activity must be considered as well. A small amorphous group of patients may develop into a crowd of threatening proportions, a tightly knit group might emerge and quietly but insidiously undermine treatment activities, or the unrest might dissipate itself after only a modicum of complaints. Once the causes and conditions of such transitory behavior are more clearly understood, the patients' irritations and seemingly erratic behavior might become more amenable to treatment or even be of therapeutic use.

The length of time the patients anticipate staying in a center, the frequency of their home visits, the quality of the center food, and the permissiveness and arbitrariness of the staff are among the issues that concern the patients. The children discuss and divide on their opinions on these matters; they challenge each other's contentions and positions. In this process of spontaneous give-and-take, various opinions are bolstered, modified, and incorporated with others. Though consensus may not be developed among the children, enough accord is usually reached for them to get along with each other and to be in some unanimity. Sometimes, however, this willingness to discuss their differences in a spirit of compromise may not be present. The group may be unable to declare a collective opinion, and divergent ideas may become exacerbated until wild shouting or even fights break out.

Research on patient center opinion might focus on its development including the types of issues that receive attention, the consistency or shift in the group membership of those who become involved, and the formulation and debate of issues. Those aspects of the process that contribute to the development of a positive milieu might be identified for deliberate use in treatment. Those that result in dramatically disruptive behavior could also be determined in the interest of prevention.

Breakdown in Organized Group Life

Breakdowns in organized group life — in the school, in the cottages, in the dining room, on the recreational field — are significant for the understanding of the individuals involved, the group life of the center as a whole, and the interaction between these two. The noninvolvement of ungrouped patients and patient runaways are sketched here as examples of breakdowns that could be studied in detail.

Some patients are not intimately related to any

particular group in the center. A few are utterly isolated, others form a loose collectivity, and some attach themselves to well-organized groups without becoming involved in their intimacies. Investigation of the various circumstances that tend to encourage and sustain the isolates in relationship to others should produce information that could be used in treatment. Thus special staff and other patient interpersonal techniques might be developed to aid in this. Also, particular rules and even rituals might be devised for certain problematic situations. Unique ways of involving the isolates in planning and activities and innovative methods of communicating with them, including entering their fantasy life, might be designed. In addition, study should consider which individuals are affected and to what degree by the particular forces that encourage and sustain atomization.

Runaways may not be a major center problem, but they too illustrate the evolution of a problem from the interaction of the psychodynamics of the patient and the dynamics of the center milieu. If the runaway is an isolated expression of a particular child's psychodynamics with little or no stimulation by the center's milieu, the behavior still affords the opportunity to understand unique, unconscious conflicts and their concomitant intense feelings and impulses. While runaways without some stimulation by the center milieu are highly unlikely, the less the milieu stimulations, the greater is the opportunity to study the psychodynamics of the act. The symbolic meaning of the escape from the milieu for the patient's unconscious and the linkages between manifest behavior and covert strivings could be explored.

When a runaway seems to result from the problems of the patient's group life, additional research questions can be raised. Do the milieu pressures and the opportunities for running away actually encourage such behavior, and if so, which specific aspects and situations do so? In conjunction with the immediate situation is the remainder of the patient's world, the area of friendships, leisure activities, and relations with the wider center. Informal associations, clubs, organizations, school, and relationships to caseworkers and psychotherapists should all be studied in relation to runaway behavior.

Attractions outside a center may also influence runaway behavior, and they, therefore, should be reviewed too. Strong familial, romantic, or friendly relationships, including neurotic ones, can have a powerful drawing attraction for the children. Precipitation can include emotionally arousing letters or visits or the failure of these expectations to be fulfilled.

Studies on Center Administration

The administration of a center is particularly complex. In addition to being responsible for the internal management of the center, the director and his colleagues are the formal link between the center and an array of interested outside parties, including referral agencies and courts, mass media, and the general public in both the immediate and outlying communities from which patients come. Further, the professional leadership is directly responsible to a board or parent agency. Inconsistent expectations of the administration may be held by groups both internal and external to the center.

Perhaps a preliminary investigation of the center director's ideas and those of his key assistants on the subject of the operation of the center would be the place to begin. Their ideas make up a loose frame of reference, often on an informal and intuitive level, that provides the *de facto* orientation for their interpretation of the problems and the administration of the programs. Such orientations create a selective perception as to what is important and what is trivial. Exploration of these orientations might indicate the types of alternatives that administrators see as available to them in connection with their perception of a center's problems. Unique ways of reorganizing activities after a breakdown and gauging the activities to meet special problems may be reflected through such a study. Nonclinical factors influencing the character of the center might become apparent and include such elements as budget limitations, "deadwood" staff remaining from previous programs, and unique pressures from non-professional board members or community agencies.

2. Unique Challenges of
Institutional Administration

Clayton E. Nordstrom

The administration of institutions offers some of the most unique, exciting, and difficult challenges that can be found in the field of social welfare. These are challenges that cannot be found to the same degree, if at all, in noninstitutional agency programs because the institution is a complex and ever changing pattern of interacting individuals and group, staff members and clients, which must constantly be evaluated and amplified or modified to meet the needs of the institution's clients. Institutional administration is also unique because in no other social welfare setting are the administrator's personality, knowledge, and skills so directly related to the establishment of a therapeutic milieu designed for the treatment of the agency's clients. This paper will present some of the differences between administration of institutional and noninstitutional services and will place emphasis on the elements that are especially challenging because of their uniqueness to the executive's role in the administration of an institution.

For this discussion, it is assumed that an institution is a setting in which people voluntarily or involuntarily live together with agency staff in order to receive help for emotional and social problems and an opportunity for

Reprinted from *Child Welfare*, vol. 45, no. 3 (March 1966), pp. 151-57, by permission of the author and the journal.

healthy development of their natural abilities and social life. The noninstitutional program provides a service on an outpatient basis to clients while they live in their own homes. It is further assumed that the primary purpose of the institution is the individualized treatment of each resident client for his problems, utilizing the inherent and created values of group experiences and a variety of specialized services as needed by each client. The ultimate goal for each client is, whenever possible, return to family and/or community living as a healthier and happier child or adult. The fact that the writer's experience has been entirely in the child welfare field should not alter the application of the ideas presented, as the basic elements of administration are the same in all institutional settings. It makes little difference, therefore, whether a person is concerned over the administration of a training school for delinquents, a residential treatment center for emotionally disturbed children, an institution for the less disturbed child, or an institution for adults — as there will be a similarity in the basic problems and processes of administration of each and there will be elements that will be unique to the institutional settings as they will not be found in noninstitutional programs.

The institutional setting and the responsibility of the institution for the total daily life of its clients are major factors in the challenging and action-filled life of its administrator. It is the responsibility of the administrator of an institution for creating and maintaining a therapeutic and educational setting that influences the institution's clients 24 hours a day that most clearly distinguishes his responsibilities from those of the noninstitutional agency administrator. When an individual, or client, becomes a resident of an institution, he takes on a new social role in a new social climate. The administrator has the responsibility for creating this new social climate or special world that will maximize socializing and therapeutic influence toward the problems of the client. These problems are usually recognized and supported in some measure by the institutional community.

The challenge of creating a special world for the

agency's clients requires that the institutional administrator have some knowledge about the life and the problems of each client. Unless the institution is very large, the administrator usually knows most of its residents. He is involved in intake, treatment, and discharge planning and helps in defining and interpreting the agency's and therapist's role to the client. The administrator must, as far as possible, be attuned to the social climate of the institution as well as to the life of each resident, to his problems, and to his social role and must rise to the challenge of meeting the needs of the client through organizing and enabling the institution's staff to create a special "therapeutic" world for the client.

In contrast, the noninstitutional administrator may know very little about the individual clients of the agency. He may never meet clients, be involved in planning treatment, or be directly involved in working with the client. He does not have to be concerned about the total life of the individual client, who continues to carry on his usual social role in a social environment away from the agency. He does not become directly involved in the new role relationships that develop between clients and the agency and staff and which are relatively simple. The administrator's interest in the client may only be an indirect one as he may not know the client either by sight or by name. His only concern is that the therapist be enabled through his administration to provide the needed service to the client who has come to the agency for help. On the other hand, the client may never become concerned about or be aware of the administrator's role in the agency. In a family casework agency, for example, the client usually develops a primary relationship with his therapist and a secondary relationship with the agency. He comes to the agency for one hour per week, and his major contact is with his therapist. He may never meet the administrator or other members of the staff, except the receptionist. Except for group work agencies, the clients of the agency may not know each other and have little influence on each other, and the administrator's influence over the social role or social climate of the client is negligible. The client's problems may also remain as "private problems" unknown to his community. He does not, therefore, have to be concerned with the role of the administrator as it affects his treatment program and life.

In the institution, the client may quickly become aware of the administrator's role and its effect on his life. Dependent upon procedures in a children's institution, a child begins to perceive either during intake or soon after placement that the administrator is the highest authority figure in the institution. The administrator

> is responsible for the broad planning of the living arrangement for children, and for securing the necessary staff and equipment to implement these plans. He is involved in the policy decisions of the various departments which operate under his leadership. . . . In daily living, the administrator plays an important role in defining limits for both the children and the staff. He is available to the children as a "court of last resort" on all decisions, although in practice they may refer to him very infrequently.[1]

The children (just as adult residents would in an institution) often perceive, therefore, the administrator as a powerful person who can make important decisions regarding their own welfare and who can tell the staff members what or what not to do. We would not expect, of course, that every child would see the administrator in exactly the same way, as the child's past experiences and his type of pathology will influence his perceptions of any adult in the institution.

In examining the role of the administrator of a children's institution and his responsibility for having some awareness of each child's needs and the child's new social role, it becomes apparent that the administrator must be fully aware of the influence of his own role as well as of the institution's total social climate on the children in care. The institutional setting creates a complex set of roles and relationships for the children with each other and with staff members. For example, it can be demonstrated that even with three persons there can be as many as 16 different, clear-cut patterns of interaction between the three members of the group. With eight members in a group, there can be more than 5,000 possible different patterns of interaction among the group members as they act in different combinations with, for, or against each other. To count the number of possible interaction patterns in an institution with 100 or more children and staff would require the aid of an electronic computer, but it is easy to see that it is this very complex nature of group living that challenges the administrator in developing the social climate of the institution. The institutional administrator must, therefore, have a deep understanding of the dynamics of group relations. Morris F. Mayer has pointed out that

> the group living process has become an important treatment tool in itself, and as such, combined with the casework process, the education, the medical and psychiatric care, represents a therapeutic channel through which the child develops into a stronger personality.[2]

The institutional administrator must understand group process, and he must become involved in it to the extent that his leadership and enabling roles influence not only the total atmosphere of the institution but subgroupings and individuals. He must be prepared to effectively interfere with the power structure through which various individuals and subgroups attempt to take over subgroups or the total group. He must be concerned with the complexity and with the effects of roles and relationships between and with staff and resident-client subgroups and individuals on the treatment of individual clients. Gisela Konopka has clearly delineated this aspect of the administrator's position in the institution:

> In many institutions, strangely enough, the administrator actually is not looked upon as a member of the team and he does not look upon himself as such. He thinks he can delegate the responsibility for treatment to a group of outside experts. It is my contention that this is impossible. The administrator of an institution will set the climate found in the institution. His dealing with his own staff, with the youngsters or adults given into his care, and with the community around them makes

> treatment possible or impossible . . . administration
> cannot be separated from the content or the purpose for
> which the institution is created. Only the administrator
> who has a basic philosophy, conviction and knowledge
> regarding the treatment purposes of his institution can
> create the kind of atmosphere conducive to the fulfill-
> ment of this purpose.[3]

The administrator must be constantly aware of the role
he plays in the institution and find ways to evaluate his
effectiveness in helping his staff to fully utilize their
individual skills in a teamwork relationship to help the
children or adults in care. It is all too easy for the
executive to use his authoritative-parent-therapist role to
meet his own needs rather than the needs of his staff and
clients. He must, therefore, continually examine his
relationships with clients as well as with all of his staff. He
must use his role in a manner that does not negate or
interfere with the roles and responsibilities of staff
members.

> The executive functions best when, through his own
> understanding of the needs of clients, he may enable his
> staff to use their own skills to carry out their respon-
> sibilities in working with the clients of the agency. He
> has to know his staff, teach them, consult with them,
> give them full authority to carry out the details of their
> work, and assist them whenever needed.[4]

He must be able to interpret his own role and the role of
staff members to the institution's clients so they may use
each to their best advantage and so they may have the
security of knowing that the administrative lines of
responsibility are clearly defined and respected.

The role of the institutional administrator appears to be
a complex one as he serves as a leader, developer,
coordinator, supervisor, enabler, team member, employer,
decision maker — and even as a "parental" figure to the
staff and children or adults in care. The vitality, growth,
and effectiveness of an institution will depend upon the
knowledge and skills, the strengths and weaknesses of its
administrator. This implies that the administrator should
have a basic knowledge of social welfare, and child welfare

specifically if he administers a child care institution, and possess the skills necessary to carry out his major responsibilities as the executive. We cannot expect the administrator to be an expert in all the disciplines employed in an institution, but he does need to know enough about each skill required so that he can employ properly qualified staff and evaluate their work. The administrator should fully understand the contributions to be made by each staff member and be able to let each function in his own area of competence. This understanding not only allows the delegation of duties to those persons whose skills and roles in a milieu of relationships can be most helpful in the treatment of the institution's clients, but allows the administrator to devote more of his time to the study, evaluation, and development of services.

By comparison it is a more difficult task for the institutional administrator to select, train, delegate, and coordinate his staff than it is for the executive of a noninstitutional agency with a lesser number of roles played by staff in the treatment of clients. Even the child guidance clinic, which may include a psychiatrist, psychologist, caseworker, and group worker, in the treatment of a child and his parents, will require the assignment and coordination of the roles of only four or five people. This treatment team may have direct contact with the members of the family only 2 or 3 hours each week, and the family is left to fend for itself during the remaining 165 hours of the week. The institutional administrator is not concerned with a treatment team of only 4 or 5 persons as they provide a service to a particular client but with 20, 30, 50, or several hundred staff members who may comprise the treatment team of an institution. There is a greater number and a greater variety of professional and nonprofessional personnel involved in the specially created world of the institution, all of whom are directly or indirectly involved in the treatment and education of clients 24 hours a day, 7 days per week, and 52 weeks per year. Martin Gula has pointed out that in a modern institution

a "master plan" for the study and treatment of the child

and concurrent service to the family is established before or soon after his admission and is frequently reviewed and reshaped during his residence. This diagnostic and treatment plan evolves from the joint thinking of all staff members who are treating the child and working with the parents. It is not a simple prescription given to the residential staff by the psychiatric, medical, or casework staff. Moreover, procedures are established to coordinate effectively the activity of various staff members for the benefit of the child and his parents at various stages of the child's treatment. Each staff member becomes a part of a total effort in behalf of the child.[5]

The executive, houseparents or child care workers, psychiatrists, caseworkers, group workers, teachers, maintenance staff, clerical workers, volunteers, and others are all a part of the team of professional and nonprofessional workers in the institution. It is a team that may also include the faculties of nearby community schools and the community itself, as the institution must maintain a close and congenial relationship with them to meet the needs of its clients.

Without a doubt some of the most difficult tasks of the institutional administrator include the employment, training and coordination of his staff. These tasks present problems that multiply rapidly as the size of the institution grows in number of staff and residents, but whether the institution is large or small, there seems to be none in which the administrator does not have difficulties in finding suit-. able staff members. It is incumbent upon the institutional administrator, therefore, to continually seek employees with the potential for contributing to his agency's program.

He begins the difficult task of building his institutional team through defining the purpose and goals of the institution, through establishing the size and kind of staff needed, and through the preparation of job descriptions that clearly define the roles and responsibilities of personnel. He will establish clear lines of responsibility and authority and define the nature of working relationships between individuals, departments, units, supervisors, and administrator. He will employ his staff not only to fill certain specified jobs but to complement and strengthen the institutional team in its subgroups as well as in its entirety. It is not enough to employ a gardener who knows how to prune shrubbery and make the grass and flowers grow — it is necessary to employ a gardener who has a positive feeling for children, especially those who might pull up his prize tulips, and who, through training, can see himself as one of a group of helpers in the treatment of disturbed children. It is not enough to employ caseworkers skilled in the diagnosis and treatment of children and adults — it is necessary to employ caseworkers who can also develop an understanding of group living and group processes and who can learn to give and take and to work as a member of a team. This requirement of employment of individuals in all professional and nonprofessional positions who can develop understanding, cooperative teamwork relationships in the treatment of clients is unique to institutional administration.

Every member of the institution's staff has some effect on its residents for, unless the institution is very large, all employees will have some kind of contact with each resident several times a week, if not every day. When a child sees a staff member the experience will have some effect on him, whether or not they speak to each other. The child may feel reassured just because he sees one or several staff members, or he may feel rejected because an individual does not speak to him. He may grow a little more each day because each staff member greets him cheerfully, or he may become more withdrawn or hostile because staff members are critical and hostile toward him. The children in an institution will be directly affected by the morale of the staff and will change for the good only when the understanding, patience, and good humor of the staff reflect the strength of their training and cooperative working relationships.

Once employed, the employee must be continually involved in a training program geared to his level of understanding, previous training and experiences, and his responsibilities in the institution. The need for continued training for the job to be performed applies to all — the child care worker, the caseworker, the cook, the psychiatrist, the administrator, and the others — for there is no one way to treat children and adults who themselves never have exactly the same kinds of problems.

Martin Gula has also very clearly summarized the important aspects of institutional administration that tie the selection and training of staff together with the treatment of an individual and the group:

> The treatment needs of children increasingly influence administrative planning such as selection of staff, grouping of children, and developing of services in the institution. In other words, the entire environment of the residential setting is constantly adapted to the treatment requirements of the child and the group.[6]

It is a difficult task to develop and carry out the inservice training program of an institution due to the wide variation in the education, experience, understanding, skills, and roles of the staff. For example, the institution's staff will include persons with levels of education from grade school through the master's and doctorate programs, and a majority of persons without any previous experience in an institution at the time of their employment. Yet each person may have a direct and important influence on the treatment of a resident. In fact, it is common to find that those employees spending the most time with the residents have the least education and preparation for their jobs prior to employment. The training program must, therefore, not only be planned to be an educational process for persons with various levels of education and experience but be adapted according to the roles played by the staff.

This means that the administrator must plan and carry out several simultaneous programs, each designed to strengthen the roles and understanding of various segments of the total staff. This is difficult because we do not yet fully understand the meaning of social roles and experience in the treatment of emotionally disturbed individuals, and we do not know the most effective method in teaching the knowledge and methods we now have in residential treatment. There is much to challenge the administrator in deciding who should do the training, the proper grouping of staff for training purposes, what the content of training programs should be, and the methods to be used in the training process.

It seems that as the training of institutional personnel increases, the greater the effort must be to designate and coordinate the roles of the staff. In a noninstitutional agency where there are fewer types of roles involved in carrying out the purpose of the program, coordination of staff is relatively easy. The fact that there is less divergence in the professional training and understanding of the staff in the noninstitutional agency also creates fewer problems related to role confusion and the need for conformity to the goals and philosophies of the agency. In an institution the relationship between the degree of training and degree of coordination of staff revolves around the goals of the institution as seen by the administration and staff. As the goals of institutions have gradually shifted through the years from custodial care, control, protection, and broad social training of groups of dependent, delinquent, retarded, or emotionally disturbed children and adults to the goal of treatment and education of the individual according to his own problems, needs, and potentialities, the need for training and coordination of staff has received much attention. When a child care institution had, for example, the same goals for all its children and used the same rigid approach for all in care, it was relatively simple to train and coordinate the staff. Emphasis was on demanding total group conformity through submission to adult authority and the rules of the institution rather than on helping each child to accept and follow the rules of the institution and the broader community according to his readiness and ability to form positive relationships with adults and society.

,The emphasis on individualized treatment through the use of one-to-one relationships as well as the total milieu of the institution requires more administrative control over the activities of professional, as well as nonprofessional employees, than is found necessary in a noninstitutional setting.

As treatment agencies become more complex they tend
to employ members of several — sometimes many —
professional groups. This presents new problems in
defining the appropriate division of effort and allocation
of authority among these groups. Competing claims are
presented with respect to the essential skills, preferred
tasks, and appropriate statuses within the organization.[7]

Robert Vinter has further described the nature of
administrative responsibility for keeping a balance between
the exercise of professional autonomy and the control of
individual behavior in achieving the goal of the
organization:

Professionals in treatment organizations also assert the
principle of autonomy in exercise of their special skills.
They value independence and initiative in the use of
these skills, especially in the primary areas of decision
and transactions with clientele. The more complex and
esoteric the technology utilized, the less possible it
becomes to control behavior directly through administrative rules or close supervision. The treatment organization must, nevertheless, insure that staff behavior is in
conformity with its general purposes, and that staff
actions are coordinated. Certain mechanisms are developed, therefore, to achieve the necessary controls
while respecting professional claims to autonomy.[8]

The administrator of the treatment institution has a very
special challenge in the task of developing the mechanisms
to achieve necessary controls over divergent action that
could interfere with the total social climate and goals of
the institution. He also faces a special challenge in making
it possible for the staff to exercise enough autonomy over
their actions that they will feel a professional responsibility for making many of their own decisions and for
developing new ideas and methods of treatment. Otherwise, initiative and experimentation will be sacrificed for a
rigid conformity to rules and regulations that nullifies
growth in the agency's program.

An integral part of the ongoing process of maintaining a
therapeutic living environment, employment and training
of staff, and of permitting initiative and flexibility of
individual action within a controlled organization is the
process of communication. The literature in the field of
administration is filled with importance of communica-

tions in any organization between the executive and the employee, individuals, departments, producer and consumer, and the producer and the general public. The importance and the problems of communication increase rapidly as the size of an organization increases in the number and roles of its membership. In social welfare, the noninstitutional program with 20 employees will find it easier to handle communication problems because it involves fewer and less complicated role relationships than does the same size institutional program. The institution presents so many problems in communication that the administrator is constantly examining these problems with the hope of finding more effective and efficient methods of getting information to the right people at the right time. Communication is a problem in an institution because it involves not only the administrator and his staff but the children or adults in care as well. It has often been said that the best and quickest way to get information to the children in an institution is to swear the staff to secrecy in a meeting behind locked doors when all the children are away from the campus. They seem to get information more quickly, although it may be less accurate this way than through the more organized methods of communication.

Communication is important:

> When the staff at every level accepts wholeheartedly the philosophy and purposes of management, when accurate, uncensored reporting of what is actually happening flows upward, and when there is a dynamic flow of management's philosophy and purposes down the line to all personnel and on to the children, then it can be said that communication is well established. Open channels of communication to the superintendent are particularly important. The more accessible he is to suggestions from all his staff, the more likely he is to know what is really going on in the institution.[9]

The administrator must keep himself accessible not only to his staff but to the residents of the institution through formal and informal channels of communication. He is then more able to get a firsthand feel of the "state of health" of the institution as it fluctuates from day to day, to reduce conflicts, and to focus the energies of staff and residents on the institution's goal. [10]

The responsibility of the administrator for the "state of health" of the institution is also unique to the institutional setting. It is a responsibility that goes on 24 hours a day, 7 days per week, and even with the most competent staff, the administrator always carries with him a deep concern for the welfare of his agency's clients. Unlike the administrator of a noninstitutional agency service who does not have reponsibility for knowing about how clients are doing away from the agency or what is happening to his staff, the institutional administrator must be concerned over the health, safety, and emotional state of his staff and residents at all times, for what happens to one individual may affect everyone in his institution.

The institutional administrator has more emergencies to meet and more decisions to make. When a staff member is sick, for example, the clients of an institution cannot be sent home, and someone or some arrangement must be found to meet their needs for care, for control, for education, for recreation, or for counseling. An acting-out child, or group, may require the direct intervention of the administrator in order to restore order in the life of the child, the group, the staff, and in the institution as a whole. A fire, an epidemic, a runaway, and a host of other situations may cause emergencies at any time of the day or night requiring administrative decisions and direction. These emergencies plus the everyday demands of residents and staff are elements of administration that are unique to the institutional setting. They often seem to interfere with the orderly accomplishment of the administrator's work, and he must constantly reorganize himself in meeting his administrative goals.

The orderly accomplishment of the administrator's work is not only related to how well he can organize his daily, weekly, monthly, and yearly schedules but is also directly related to the size and administrative structure of the organization. The experienced institutional worker will have recognized that much of what has been said in this paper about the administrator's relationships to the institution's clients and staff is most directly applicable in a small institution. Even the small institution with less than 50 residents requires subadministrative personnel to supervise various departments of the staff and to insure adequate attention to the needs of individual clients. With larger institutions, subadministrative personnel are required to supervise units of staff and residents to promote a therapeutic living environment and to keep efforts of the staff directed toward individuals as well as toward the various groups. The administrator of the large institution cannot know every resident or staff member, but working through the knowledge of others he can keep attuned to the climate and the program of his institution, and effect changes as they are needed.

The institutional administrator often has a relationship to his Board of Directors that is unique to institutional programs and that also interferes very directly with the orderly accomplishment of his administrative tasks. Board members of private institutions may through tradition be involved with program, clients, maintenance of property, and staff. Board members of noninstitutional services may seldom, if ever, see clients, so they do not get involved with them and are not overly concerned with offices that may be rented by the agency. The institutional board member may feel comfortable with that which he knows well and strongly resist changes in the agency's facilities or program, or in its own role. The institutional administrator may, therefore, find that he must take more initiative in defining the role of board member, in guiding them in their work, and in interpreting the need for change in services. He must spend more of his time that the noninstitutional administrator does in blending the roles of staff, administrator, and board so that their roles do not interfere with but complement each other. This is a task that takes courage and conviction to accomplish because it often involves a very delicate relationship with the board or with individual board members.

There is a quality in the relationship between the institution and the general community that resembles the uniqueness of the relationship between the administrator and the Board of Directors. The community, to a lesser degree than a Board of Directors, has similar relationships to and understanding of institutional and noninstitutional services. The family casework agency provides a service that may not be easily recognized, accepted, and supported. For example, preplacement planning with unwed mothers may not be so readily supported as payment for the seclusion of the mother in an institution, medical fees for delivery, or foster care for the child. The institution, however, fulfills a community need that is more easily recognized by the community, such as the care of neglected children, control of delinquents, and care of the mentally ill. Support of the institution may, therefore, be more easily obtained from the community to fulfill those functions of which the community approves.

The seeming nearness of the community to the institution's buildings, program, and clients which may promote public support may also interfere with plans to change various aspects of its program. The institution has certain traditions in the community which the public understands and with which it feels comfortable. [11] Innovations in the program of the institution may not be easily understood or accepted because they offend the expectations of the community, and the community may protest against racial integration, replacing orphans with disturbed or delinquent children, or even replacing the "old brick orphanages" with modern cottages. The administrator of the institution must carefully prepare the community for changes and be prepared himself to defend as well as to promote changes when they do take place.

The administrator of an institution must be especially careful not to isolate himself and the institution from the community on which the agency is dependent for support and cooperative services. Because the institution may seem to offer a total service in meeting the physical, educational, social, and emotional needs of its clients, there may be less awareness of mutual interdependence with other social agencies in giving day-to-day service to clients. The noninstitutional agency offers only a partial service in meeting total human needs, so it has a greater awareness of the mutual interdependence of agencies in meeting the needs of clients. It will, therefore, have more opportunities for developing strong interagency relationships.

The institution must also develop strong relationships with other private and public agencies in the community if it is to be most effective in serving individuals and families with special needs. The institution may not be able to help all members of a family with their problems, and, in most cases, the clients of the institution are expected to return to community living. A friendly, knowledgeable, active, and cooperative relationship with other agencies will serve to strengthen the program as well as the position of the institution in the community.

It can be seen that administration of institutions presents some very unique challenges that arise from the complexity of relationships between the administrator, staff, clients, Board of Directors, and community. There is probably no role in social work that is more demanding than that of the executive of an institution as he is asked to carry out his responsibility for the total daily lives of children or adults. In one day he may be called upon to be a counselor, plumber, recreation worker, peacemaker, nurse, houseparent, and administrator. He must keep attuned to the social climate of the institution. He is constantly under pressure from his staff and the institution's clients to solve their problems. He is "on call" 24 hours a day, 7 days a week, and may be called upon to make important decisions both day and night. He is constantly involved in the evaluation of his role, the roles of others, and the methods used to carry out the goals of the institution. These are challenges that make institutional administration exciting and full of anticipation of problems yet to be solved and of the tasks yet to be done.

NOTES

1. Donald A. Bloch and Earle Silber, "The Role of the Administrator in Relation to Individual Psychotherapy in a Residential Treatment Setting," *American Journal of Orthopsychiatry* (January 1957): 67-70.
2. Morris F. Mayer, "The Houseparents and the Group Living Process," in *Creative Group Living in a Children's Institution*, ed.

Susanne Schulze (New York: Association Press, 1951), p. 97.

3. Gisela Konopka, *Group Work in the Institution* (New York: Whiteside & William Morrow & Co., 1954), pp. 12-13.

4. Clayton E. Nordstrom, "Introduction of Casework Service to a Children's Institution and Its Effect on the Executive," *Child Welfare* (March 1962): p. 115.

5. Martin Gula, *Child-Caring Institutions* (Washington, D.C.: U.S. Department of Health, Education, and Welfare, Children's Bureau, 1958), p. 16.

6. Ibid, pp. 16-17.

7. Alvin F. Zander, Arthur R. Cohen, and Ezra Stotland, *Role Relations in Mental Health Professions* (Ann Arbor, Mich.: University of Michigan Press, 1957), chap. 4.

8. Robert D. Vinter, "Analysis of Treatment Organizations," *Journal of Social Work* (July 1963): 10.

9. *Institutions Serving Delinquent Children* (Washington, D.C.: U.S. Department of Health, Eudcation, and Welfare, Children's Bureau, 1957), p. 21.

10. *Administration and Staff Training in Institutions for Juvenile Delinquents* (Washington, D.C.: U.S. Department of Health, Education, and Welfare, Children's Bureau, 1959), p. 11.

11. Kathryn Mahlin, "The Introduction of Innovations in Social Agencies" (unpublished paper, 1964).

3. Residential Programs: Their Component and Organizing Theories

George H. Weber and Bernard J. Haberlein

Only through rather arbitrary definition could residential treatment centers be easily placed in the overall context of child care institutions. There is considerable similarity between residential treatment centers, group homes, training schools, inpatient psychiatric units, and even boarding schools. Each professes humanism, particularly a concern for children and helping them. In assuming 24-hour-a-day care for the youngsters, they all take responsibility for their proper feeding, adequate clothing, and personal hygiene. Leisure-time activities and some education for school-age groups are provided. Furthermore, most institutions have direct access to clinical thinking, psychiatry, psychology, social work, and special education from their staff or from outside consultation. Thus, professional orientations and techniques are manifest in these different types of institutions.

The task of identifying residential treatment centers is further confounded because institutions that designate themselves as such differ substantially in their theories to explain emotional disturbances and techniques on how the children ought to be treated. Moreover, they have different administrative auspices and differ on the number and type of children they admit and the number, type, and skill of staff they employ.

In spite of the aforementioned difficulties, residential treatment settings have some identifiable characteristics that differentiate them from other children's institutions. The prescriptive criteria that follow are by no means absolute; however, they may serve as guidelines for identifying residential treatment centers and for placing into some context the articles that comprise the body of this volume.

1. Residential centers aim to deal with children's maladaptive behavior. Moreover, they have a theory and technique, even though these may vary from one center to another. For example, some base their techniques upon psychoanalytic theory; others base their techniques on operant conditioning principles, while still others have eclectic theories and techniques. But residential treatment centers have deliberate theories and techniques as they try to help the patients improve their maladaptive behavior. Intuition, clinical skill, and other elements of the "human equation" play key roles in the treatment; however, even these elements are identified, organized, and practiced within a theoretical framework.

2. Residential treatment centers deal with a population that is defined as being deviant along some behavioral or psychiatric continuum. Irrespective of a center's diagnostic perspective on children's problems — for example, whether it seeks unconscious conflicts for resolution or problematic behaviors for extinction — centers usually are not equipped to accept persons with records of antisocial behavior, at least not if their antisocial behavior has been brazen, shrewd, and unaccompanied by anxiety.

3. Residential treatment centers select their patients through diagnostic procedures that assess their "make up" and behavior. While the diagnostic descriptions of the children vary, depending on the theoretical and diagnostic orientations of the center, descriptions point to the patients' problems and their home and community circumstances. These findings are then translated into the specifics of the residential treatment. Psychological tests, various types of interviews, neurological examinations, social and developmental histories, and baseline measures of specific types of behavior are among the diagnostic tools used to select the patients and specify their

treatment goals and procedures.

4. Patients are selected for the purpose of treatment. While care and custody, education and training, *in loco parentis* may be important services of a center, both their existence and significance are derived from their role in the child's total treatment. Tailored to both therapeutic and developmental needs, such treatment is often a combination of individual and group techniques designed specifically for each child on the basis of careful diagnostic study. Its goal is personality change through action on both the "causes" and manifestations of problems. The focus may include individual elements of behavior, attitudes, feelings, motivations, and conflicts, as well as external influences such as the family and other significant figures in the child's life.

5. Residential centers purposefully integrate various program activities into the stream of each child's daily living experiences. All program elements ranging from recreation to one-to-one treatment and from the routines of daily living to group therapy must be interrelated to create an overall positive impact on the child during his stay in residence.

6. The residential treatment maximizes attention to the individual needs of its population. This extraordinarily complex task is simplified to some extent through limitations on the types of children that are admitted to a center and placement of them in relatively homogeneous groups after admission. Thus children of approximately the same developmental and intellectual levels, chronological ages, verbal and physical skills, and ways of behaving are placed together in living units, activity groups, and educational classes to facilitate programs for groups. Even a relatively homogeneous population and grouping, combined with programs on the group level, will leave problems to be approached through individual techniques. Some children whose behavior is the same may have different dynamics for it. Then too, even homogeneous groups of children have a range of responses to a program.

To facilitate the development of individual treatment goals and procedures, centers begin with assessing the child's complaints and complaints about him presented at intake by parents and referring agencies. Using this and other diagnostic information, clinical judgments are made in setting up a child's program. Activities of the overall program are drawn on. In addition, such nuances of treatment as staff attitudes and actions to be taken with specific children in various circumstances are prescribed. Moreover, the center must make periodic reevaluations of the patient's status and adjust its program accordingly.

7. The residential treatment center is flexible in planning for the length of a youngster's treatment. The initial estimate of a child's length of stay is based upon his diagnostic study and a center's general knowledge of treating such cases. The initial estimate may change as the staff scrutinizes the child's response to treatment. Also, a change in the patient's home situation may vary radically thereby altering his progress and, consequently, his length of stay in a center. Efforts are directed toward returning the youngster to the community where he can participate in the normal activities of youth, although there well may be the need for continued assistance.

The discharge of a child from a center should rest mainly on his behavior and attitude, indeed upon substantially having "solved" the problems that brought him into the program. Since his problems, however, were not independent of his home and school, these and other significant institutions have to be assessed for their capability to take the child back.

Even when residential centers have court or welfare cases, which may constrain a center's decision making, they, rather than the court, or welfare department, should determine the character of the child's program and his length of stay.

8. The residential treatment center employs clinically trained personnel: psychiatrists, psychologists, social workers, occupational therapists, and special educators. These specialists conduct diagnostic studies, carry children in individual and group therapy, and consult with or supervise child care workers and others who interact with the children. They also participate in a center's policy

discussions and decision making, and provide inservice training to child care workers, teachers, and others. Through such activities, the clinicians contribute to the development of the treatment program and plans for individual children and the implementation of them. In some instances certain professionals work in cottages or recreational activities. For example, in some centers, social group workers will be responsible for the overall management of the living units as well as work in them.

The professionals' skill, innovativeness, and energy are generally the major factors that determine their impact on the children as well as the administration of the institution.

9. The skills of the child care and related workers must be at a high level. These workers having intimate and continuous contact with the children are key in their treatment. In view of this, it is important that they be optimally trained, receive skilled supervision from the professionals, and maintain a cooperative working relation with them.

10. The parents are required to participate in the child's program. Their participation is gauged to be of immediate assistance to the child by providing information about him, visiting and encouraging him, and planning for his return to the family. It is also gauged to help the parents relate to him more harmoniously. Since parental behavior is usually intimately related to the child's problems, plans may have to be developed to help the parents cope with their own problems.

11. Residential treatment centers are relatively open settings. Within their planned schedules, the children are given considerable autonomy of movement. If the program is functioning adequately, there is very little need for locked doors and fenced grounds. Staff and their relationships to the children and programmed activities should provide the necessary security and control. With such an approach the children will neither feel the need to run away nor will they require constant surveillance to keep them from running. "Containment cottages" or closed wards may be used temporarily to traverse particularly

difficult periods in the child's treatment. Such programming must be distinguished from removing a rebellious child from a group for a short period of time. A containment cottage or closed ward, along with having a specific program for the children who are out of control, will have the restraints of a physical enclosure.

The openness of the center extends into the community. Children will make shopping trips, attend movies, and in some instances will attend school in the community.

12. The residential treatment center includes procedures to evaluate its work. Moreover, the insights and criticisms that emerge from this are faced, and corrections are made in the program. Thus, center goals and means to achieve them must be specified, and measures to assess the effectiveness of means must be developed.

Provisions for systematic data collection and analysis have to be made. Basically, questions such as the following should be asked: What are the aims of treatment? What are the means to achieve the desired improvement? What will be the indicators of the improvement, and how will they be measured? How can one be sure that the measurement is related to that which took place in the treatment? What are the implications of the findings for program improvement?

THE COMPONENTS AND ORGANIZATION OF RESIDENTIAL PROGRAMS

A residential treatment center combines a number of activities that attempt to meet the children's needs. Recapitulating briefly, these activities include: (1) group living, particularly as it takes place in cottages; (2) an educational program directed toward offering academic work appropriate to the children's achievements, interests, and intellectual potential; (3) recreation and leisure-time activities, such as arts, crafts, and games that are carried out in the school, living units, and perhaps in a centralized recreational unit for the center; and (4) intensive diagnostic and treatment services offered or directed by psychologists, psychiatrists, and social workers.

Residential treatment centers develop certain structures and modes of operation to encompass their programs and direct them toward the achievement of their goals. Through a combination of rational planning, spontaneous and *post hoc* actions, the mission of a center and its program and organization come into being. More specifically, a center's pattern of authority, division of work, way of communicating, and efforts to reward its staff are developed into formal statements and informal understanding. Among the more important influences determining a center's structure is its theory of treatment. Complex in nature, a theory governs the manner in which the children's problems are viewed, diagnosed, and treated, and how a center organizes itself to carry out these views and procedures.

Milieu therapy, for example, seeks to change patients through the influences of a center environment, its activities and relationships with the staff and other children. Thus, teachers, child care workers, arts, crafts, and recreational people, custodial workers, and even patients become environmental treatment agents, and substantial responsibility is delegated, at least to the previously mentioned staff. Psychotherapy and other intensive interviewing therapies are offered to a limited number of patients, and are seen as one component in the overall program. With the aforementioned delegation of responsibility, the subordination of nonclinical occupational groups is minimized, and an equalitarian philosophy has an opportunity of functioning. At any rate, information is exchanged as a mutual activity, and the staff instruct each other. Though considerable authority accompanies this delegation of responsibility and work, the task of directing and coordinating the treatment effort remains with the clinical staff. However, the direction and coordination responsibilities assumed by the clinical staff turn their work to administration, training, and consultation. Their focus will include such center problems as communication barriers and interpersonal conflicts between different groups of personnel, between staff and patients, and between patients.

Another theory of therapy, individual psychotherapy with the milieu as adjunctive, may further illustrate the impact of a theory of treatment on the organization of a center. Though typification of individual psychotherapy is somewhat difficult because of the several types and their various permutations, two contrasting general types stand out: (1) psychodynamic psychotherapies, particularly as they derive their procedures from psychoanalysis; and (2) the behavioral modification approaches which are based on learning theory. Each has a different impact on center organization.

First, psychodynamic therapy aims to help the children resolve their intrapsychic conflicts, especially the unconscious ones, and modify and strengthen their defenses. To achieve these ends the authority and direction of the program is centralized and rests with the clinicians. They conduct the diagnosis and individual and group therapy and direct the tasks of such others as child care workers and teachers, if not directly then through their supervisors. Reports of the children's behavior in their living units, classrooms, and recreation are given to the clinicians who use them to evaluate the child's progress and relate to their observations of the child's progress in psychotherapy. The complexity of the diagnostic terminology and language of psychoanalytic and ego psychology would tend to reinforce the authority of the clinicians because those without training in those areas will have serious difficulty in understanding technical discussions and thereby be limited in participating. Though there may be a concentration of authority and technical information with the clinicians in this approach, substantial responsibility for the children falls to the teaching and recreational staff. However, these responsibilities are restricted to providing care, nurture, instruction, and activities. Counseling on sensitive personal problems is generally discouraged. Rather, those in immediate contact with the children are encouraged to keep their conversations with the children on the routines and problems of center living and to refer the children's personal problems to the clinicians.

As suggested earlier, a behavioral approach provides a contrasting model of residential treatment. It is probably more directly related to an environmental approach than other psychotherapies. This characteristic stems from learning theory, particularly as the theory seeks to specify the relation between behavior and the significant factors in the environment. Contingency management, an important technique of behavior modification, arranges the rewards and punishments in the patients' milieu to encourage and discourage specific ways of behaving. As such, it can serve to illustrate the impact that this model of treatment has on a center organization.

In developing a contingency management system, the clinicians develop baseline data of the child's behavior, particularly on the reported problem behaviors. Identifying the child's problem behaviors and counting their frequency, and specifying the settings in which they occur, involve the child care workers, teachers, and others. Though they get direction from the clinicians, these workers do the actual observing and enumerating. Once the baseline measures are drawn, the clinicians again turn to those working in the environment to plan the child's contingency management. As in the diagnostic work planning, the child's management involves these people in very specific activities. In planning the child's management, the clinicians include the child care workers and others to decide how they will work with the child. For example, the clinicians in conjunction with the staff in the environment will decide which of the child's behaviors are to be encouraged, supported, and rewarded and which behaviors are to be discouraged, stopped, and punished. The specificity and closeness of relationship is maintained as the contingency management program is initiated and maintained. Moreover, periodic evaluation of the impact of the management techniques on the child's behavior requires further clinician, teacher, and child care worker collaboration. The problematic behaviors enumerated initially are observed and counted again, and compared with the earlier baseline measures.

Authority on diagnostic and treatment matters is

dispersed in association with this division of work and way of working. Final authority remains centralized with the clinicians; however, a great deal of authority is distributed to the staff in the child's immediate environment. The mechanics of developing and maintaining the contingency management requires frequent face-to-face contact. Thus, the clinicians and other staff are closely linked together. To the extent that this interface is personable, their communication and cooperation should be enhanced.

Part II
Some Treatment Issues

OVERVIEW

The technical problems of treating children in residential centers are manifold. For example, there are those that emerge from separating children from parents, developing therapeutic relationships with the children, treating the children's conflicts, including their sexual aberrations, parental visiting, and terminating treatment. Such concrete problems as home sickness, runaways, crying, rage outbursts, bullying other patients, withdrawal and uncommunicativeness, and homosexual behavior challenge the staff.

Characteristically, many of these problems are viewed as functions of the children's psychopathology. However, the character of the psychopathology is not always clear, nor is the linkage between the pathology and the behavior. Seemingly similar behavior has different intrapsychic dynamics, and some seemingly different behavior has similar intrapsychic machinations. However, the problems of the children do not emerge from their psychopathology alone. Indeed, a center's milieu may stimulate some problems. Such may occur, for example, by the lack of spelled-out rules governing the children's behavior. Nevertheless, problems do occur, and several illustrative problems are presented in the articles in this section. They include: Mandelbaum ("Parent-Child Separation: It's Significance to Parents"), McNeil and Morse ("The Institutional Management of Sex in Emotionally Disturbed Children"), Adessa and Laatsch ("Therapeutic Use of Visiting in Residential Treatment"), and Hirschberg ("Termination of Residential Treatment of Children").

4. Parent-Child Separation:
Its Significance to Parents

Arthur Mandelbaum

Understanding the anxieties that parents suffer in separating from a child is essential if parents and child are to be helped. This paper is particularly concerned with the significance of separation to parents in the residential treatment of children. Of all problems the social worker encounters in casework with parents and children, none is more significant than separation. But is it not true that separation is central to all life experiences?

Albert Camus stated, "Separation is characteristic of the human condition. It is often the rule of the world....It is in the essence of things that all who love should be separated."[1] Of course, Camus was speaking of the separation that inevitably accompanies all growth and development and is therefore impossible to resist: birth, infancy, childhood, adolescence, adulthood, old age, and death. Throughout each stage of this growth and development, from birth to death, there is a gradual giving-up of the old for the new in an orderly sequence within which there may be great variation but where the pattern follows a major form. Separation through growth and development is a process whereby parents and child learn to differentiate themselves from each other and to part gradually—a process made possible by the satisfactions experienced by each individual in the family which bring a sense of

Reprinted from *Social Work*, vol. 7, no. 4 (October 1962), pp. 26-34, by permission of the author and the journal.

growth, achievement, and contentment. The transition from one developmental period to the next during the early years is smoothed by the ever consistent, ever present parents, who create a sense of outer continuity, predictability, and harmony which becomes transformed in the child into a sense of inner security. Erikson has described this as essential for giving the child an identity and a sense of inner goodness and basic trust.[2]

The mother, who gives early essential nurturing experience to the child, is assisted by biological, social, and cultural factors. After the child is separated from her body, holding him close and feeling his softness and warmth comfort her for the loss of sensations and unity that she experienced prior to his birth. The encompassing love of her husband and his consistent support and attention mean that the child is loved as well, because now, although the biological unity is gone, she and the child are, in the emotional sense, still one. The culture approves of her caring for the child and sanctions her motherhood as the major priority. If she is always present for the child, alert and responsive to his needs, and if he is somewhere within the circle of whatever major interests occupy her, then he will absorb into himself an image of his mother that will become deeply etched into his personality. He will then go on to relate himself to his father and others who enter his life. Wherever he goes, he will carry an image of his parents that will remain unshaken; because he knows he belongs to them, he does not have to be physically bolted to them. Such a child will be able to separate. Psychoanalyst Christine Olden has stated, "It could be that you renounce complete possession of the baby more easily if these first months were a satisfactory experience, if you are satiated and feel free to go on to different joys with your child."[8][3]

This long satiation experience of nurturing and dependency between mother and child is characteristic of the human species, in contrast to the pattern in lower animal life. With the latter, instincts transmitted from one generation to the other enable the mother to force a separation from her young after a relatively short period of time; then, instinctively, the young know how to survive and care for themselves. But the human infant, who is so long dependent on his parents, develops slowly and painstakingly, acquiring in the process a permanent capacity to learn from experience, which is a more creative and flexible way of existence.

> Without a protected childhood in which there is time for play, mankind would probably never have arisen above an animal existence. Perhaps in the future, the playing of children will be recognized as more important than technical developments, wars and revolutions. . . .it was precisely the protection of children from the struggle to survive which favored learning and new developments.[4]

Some fear of separation is universal to children and their parents. When the young child enters kindergarten or when the young adult goes away to college, parents experience vague apprehensions and anxieties. In a study of a group of normal parents whose children were to begin school for the first time, the parents expressed concern that the streets were busy with traffic, the child would be bullied by older children, he would come home with ugly words expressing dangerous aggressive and sexual thoughts, he might even eulogize the teacher as attractive, competent, and omniscient. Many mothers expressed a sense of loneliness after the first few days of school, and both parents shared some concern that now there would be a real test as to whether they had done a good job of rearing their children during those first five years when they were all theirs.[5] Harry Golden, with great sensitivity and insight, expresses the dilemma of parents upon separation:

> I believe the most stirring moment in this experience of a parent comes on the day he leaves the child in school for the first time. This can be so sharp an experience that, where there are two or three children, this ritual has to be alternated between parents. I remember leaving one of mine there all starched up with a look of bewilderment on his face such as I never want to witness again. I held his little hand and got him registered. As we walked through the yard and corridors of the school he never took his eyes off me and never said a word: Then

came the moment to put him in a line and—leave him.

I tried to be nonchalant as I walked away but I quickly hid behind a pillar; he had never taken his eyes off me. He just looked and looked, but I could see that he filled up, but, since I am bigger, I filled up more. What an ordeal! Yet I know that the final decision could not be delayed for long. There was no law that forced me to keep watching him. I turned my back and started out slowly and then I practically ran out the door. You have to make a break.[6]

THE DISTURBED CHILD

The child who is considered a suitable candidate for residential treatment is not likely to have had the long satiation experience of nurturing and security essential to the development of identity and basic trust. His world has been chaotic, inconsistent, uncertain. His family has suffered breakdown because of events happening to his parents: separation, divorce, death, physical or emotional illness, or imprisonment. He himself may contribute to family breakdown through physical or emotional illness, severe retardation, acts of delinquency, or a combination of some or many of these factors which in their interaction are so intense and malevolent that the family can no longer tolerate or endure their impact.

One outstanding characteristic of a disturbed child is that he cannot relate to his parents without demanding infantile, primitive gratifications. He explodes with rage and aggression when these needs are frustrated. His world is filled with glaring hatred, disorganized behavior, wildly fluctuating ego states, bizarre symptoms, and distorted realities. This child cannot bear separation except to withdraw into the loneliness of himself where the dangers of abandonment are less likely and where he does not have to depend on the whim and uncertainty of adults and their world of terror. Because of the illness within him and in the parent-child relationship, he requires residential treatment.

The purpose of residential treatment is to arrange life sensibly for those children whose lives have not been sensible, to bring order to lives that have not had order, to give an experience within a new framework of security where the events of each day and the child's reaction to them are examined for meanings that gradually will appear consistent and logical to him. George Santayana said that those who cannot remember the past are condemned to repeat it.[7] In residential treatment the child repeats his past—it is the only behavior he knows. But he repeats it to have it examined by himself and others in a heightened, ordered way so that he can take up once again the torn threads of his interrupted and halted development and, from the fragment left of his life, revitalize himself into a whole human being.

> The essence of the residential process is that as each child projects his inner world against the macrocosm of the residence, by and large the staff will find from each other and within each other, the strength to resist stepping into the role of the feared parents, and give the child the nurturing and protection he needs to restore his faith in himself.[8]

It is this knowledge and conviction about the purpose and value of residential treatment that the social worker brings into his process with the parents.

FACING THE NEED
FOR RESIDENTIAL TREATMENT

As the parents face the formidable question of the child's need for residential treatment, their great fear of separation brings a feeling of isolation and loneliness. Their impulse to act, to agree quickly to place the child, to make this profound decision impulsively, is slowed and eased in casework. Indeed, it is characteristic of resistance to placement that the parents wish to bypass an understanding of the child's difficulties and the problems that exist in their relationship with him as unfolded by the study. To understand the child and their problems with him is to understand themselves, and there is a wish to avoid this pain. But there is also a wish to avoid understanding the fearful recommendation of placement—to run quickly from the child and leave him behind. The decision to run away seems less intolerable than facing thoughts about losing him, and later the parents must undo their act by returning to claim the child.

The study process, which every family is required to go through prior to any admission, aims not at a decision for residential treatment but rather at a beginning understanding of the nature of the total problem. Once the parents understand this as the first goal, the first essential, they will not feel urged or pushed, and a major part of their anxiety will be relieved with their realization that their child will not be placed until he is understood and until they share in that understanding. It is only from such a process that the importance of the need for this kind of total inpatient care begins to crystallize. When the study process deeply involves the parents and when their rights for making any decision are held foremost, treatment once embarked upon is less likely to suffer disruption. Since residential treatment is a contractual arrangement involving considerable time and expense, there must be as much assurance as possible prior to placement that both the parents and the treatment center will abide by the treatment. The important questions are consistently examined: "Can the child live with you at home?" "Can you live with him?" "If not, can you find the strength in yourself to permit the child, for an indefinite period of time, to live without you?" "But can you also see it as more than a matter of living—that it is a matter of growth, too?"

If these questions are not carefully deliberated, there will be treatment disruption at the first sign of stress. When this occurs it constitutes additional trauma for the parents, the child, the staff of the treatment center, and the children already in residence (who suffer when one of them comes and goes unexpectedly and abruptly and then begin to doubt the power and wisdom of the setting to give them protection from disruption and the logic and predictability their lives require).

The study process is not accomplished by one or two hours of work. To think that it could be is to depreciate the many-faceted aspects of the parents' thoughts and emotions and the depths of their concerns; it is also to overevaluate casework, expecting a persuasive power and magic from it which can then only bring disillusionment and a futile search for new and magical treatment methods. The process begins from the moment the parents make contact with the setting. It continues through the evaluation and study of the child, in which both parents must be deeply involved. It lasts until the parents have given enough consideration to their conflicting feelings and have arrived at sufficient understanding to risk separation.

BEFORE AND AFTER PLACEMENT

What are the feelings of parents who face the prospect of residential treatment for their child? During the study and later, during the admission procedure, a universal reaction is that the child's need of residential treatment reveals their inadequacy as parents. They have been found deficient in qualities of goodness. Their past and present anger has been evil and destructive to the child; their power to hurt him is unlimited. This anger has assumed such power, they believe, that it has damaged the child beyond repair and he will never recover. There is also anger at the recommendations (but perhaps relief, too) and a secret hope that the treatment center will fail, for if it succeeds, and the child succeeds, it will mean they have solved things in the past in the wrong way. These are forbidden thoughts that arouse guilt and the fear that if discerned further disapprobation will be brought on themselves and they will be rejected as worthless. On the other hand, if the treatment center should fail, it will mean that their own failure is less, for the child is beyond anyone's power to help.

Many parents consider residential treatment as meaning they have been of no value to their child whatsoever. The good things they have done for him, the warm, tender moments, are swept away by the totality of their bitter thoughts. They no longer have a useful function; their parental rights are entirely severed. They feel that the treatment center will now do all the work, and this confirms their helplessness, their inadequacy, and their feelings of being unwanted. They feel that even if the child is given the opportunity to grow, to get well, he may fail, and perhaps it would be better not to risk this failure after a series of so many—why gamble and risk finding out that there is no hope whatsoever? And because some parents tend to undervalue themselves, they depreciate the child and his potential strength or undervalue the child and thus themselves.

Separation from the child means that he is irretrievably lost. "Out of sight, out of mind" was the expression used by one parent. The disorganized parent, whose internal personality organization is fluid and fragmented, fears that he will lose the image of his child (the inner picture-making mechanism is broken), and this is equivalent to death. Because he feels his inner self is so chaotic, he fears that the child has similar problems of disorganization and that during the child's absence from his parents he will lose his image of them, which is the equivalent of their death. They will die and he will die.

During the interim period (after the study of the family and before admission), the social worker continues to explore with the parents the meanings of their fears, doubts, and expectations. They learn to look forward to residential treatment with hope that this, at last, is the long-hoped-for solution. They see it as having value for the relief it will give from the intolerable demands the child makes on them, and perhaps the demands they make on the child. They partially recognize that some of the chains that bind them to the child are forged with anger and guilt. These feelings are so strong that the act of giving the child into someone else's care is felt to be an act of aggression on their part. They see this reflected in the anger and doubts of the child about leaving home and their fear that as he grows big and powerful he will retaliate and destroy them. But this is because they see the child as having failed to renounce the pleasures of his instinctual life and feel that they have failed to help him move in this direction.

As the parents continue to exchange thoughts with the

social worker during this period, it becomes clear to them that they have one direct way to assist the child to begin the education of his instinctual life: by separating from him. This step calls for their work and sacrifice, the renunciation of whatever unhappy gratifications they have from the primitive aspects of the child's behavior. This renunciation is the decision for placement. Through carefully planned admission procedures in which grief reactions and depression are expressed, the social worker continues to help them understand and master their feelings. Once these are mastered, the parents are rewarded by the gradual recognition that they have accomplished something good for their child, because it brought him growth and growth to themselves as well.

After placement the parents fear that the great force, the great energy they have put into the struggle, will now be gone and that the vacuum created in their lives because of the child's absence will cause them to lose their momentum, their reason for struggle, their reason for existence. One mother said that her son was like a great wind against which she could lean and remain upright and strong; now, with him gone, she would collapse. Another mother wrote her son shortly after admission:

> Hello Honey,
>   Well, we have had it around here. Workmen all over the place. And now the roof is falling in. Then the painters again. Then the gardener. If you lose me, just check the local nut houses—that's where I'll be!
>   I missed you yesterday. . . . there is no news here . . . worth listening to that is. I forgot to tell you my bathroom window is disintegrating and both balconies are gone. I tell you, Allan, I'm getting tireder and tireder. If there is no such word as "tireder" you can take your choice and you can have it. I love you.

The parents are also afraid that they who are "bad" parents will be replaced by "good" parents. This fear is sometimes reinforced by the residential staff.

> And it will be found that categorizations of good and bad, loving and rejecting, eager to help and uncooperative, which are used subtly to dichotomize treatment

staff and parents are current in some measure in all settings where children are treated. . . . Some of the many seemingly insuperable difficulties which frequently beset the relationship between the real parents and the residential center can be linked to these feelings. Generally children who have endured a particularly unhappy life experience, or whose conditions call forth immediate pity, are more likely to evoke these fantasies and feelings in total staff with extraordinary swiftness and intensity.[9]

When rescue fantasies from the "bad" parents do occur among staff, these are accompanied by feelings of righteous indignation and passion, with the result that diagnostic and treatment goals are blurred. The parents, alert to negative attitudes, can only react with a deeper pessimism about themselves. They fear the residential staff will alienate the child from them with these hostile feelings. And attitudes of contempt for the parents are sensed by the child as an estimate of him, for he feels himself a part of his mother and father. The parents may soon develop counterrescue fantasies and wish to remove the child from the "bad, critical place," especially as the child in correspondence and during visits describes his anger toward staff, his loneliness, his wish to be withdrawn. The strength of the parents to resist the temptation to return to the former unhealthy relationship with the child is sorely tested. If these elements in the separation are carefully predicted in advance, if the parents are prepared for these actions by the child, and if the meanings of the actions are correctly interpreted, they are then able to sustain the treatment.

Some parents communicate their distress after the child is admitted by excessive letter writing and a constant stream of gifts and clothing. These mean to the child, "Do not forget me," or "I am sorry that I have sent you away, please forgive me," or "I do not wish you to forget that I am the major person in your life, you need me, I need you and I do not want you to relate yourself to others; please stay young for it is the way I love you best."

These expressions may also indicate to the child that he remains the only source of gratification for his parents, the only reason for their existence, and that they have no other avenues available to them for satisfactions and a fruitful life. Thus, loyalty struggles become inextricably confused in the process of separation. If the child is to get well, he must have his parents' permission and be sure of their conviction that it is all right for him to love others, to have regard for himself, and, finally, to regard his parents with esteem, dignity, and without fear that they will withdraw from this healthy, mature expression of his need and love for them.

WORKING WITH STAFF AND PARENTS

It is one of the essential responsibilities of the social worker to convey to all staff his knowledge and feeling about the parents, giving a whole picture of them as they really are—vital, human, and tormented. Social workers may become angry when a child's spirit is mutilated, but if they go to the other extreme and turn this anger against the parents they fail to see the mutilation of the parents' spirits, and the negative effects on their own spirits as well. When the social worker succeeds in identifying himself sufficiently with the suffering of the parents and can catch a glimpse of the extent of their terror, he is better able to provide staff with a framework of understanding. Staff will thus know better what the child carries within himself of his parents, what his life has been before he came, and what he is likely to do and repeat; they will know what the parents have within themselves that corresponds to what is in the child and, then, how these forces continue to interact even though there is physical separation.

> Mrs. B. recalled that as a youngster she had been like the patient, whining and clinging to her mother, frightened of separation. When Mrs. B. left her son with us, she was depressed, and at home she felt confused, disorganized, helpless, and without strength to do much. In the residence, a child care worker who had noticed Mr. B.'s son meandering aimlessly and morosely about reported: "Instinctively I put my hand on Ben's shoulder. He spun around and embraced me tightly. I sat down and still holding on he sat on my lap. He squeezed

me for a moment and I commented on his wish to be small. He said, 'I'd like to be smaller than the youngest child here. I'd like to be one year old. No! I'd rather be no months old and be small enough to crawl back in my mother's stomach.'

"At this point he moved off my lap and sitting next to me continued, 'I'd like to be smaller than a dot.' I said, 'Maybe you'd like to start all over again.'

"Ben said, 'Yes I would so I could be in my mother's stomach and she would eat and eat and I'd get bigger and she'd get fatter and fatter; so fat, two by four, can't get throught the bathroom door. And she'd try and try and she'd break down the wall of Southard School and get into the bathroom and then I could start all over and I wouldn't have to come to Southard School.'"

During the first months of residential treatment, the social worker listens to what the parents say, write, or telephone to him, translating back to them the essence of their concerns. Hannah Arendt has written, "True understanding does not tire of interminable dialogue and 'vicious circles,' because it trusts that imagination will eventually catch at least a glimpse of the frightening light of truth."[10] And if the social worker translates this light of truth with kindness, warmth, clarity, and intelligence, it will become clear that there are no absolutes. Placement is an intervention which at first may seem all injury, all loss. As the child struggles to be without his parents and solve his problems and as they struggle to live without him, antagonism and despair seem paramount. This is often revealed through correspondence.

Dear Dr. W.,
    Would it be possible for me to visit. It's hard not hearing from Don himself. I get the feeling that I have to see him before something snaps. Who says the world is round? Don is way out in Kansas and that may be beyond the edge of the disc, where things drop off.
    One if by land and two if by sea!

Dear Mousie,
    Those hamsters are as smart as they can be. I guess it gripes them that we are just a little bit smarter. They have discovered that if they work real hard they can squeeze out of their cage. I had them out in the patio yesterday. . . . All of a sudden, one of the little monsters escaped. . . . Finally Daddy looked behind the wall, and

there the little thing was trembling and looking all around. I guess he was kind of scared, being out in the big world all alone. Served him right . . . because now I won't let them out of the house again.

Dear Cindy,
It has been a tough day. I believe that I am getting old for somehow I get more tired more easily. . . . What is more those things which used to act as incentives no longer do so. . . . I am dog tired. It just seems as though things just pile up. Believe me Cindy, it is a tough life and no one knows it better than you do.

The feeling that all is lost is an extremely egocentric one. The parents attach to their feelings an absolute value that obscures everything but their own dilemma. This position is a massive defense, and as long as it exists there is a stalemate in which no forward action is conceived as possible. When the worker indicates that placement is not the end but the beginning, that their involvement is not only desired but necessary, the parents are relieved; but anger comes from the opposite extreme position—that placement in and of itself does not absolve the parents of struggle, of the need to understand the child and themselves and to come together with him when there is a strategic need to do so. Slowly, parents are able to reenter the struggle, but now from the designed, protected position of carefully timed contacts in which there is no overloading of such severe emotional intensity that the parents and child are injured. It is as if once powerful magnets came together with such force that separation meant a ripping-apart rather than a coming-together and leaving when the life situation demanded it.

Dear Mr. M.:
Nice to see you and talk with you again. I did have a good visit with Harry. Feel much better about him. At times he displays a good deal of hostility toward me. If he has that much then it is better that he can display it, although it is a little difficult to take at times. He is mighty precious to us, and we are so glad that you people took him. He would not have had a chance otherwise. Usually when I return, I am depressed for several days, sometimes for weeks. Now it is different. I get over things much more quickly. Each time I have more strength to walk. This was the best yet. I believe that slowly I am emerging from the woods.

Absence from the child is more than a matter of suspended animation, a continuation of old routines; it is a matter of healing and growth, too. For absence, sustained by the relationship with the social worker, has a healing power. When the parents are encouraged to assure the child that as he grows stronger they do not get weaker, and that he is not expected to return home in order to take care of them, they will examine this need and expectation from their child and trace its irrational sources. For some parents, the closeness to the child has served to ward off their fear of facing other relationships in which their own inadequacies might be uncovered; a fear of facing life situations whose demands would be too harsh, too perfectionistic. Placement gives the parents the needed opportunity and freedom to seek a reunion with each other, to test carefully available strengths, to relate to others, to enter new activities and pursuits. To their surprise, the collapse they expected to undergo does not occur. Much of the resistance of professional people to separation of the child from his family for the purpose of residential treatment is based on the fear that the family will disintegrate. The current crisis in the family brings so much to the fore that is regressive that underlying strengths of parents to sustain themselves are covered over and underestimated.

When the parents reveal their feelings that it is *they* who have been abandoned, these feelings are gently highlighted by the worker. The perception of the parents is then widened to permit them to assure the child that he has not been abandoned and that he has their permission to feel less lonely for them. Much of the unconscious protest of the parents about the child's growth seems based on the fear that should he achieve levels of maturity they have not been able to gain he will then be beyond their control and his power will be used destructively. Thus, sexual strivings are feared lest they go awry, and aggression and learning are feared because they might be turned into delinquent activities—all this corresponding to what is tenuous and poorly integrated in the personality of the parents. But it is possible to master these fears as the parents observe the child mastering them in his new environment. And as they understand some of the barriers overcome by the child, to some extent they overcome their own.

What further gives the child freedom to move on is the confidence that his parents have other gratifications in their lives that occupy them. He is not the center of their universe, and they are not totally stricken at his loss. The knowledge that he can crush his parents because he is everything in their lives is too awesome a power for any child. Once he is relieved of this power, a tremendous burden is lifted from his shoulders, and he is no longer an omnivorous monster but a small child who wants care from powerful but safe adults. Further, the child must have his parents' optimism that a new world is offered him and that they are not jealous or resentful of it. "After all there is freedom in not being loved too deeply, in not being thought of too often. Possessive love makes most of the complication and nearly all of the unhappiness in the world." [11]

LIFE — NOT DEATH

The interpretation in casework of these feelings in the parents does not deal with their unconscious. True, these are deep feelings, but they are sharply apparent as the parents react. They are expressed directly or through metaphor, analogy, displacements, and projections, but very close to the surface of awareness. As the worker urges the parents to think with him, cross-lacing back and forth what the child does and its consequences to them, and what they do and its consequences to the child, the worker couches his language, thoughts, and feelings in terms of what is logical and consistent with societal expectations. And if these societal expectations are logical and consistent, they are consonant with principles of healthy growth and development. Through such a process, strength and positive feelings gain ascendancy. And as the parents lose their exclusive self-preoccupation and turn outward toward the child and toward work and friends as other sources of gratification, they do not fear loneliness.

Separation is then not an act of death, but of life and growth. This is the contribution of the social worker in helping heal the parents. His efforts coincide and intertwine with those of other disciplines invested in residential treatment, where united energy in a collective enterprise frees the human gifts in parents and their children.

NOTES

1. Philip Thody, *Albert Camus* (London: Hamish Hamilton, 1957), p. 28.
2. Erik Erikson, *Childhood and Society* (New York: W. W. Norton & Co., 1950), p. 219
3. "Notes on the Development of Empathy," in *The Psychoanalytic Study of the Child,* vol. 13 (New York: International Universities Press, 1958), p. 515.
4. Henno Martin, *The Sheltering Desert* (New York: Thomas Nelson & Sons, 1958), p. 140.
5. Donald C. Klein and Ann Ross, "Kindergarten Entry: A Study of Role Transition," in *Orthopsychiatry and the School,* ed. Morris Krugman (New York: American Orthopsychiatric Association, 1958).
6. Harry Golden, *Only in America* (Cleveland: World Publishing Co., 1958), p. 49.
7. Clifton Fadiman, *The Lifetime Reading Plan* (Cleveland: World Publishing Co., 1960), p. 14.
8. Rudolf Ekstein, Judith Wallerstein, and Arthur Mandelbaum, "Countertransference in the Residential Treatment of Children," in *The Psychoanalytic Study of the Child,* vol. 14 (New York: International Universities Press, 1959), p. 186.
9. *Ibid.,* p. 189.
10. Hannah Arendt, "Understanding and Politics," *Partisan Review,* vol. 20 (July-August 1953): p. 392.
11. Ellen Glasgow, *The Sheltered Life* (Garden City, N.Y.: Doubleday, 1932), p. 252.

5. The Institutional Management of Sex in Emotionally Disturbed Children

Elton B. McNeil and William C. Morse

Surprisingly, the many volumes written about the institutional care of emotionally disturbed children rarely make systematic reference to the problems of dealing with sex. An examination of the indexes of such books would give little clue to the seriousness of the problem of behavior among institutionalized children. While sex is discussed and commented on, it is not delineated as systematically as are other impulse systems such as aggression. Most descriptions of sexual attitudes, feelings, or behavior are limited to the confines of a case history format and suggest that problems, when they occur, are individual rather than group issues. The paradox presented by this relative lack of attention arises from the fact that professionals experienced in caring for emotionally disturbed children regularly report that sexual behavior is a delicate and difficult psychological problem requiring sensitive management by responsible adults. In theory, sex is accorded the role of prime mover; in the literature of practice it does not seem to be accorded this status.

In rare instances, clear and detailed accounts are given both of the nature of sexual behavior among

Reprinted from the *American Journal of Orthopsychiatry*, vol. 34, no. 1 (January 1964), pp. 115-24, by permission of the authors and the journal.

institutionalized children and of the techniques and principles of adult response to it. There is substantial question whether these reports reflect practices typical of most institutions, but the norms for comparison are not readily available. Probably the most extreme statement of practice and belief is to be found in A. S. Neill's description of Summerhill. He maintains, for example, that "sex is the basis of all negative attitudes toward life,"[2] that "heterosexual play in childhood is the royal road . . . to a healthy, balanced adult sex life,"[3] and that "at Summerhill, nothing is unmentionable and no one is shockable."[4] The discrepancy between his theory and practice is made clear when he notes, "If in Summerhill I approved of my adolescent pupils sleeping together, my school would be suppressed by the authorities."[5] It is difficult to find a modern, systematic, and detailed representation of the more conservative point of view, which probably characterizes the average institution.

The scarcity of careful delineation of the principles of institutional management of sex in emotionally disturbed children exists with good reason. In part, it occurs because professional views of the sexual attitudes and behavior of children are probably more "radical" and "permissive" than those held by the average member of society. Then too, institutional life is a highly artificial subsociety that has unique needs and demands that must be met if it is to maintain an operational stability. A vital additional force promoting the avoidance of this aspect of clinical management can be traced to the fact that, even among professionally "liberated" childcare workers, sexual behavior in children is not responded to with as much psychological comfort as are other forms of behavior. Finally, there is an illusion that extensive agreement exists regarding a psychologically healthy approach to sex education for children—an illusion that retains its apparent substance by avoiding close scrutiny.

THE VARIETIES OF SEXUAL EXPRESSION

As an example of the problems of institutional

management of sex, we will refer to some aspects of the behavior of the population of emotionally disturbed boys who attend the University of Michigan Fresh Air Camp. The camp is a clinical training center for graduate students drawn from the fields of clinical psychology, psychiatric nursing, psychiatric social work, and special education; the campers are boys recruited from detention homes, training schools, mental hospitals, and clinics throughout the state of Michigan. As a short-term diagnostic and therapeutic training center, we deal with a broad spectrum of symptoms and degrees of emotional distubance.

The range of sexual behavior that may eventually emerge among some campers in this setting includes sexual language and gestures, "playing the dozens,"[7] group and individual masturbation, homosexuality, exhibitionism, attempts to promote heterosexual experience, and some standard and not-so-standard perversions. Lest the wrong interpretation be made, it should be noted that this kaleidoscope of sexuality is a range of behaviors and not the mode.

Unlike a "closed" institution, the camp is an "open" setting, which tends to exaggerate or highlight the range, frequency, and intensity of sexual expression. The camp community is effectively isolated from the traffic of persons who usually enter and exit from the typical hospital ward while performing their specialized duties. The pattern of shift working is less pronounced, and 24-hour-a-day contact through the sharing of meals and recreation areas breeds a quick familiarity among all community members. Thus, while a clinical camp for disturbed children is not representative of other institutions, the uniqueness of its social and psychological structure is particularly advantageous for the study of sexual behavior in its full-blown form.

At camp, the first few days constitute a nonsexual "honeymoon." During this time of ferreting out the social and sexual mores of the institution, a polite facade masks the underlying motives of some campers. Before long, there is an outburst of rage on the part of one of the children, and this rage is accompanied, naturally, by profanity or sexual reference directed at a fellow camper or restraining counselor. The ripple of shock that accompanies this action is apparent in the other campers even when it is treated casually by the counselors. The ability to shock or to take others aback carries with it a substantial prestige value, and what was done in rage soon becomes the product of cold calculation. Rapidly, sexual reference is employed in behalf of aggression, resistance, and defiance of adult authority, and the degree of contagion is substantial. While many of the younger children know the words but not the music of sexual swearing, its spread and elevation to the commonplace is rapid.

Sexual language, when repeated with sufficient frequency, tends to bleach out the affect associated with it. It soon suffers the impotence of the commonplace, and thus the originator is forced to a new level of innovation. This often takes the form of sexual gestures. The advantage accruing to these manifestations of sex lies in the space-conquering capacity. An emotionally disturbed child can signal some insult across the length of a dining hall and accomplish his nefarious ends at long distance. Any form of sexual expression at these lower levels must be promoted constantly to a new, more complex, and more dazzling achievement if it is to maintain the interest of the peer audience. Sexual language may evolve into "playing the dozens" as an exercise in verbal sexual proficiency, it may take the form of peer sexual invitation, or it may find its outlet in an exhibitionistic display of sexuality on the part of the child. Sexual conversations often focus on fantasies about adult sexual behavior, and it is apparent that these contain thinly veiled anxiety and curiosity about parents, rather than adults in general. For the child, aggression has become a paramount issue, and sex is pressed into its service. Physiological events such as enuresis and encopresis become suspect as subtle sexual expressions (or at least complications in the direct expression of sexuality) and, because of the varying levels of psychological and psychosexual maturity among the witnessing children, confusion reigns.

What was an individual sexual enterprise often becomes

a group phenomenon within small subgroups. The level of dynamic group excitement that can be provoked by sexual overtures is unparalleled. The final phase of this burgeoning sexuality for the minority of the children expresses itself in two fashions: (1) an intense concern with the personal life (translated "sexual life") of the counselors and (2) an attempt to promote sexual experience with the female counselors. This latter has a quality reminiscent of the early 1900s about it. The male children view the female sex impulse as something akin to a raging beast that needs only to have the bars of its cage rattled. Sex talk and exhibitionism (pulling down one another's trousers, provocative dances, and the like) are viewed as potent stimuli that will somehow sexually excite the female of the species. The fact that the reality never matches the fantasy does not deter a child who may be acting out a seduction fantasy.

It must be emphasized that sex constitutes only one of the huge variety of problems we deal with among our disturbed boys. There are many of our 70 clients who *never* get involved sexually at any level, and while a steady undercurrent of sexuality may exist for some cabin groups it may remain fairly quiescent in its expression, flaring up only occasionally. Our clinical efforts are directed, primarily, toward the management of aggression and in dealing with a number of kinds of neurotic conflict.

The management problems posed by these sexual expressions can be arranged under three broad headings: (1) the management of sexuality, (2) the fusion of sex and aggression, and (3) the adult response to various sexual actions.

THE MANAGEMENT OF SEXUALITY

Perhaps the single greatest error made by adults dealing with distrubed children is underestimating the amount of guilt and anxiety that is generated by sexual activities and thoughts. These emotions complicate the process of management, since they serve to produce an emotional hangover which, in turn, becomes motivation in other situations. It is difficult to deal with sexual events and achieve closure for specific incidents in the short run. In most institutions the child comes into continuous contact with a variety of persons, and a sexual situation mishandled by one adult can trigger a chain of emotional outbursts the source of which is almost undetectable. The subsequent mishandling compounds and complicates the original event.

The attempt to shortcut the intensification of psychological distress follows a general set of principles at the Fresh Air Camp. We start with an assumption of the naturalness of the urge to sexual expression, an awareness of the extensive social prohibitions that apply to it, and a wariness about the overdetermination of sexual behavior. Sexual language, for example, is not reacted to with shock or surprise, but it is *not* encouraged by any staff member. Since such behavior is socially unacceptable, attempts are made to analyze its source, to help the child understand the motivation behind it, to substitute some more acceptable form of expression, and to restrict its appearance to private situations if it does not abate. The logic of this modified form of social control is that public sexual language, or behavior for that matter, infringes on the freedom of others, is socially disapproved, and produces emotional difficulties for other disturbed children. Thus, although the fact of sexuality is not disapproved, it is classified as a private activity, and the source and nature of public views of sex are explained. Children—even most emotionally disturbed ones—seem to be able to comprehend the logic of firm but understanding social control of sex. This is not to say, of course, that this necessarily results in adequate control.

Sexual information is supplied to the children whenever it is requested and the request is deemed legitimate. More than once our graduate student counselors have been duped by the children in this respect. The counselors' emotional investment in education, learning, and the "facts" of life makes them leap to the unwarranted conclusion that childish ignorance is the prime offender and prime source of sexual activity. Disturbed children as

well as normal ones can use a sex education lecture as a
sniggering, leering, vicarious source of sexual excitement.
While there is a vast amount of misinformation mixed with
patches of sophistication, even the child who needs
information needs more than that. He needs a thorough
exploration of his attitudes, beliefs, and feelings, since it is
in that area that he suffers most.

A usual device for the management of sexuality is to
reduce the level of temptation to which the child is
exposed. This need not be perceived as "spying" or
"patrolling" by the children although, in fact, it achieves
this end. The presence of adults during most of the waking
hours of the child, if it is not restrictive, helps him past
times he could not otherwise manage comfortably. These
adults ought to be able to deal with sex in a calm,
unemotional, and intelligent way.

FUSION OF SEX AND AGGRESSION

The problems of controlling sexual behavior and its
attendant anxiety and guilt come primarily as a consequence of the fusion of sex and aggression. Among
disturbed boys, both the sexual behavior and its con-
comitants soon are tinged with aggressive overtones. The
camp specializes in "children who hate," and most of their
psychological problems sooner or later become focused on
aggression, yet any disturbed child is an easy prey for this
admixture of motives. The male sexual role is normally
one of enterprise and domination, and its regulation and
balance require a high degree of sensitivity to the more
passive female partner. The blunted sensibility of damaged
children blurs the distinction between self-assertion and
hostility; in this way, sex and aggression become almost
indistinguishable. Whether his excursions are homosexual,
heterosexual, or exhibitionistic, they have an assaultive
quality about them. Sex language and gesture become
almost desexualized in these children as they use them to
offend adults and peers alike. The child who hates adults,
who have always been viewed as punishing, finds sexual
acting out a natural weapon.

The sorting out of sex and aggression is difficult for both the therapist and the child since sex has a physically pleasurable side to it. The child maintains that the excitement and gratification is a sufficient end in itself, and the attempt to outline its aggressive components meets a wall of resistance. Adults suffer the same confusion of interpretation of motives, and this complicates the task of therapy of sex problems. It is necessary to distinguish clearly between these motives since control is otherwise impossible.

Even anger uses sex as a weapon.[8] Since the most potent taboo is that referring to incest, it comes as no surprise that in almost every culture—as well as a delinquent one—the accusation about the sexual relations between mother and son is the most provocative. We have never seen a delinquent subculture whose members were not immediately ready for combat at the imputation that one of them had intercourse with his mother. The taboo adds vitality to the level of offense, and this pattern is repeated over and over.

In much the same way, homosexuality via intercourse or fellatio usually requires substantial aggression to accomplish its aim. Acts of this sort are dealt with as one part of the total manifestation of the sexual impulse, but their socially disapproved nature is made quite clear. An attempt is made to teach the child—without criticism—the reality of social life, and it is usually a tempered version of middle-class reality.

ADULT RESPONSE TO SEXUAL BEHAVIOR

Some of the general principles involved in adult reactions to sexuality can be described even though an exhaustive list is beyond the scope of this paper.

The Dangers of Suppression

The most common method used by child care workers in institutions as a whole takes the form of a generalized suppression of sexual behavior in the child. While motives for this action may be credible, its effect is seldom therapeutic. It acts first to ignore the meaning of the sexual act. Any such single remedy must neccessarily omit consideration of the causes and be ill adapted to the individual case. There is much too thin a line between "you shouldn't" and "it is wrong" for the child to discern, and the ease with which such adult actions can be misinterpreted by the disturbed child is too great a risk to take. Suppression, too, is self-defeating, since it attempts to cover up symptoms rather than to deal with causes and sets the stage for a much greater outburst at some later time.

Protection of the Innocent

This becomes the basic reason for dealing in detail with disapproved forms of sexual expression, and there are many "innocents" to be protected. Innocence in this respect can refer to the kind, quality, and timing of the child's previous experience. The unsophisticated child who is introduced to advanced levels of sexuality without comprehending what it is all about cannot put the experience into a meaningful or reasonable perspective. In such circumstances the emotions he will experience will not match the behavior he displays or to which he is exposed.

Among the innocents are the adults whose own adjustment may be perilous in the sexual area and for whom such events are a threat to their personal defenses. The child can provoke highly negative counterbehavior in the adult and then use this as a source for subtle and unspecified psychological blackmail in future interpersonal transactions. Parents of institutionalized children who witness or hear reports of overt sexual expression in the institution can use this as the basis for countermeasures directed against the institution and its staff, and this continuing threat undermines the child care worker's resolve to deal dispassionately with youthful sexual expression. Objections to the sexual acting out of institutionalized children may even come from professionals unacquainted with the facts of life of living with disturbed children and not just from disturbed parents. All sexual incidents are potentially explosive since they may produce so much injury to "innocent bystanders."

Criterion for Intercession in Sexual Behavior

It is apparent that all the usual concerns about understanding the individual child should be invoked here, but the question of determing the exact moment of interference has ramifications that go beyond the individual case. If the effect on the group is the determining factor rather than the act itself, then we must consider dimensions such as the cohesion of the group, its leadership structure, the role of the child in the group, the social class of the group's members, and the sociometric character of the interaction of the individuals.[9] The life style of the group and the group mechanisms for meeting threatening situations must all be considered. It is apparent that an act that would be dangerous if viewed solely from the vantage point of the individual case history may be rendered innocuous by group support. The decision to intercede and the timing and technique for doing so are, of course, functions of the clinical experience and philosophy of the worker. No rule of thumb is applicable, but a general tendency to ignore the structure of the peer group in such decisions is too widespread for comfort.

The Role of Neutrality

It is axiomatic that there is no neutral zone for adults dealing with the sexual expressions of children. Adults who lean too heavily on a device such as ignoring low-level expressions of sex will soon find the child taking advantage of this tacit permission to promote a more advanced form of behavior. Too, adults react to sex as though legal rules of evidence were necessary for it to be discussed. Where a child will be queried about the possibility that he stole or aggressed against another child, adults may require incontrovertible evidence before initiating an inquiry about sexual misbehavior; the children capitalize on the adult's reluctance to probe the area of sexual behavior and use this lack of adult attention as a lever against the adult. Exploration of possible sexual incidents is, of course, an extremely tortuous task. Children obfuscate, lie, cover up, and deny with an unspoken agreement to maintain a wall of silence toward the controlling adults. The tentativeness of the adult's approach to the task often is a sufficient cue for the child, and he reacts accordingly; that is, he launches his most powerful weapons at what he detects to be a flaw in the adult psychological structure. Adult neutrality most often is a defensive avoidance of sex; true neutrality is an infinitely complex therapeutic maneuver.

Combined Individual and Group Management

Sooner or later in every institution, pairs of children or small groups of children will present the staff with a problem of management of sexuality. The jumble of accusation and counteraccusation that usually emerges from the attempt to "get the facts" requires a substantial amount of time to straighten out, and the group structure must be put back together after its chaotic falling apart over such incidents. The children must continue to live with one another, and a shared, public, group understanding must be reached. Each member of the group must be aware of what every other member of the group has agreed to and now understands about the situation, if further group decay is to be warded off.[10]

Achieving a group understanding is only the first step in the process. The individual reaction of each child must be dealt with, since he views his relationship with the group in a highly personalized way. His emotions must be "mopped up," and the impact of the group incident must be interpreted in terms of the details of his individual case history. There are always a host of personal reactions that cannot comfortably be exposed before the other members of the group without jeopardizing his standing in it and his relationship to its power structure. This is a step that may be neglected only at considerable cost to the future of adult-child therapeutic transactions, yet it may easily be omitted under the press of time that combined group and individual working-through requires. It is our impression that, on the average, less than the necessary time is devoted to exploring all the ramifications of sexual incidents and that they are inadequately handled as a consequence.

Adult Denial of Reality

There remains the estimation of relative risk in having the adult overreact to sexuality or having him deny its existence. Denial differs from being neutral in that its appearance is seemingly unconscious. Evidences of sexual activity that would set off an alarm bell in the consciousness of an experienced worker most often are overlooked by novices. It often seems that those closest to (that is, have a relationship with) the child are unaware of sexual material that seems blatant to an outside observer. Most often, erotic arousal in the child is "therapeutically" permitted with an unclear view of what is therapeutic about the passive acceptance of overt sexual expression. The distinction between acceptance and permission is an indistinct one, and when an adult is willing to sanction moderate sexual expression, he may not always be willing to sanction the excess to which it may shortly lead. The subtle encouragement provided by remaining passive at the first stages of such expression always exists as a high contrast to the later restrictiveness that appears when the bounds of "propriety" have been trespassed.

Sex Education

We have followed a frequent institutional practice of calling on the pediatrician or medical representative for educational efforts around the topic of sex. While it would seem that the weight of medical authority would ease the tensions in such a situation, we have met with variable success with such an approach. It is lamentable that sex should be classified as a physiological problem in such a cavalier fashion. It may be that if we are to be completely honest with children we ought to teach them sex at the level the average childcare worker understands it rather than at the sometimes awkward, esoteric, and somewhat clinical and anatomical level of the medical specialist.

The continuing effort to substitute obscure, Latin-derived terminology for sexual parts and functions is again some measure of our own inability to face the reality of sex as adults know it. It seems more rational, psychologically, to rely less on clinical terminology than to use commonplace terms while focusing on the emotional and attitudinal components of sex. This seems logically to involve a frank discussion of the children's own personal sex habits and practices when called for and suggests that the average childcare worker needs more than casual instruction about the means and methods of sex education.

The most usual assumption is that every "normal" adult comes fully equipped with the capacity to educate the young in our society about such matters—an assumption that hardly seems warranted by the facts. The discomfort of adults (as well as the lack of essential vocabulary) should not be underestimated, but it regularly is, because of the discomfort most professionals feel about breeching this taboo topic. If we are truly interested in convincing disturbed children that sex is not an area of extensive taboos, then we must look to an extensive reorganization of our current methods of sex education; the reality we all know must be inserted in the sex-educational process.

The Need for Supervision

This category refers to the supervision of adult workers rather than of the children. In any institutional setting a certain amount of sexual byplay will exist between the adults, and these events are highly subject to misinterpretation by the children. Not only must the usual level of social interplay by supervised and regulated, but continuous observations of the day-by-day interaction of adults and children ought to be subject to scrutiny. The stimulus value of an attractive female with an unconsciously provocative manner should not be overlooked. The contagion of sexual behavior is great, and an originally innocent action can trigger a totally disproportionate reaction in a group of disturbed children. We have found again and again that female childcare workers make friendly overtures to male children in a manner that may be indistinguishable from the seductiveness that is more appropriately expended on male courting partners. In much the same fashion, male adult childcare workers can fall easily into a pattern of relationship that closely resembles that of a peer member of the "gang." Swapping tales of early sexual experiences and using a "one of the boys" approach has its dangers if it is not lodged in a properly mature adult worker.

Consciously or unconsciously, the male and female childcare workers may slip into a form of relationship that is hardly calculated to contribute to the development and growth of the child. It is in this area that careful supervision is an absolute essential and, at the same time, it is an area that may be neglected. Adults need to distinguish between these personal and clinical sex attitudes and come to some understanding of the congruence between them.

The Balance of Freedom and Restraint

A working institutional code always must walk the tightrope of freedom and restraint. In institutions dominated by the personality of a single outstanding theorist or director, for better or for worse, policy becomes clear if not always coherent. Most institutions are not organized in such a hierarchical fashion, and practice becomes the fashioner of theory. For whichever side of the freedom-restraint continuum the policy leans, reasonable theoretical justification can be found, since the objective facts are so hard to ascertain.

The credible arguments for controlling and restraining the overt appearance of sexuality in children tend to focus on the acting-out quality of such expresions. The point is made that institutionalized children (particularly those in psychiatric institutions) usually suffer a substantial degree of regression to begin with, and sexual acting out serves only to drive them deeper into their regressed state. These children need to be protected from the confusion, guilt, and anxiety attendant on the deepening regression. The suggestion is made that children need and want to be controlled until they are capable of managing themselves, and to deny this control is to abandon the child to his pathology and its destructive effects. While sexual acting out may be cathartic, such expressions may defeat the therapeutic goal of substituting thought processes for socially disapproved action. This line of reasoning suggests that the institution's responsibility for establishing a socially acceptable patterning of child behavior requires that from the beginning it make such behavior ego-alien, not ego-syntonic. An equally cogent set of theoretical principles can be used to defend just the opposite institutional policy; it is this adult theoretical uncertainty that encourages a vacillating policy that shifts with the fashions of the times.

The Circle of Guilt

It has been noted that sex can be pressed into the service of aggression and thus become a two-headed therapeutic issue. Perhaps a source of equal difficulty is to be found in the regularity with which sexual expression induces a guilt that can be assuaged only by some concrete punishment. Confession and discussion may not seem adequate atonement for what the child may see as the enormity of his transgression. In the magical thinking of the unconscious, the violation of a powerful taboo can be cleansed only by an antidote of equal power. In such instances the offending child may embark on a program of violence and provocation calculated to force the adult to punish and thus "even" his psychic score. The almost compulsive nature of the child's relentless search for freedom from guilt and anxiety can continue until his goal is reached and the adult finally disciplines the child (perhaps days later) for (in the child's mind) his sexual infraction. By this time in the child's sequence of behavior, he may have provoked so much anger and resentment among his peers or adults that the whole issue circles back on itself in a prolonged series of retaliations and counter-retaliations that can be traced to the original sexual transgression.

In much the same fashion, children who commit sexual acts that produce substantial feelings of guilt may redouble sexual as well as aggressive activity in an attempt to relieve guilt by sharing it with many others. The psychic isolation of being the lone offender is intolerable to most children, and they feel less guilt-ridden if others share their plight.

CONCLUSION

At the very least it must be concluded that the institutional management of sexual expression among institutionalized children has not received the theoretical attention so vital a topic warrants. It seems evident that the social taboos decried by professionals as prime sources of emotional disturbance have their counterpart among professionals in institutional life. The taboos appear in various guises ranging from the absence of professional concern in the literature through the lack of provision for training of childcare workers to the inadequate supervision of workers who make important daily decisions about managing sex in the institution. The illusion that there exists a high degree of agreement about the principles of hygienic management of sex would be dispelled quickly by any concerted attempt to discuss the issue.

NOTES

1. A. Aichorn, *Wayward Youth* (New York: Viking Press, 1935); H. Alt, *Residential Treatment for the Disturbed Child* (New York: International Universities Press, 1960); E. M. Baylor and E. D. Monachesi, *The Rehabilitation of Children* (New York: Harper & Bros., 1939); B. Bettelhiem, *Love Is Not Enough* (Glencoe, Ill.: Free Press, 1950); idem, *Truants from Life* (Glencoe, Ill.: Free

Press, 1955); F. J. Cohen, *Children in Trouble: An Experiment in Institutional Child Care* (New York: W. W. Norton & Co., 1952); G. Konopka, *Group Work in the Institution: A Modern Challenge* (New York: William Morrow & Co., 1954); M. F. Mayer, *A Guide for Child-Care Workers* (New York: Child Welfare League of America, 1958); F. Redl and D. Wineman, *Children Who Hate* (Glencoe, Ill.: Allen & Unwin, 1951); idem, *Controls from Within* (Glencoe, Ill.: Free Press, 1952); A. Weaver, *They Steal for Love* (New York: International Universities Press, 1959).

2. A. S. Neill, *Summerhill* (New York: Hart Publishing Co., 1960), p. 206.
3. Ibid.
4. Ibid., p. 233.
5. Ibid., p. 209.
6. E. B. McNeil, ed., "Therapeutic Camping for Disturbed Youth," *Journal of Social Issues* 13, no. 1 (1957): 1-64; E. B. McNeil and R. J. Cohler, Jr., "Adult Aggression in the Management of Disturbed Children," *Child Developments* 24, no. 4 (1958): 45-61; W. C. Morse and D. Wineman, "Group Interviewing in a Camp for Disturbed Boys," *Journal of Social Issues* 13, no. 1 (1957): 23-32; idem, "The Therapeutic Use of Social Isolation in a Camp for Ego-Disturbed Boys," *Journal of Social Issues* 13, no. 1 (1957): 32-40.
7. R. F. Berdie, "Playing the Dozens," *Journal of Abnormal and Social Psychology* 42 (1947): 120-21; C. L. Golightly and I. Scheiffler, "Playing the Dozens," *Journal of Abnormal and Social Psychology* 43 (1948): 104-5.
8. E. B. McNeil, "Psychology and Aggression," *Journal of Conflict Resolution* 3, no. 3 (1959): 195-293.
9. E. B. McNeil, "Two Styles of Expression: Motoric and Conceptual," in *Inner Conflict and Defense*, eds. D. R. Miller and G. E. Swanson (New York: Henry Holt & Co., 1960), pp. 337-56.
10. Morse and Wineman, "Group Interviewing," op. cit.

6. Therapeutic Use of Visiting in Residential Treatment

Sylvester Adessa and Audrey Laatsch

Most children in residential treatment centers have living parents whose direct and periodic contact with them through visiting may either aid or impede the course of therapy. Collateral treatment of parents, be it supportive or insightful, is a widely accepted accompaniment to the inpatient therapy of the child. Not yet clearly conceptualized are the therapeutic principles that are needed to guide the treatment institution in making the many decisions about visiting between parent and child.

"Visiting policies" indeed exist. Not infrequently they date from an earlier, less treatment-oriented phase in the center's development and may no longer be compatible with current treatment objectives. The disparity between overall treatment intent and actual visiting practice can and does result in subtle but serious obstacles to treatment, with staff unable to pinpoint quite what went wrong, and why.

Should parents visit each week? Should they visit at all? Are visits to be restricted to the grounds? Under what conditions should the child visit home? What safeguards can the treatment agency enforce? These and similar questions recur insistently, plaguing all levels of staff. In

Reprinted from *Child Welfare*, vol. 44, no. 5 (May 1965), pp. 245-51, by permission of the authors and the journal.

the absence of clear guideposts, they tend to be answered inconsistently or in terms of staff convenience rather than on the basis of treatment objectives. Yet visiting arrangements solidly based and carried out with conviction and average competency are essential for therapeutic gain.

The special and vivid importance of visiting arises from the fact that it repeatedly confronts the child with the primary libidinal objects linked to his deepest conflicts. Aside from inherent constitutional factors, it is the quality and duration of the child's earliest object relationships with parent figures that largely established the terms on which subsequent life experiences were met and that ultimately necessitated the major step of placement in a residential treatment unit. Each visit reactivates the conflicts and ambivalence involved in the parent-child relationship. There is no doubt that visiting is emotionally supercharged for the child and the parents — and for staff as well. Issues involved in visiting, therefore, cannot safely be left to policy making that is not based on dynamic understanding of its meaning.

In this paper we attempt to draw some generalizations of therapeutic value from the vicissitudes of visiting as experienced and worked out at Lakeside Children's Center.[1] Its population consists mainly of youngsters with weak and fragmented egos who are seriously defective in adaptive capabilities. Early and pervasive psychic trauma, frequently accompanied by actual deprivation and physical abuse, characterizes the children's histories. Clinically, about one-fourth of the children are psychotic, most of the others have character disorders or are ego-defective, and a few are basically neurotic.

It is axiomatic that seriously damaged children cannot achieve sound ego growth in a short time. The process of residential treatment is that of ego building rather than only ego rebuilding; it is more habilitative than rehabilitative. Because treatment is lengthy, children reside at Lakeside for many years — only infrequently for less than four or five. With few exceptions, children stay for as long as their individual treatment requires. The agency is viewed by children, staff, and parents as that place where the children *live*, not as a temporary way station. They reside in long-term security at an institution that tries to fulfill most of their needs, protects them from disintegrating periods of stress, and provides opportunity for growth.

BASIC PRINCIPLES UNDERLYING VISITING

In residential treatment, individual psychotherapy, therapeutic education, and the child's daily living experiences together give him maximal opportunities to overcome severe developmental fixations so that growth processes may resume. All aspects of his life-in-residence are potentially capable of having therapeutic impact. It follows, then, that the timing, handling, and arrangements of all visits to the child fall within the treating agency's responsibility. Factors of plant design, staffing pattern, and controlling auspices may make for variations in visiting arrangements among treatment institutions, but the principles on which such plans need to be based remain the same.

The basic guiding principles are: (1) visiting must preclude such stress as triggers internal conflict, defensive behavior, and ego disintegration that in magnitude and kind seriously impedes or prevents treatment (note that this formulation does not state that visiting either can or should obviate stress per se) and (2) visiting should maximize growth-producing aspects of the parent-child relationship.

Ego disintegration can best be minimized or avoided by anticipating stressful situations and then obviating them through the creative use of a variety of individualized arrangements. The center has the prerogative of varying the frequency, the duration, and the locale of visiting, as well as the people involved in visiting. The sensitive use of this prerogative provides an important lever in treatment, making it possible for the visit to produce minimal or therapeutically workable amounts of stress.

HOW VISITING PRODUCES STRESS

Stress is inherent in all visiting. The longer the visit, the greater the frequency, the larger the number of people involved, and the greater the distance from the treatment center, the more the stress potential that exists.

Even when parents are reasonably benign in their handling of the child during a visit, their very presence can reactivate the internalized conflict that originated in the earlier relationship. When this occurs, the modification of visiting arrangements can reduce stress until such time as the child comes to realize that he is responding to an internalized image rather than to his parents as they are at the moment. Treatment staff need to be aware of the distortion reactions on the part of the child, since, out of overidentification, staff may also tend to perceive the parents as bad or destructive. Direct observation of parent-child visiting by staff serves to act as a corrective measure for this propensity.

Unfortunately, visits that provide an opportunity for actual repetition of situations and interactions that contributed to the child's disturbance are the more common variety. The possibilities for acting out conflicts during a visit are almost infinite. The acting out may be initiated by either the child or the parents. For instance, a mother may stir up in a child a conflict of loyalties between the treatment agency and the parents. This can occur when, as a result of her own oral-dependent competitiveness with the child, the mother is outspokenly critical of clothing that the child has received, of the care given him, or of his therapist or his counselor. Alternatively, the child may seek to engage his mother or his grandmother in rivalry with staff over his care when, for example, this has been his lifelong protective pattern against being totally ignored. Parents sometimes use the child as a pawn in their own battles. Thus, a corruptive father may unconsciously push his son into antisocial behavior.

Stress in visiting comes about in many additional ways. A parent may be actually or potentially abusive, seductive, threatening, or depreciating toward a child. He may pass along information or gossip regarding family problems, which can often be upsetting or damaging to the child. A parent's inability during a visit to be giving, or meaningfully communicative, may well repeat earlier disappointments in the relationship. A parent who does not visit as promised, who arrives late or early, or who comes irregularly can also reinforce earlier severe disappointments. Bizarre or deviant behavior on the part of a parent can be grossly embarrassing to the child. Sibling rivalry is easily revived, particularly if the brother or sister actually comes to visit. These are but a few of the stress-creating situations that reactivate conflict within a child.

VARIABLE ELEMENTS OF VISITING

Although visiting creates stress for children, it does not follow that it is to be entirely prohibited. A child may need reassurance that his anger has not killed his parents, that they have not totally forgotten him, or that the treatment institution is not trying to deprive him of them. The elimination of visiting would produce its own stress. Consequently, more therapeutic potential exists in the variable handling of visiting arrangements than in the outright prohibition of visiting.

FREQUENCY OF VISITS

When visits are less frequent at the beginning of a child's stay the treatment center can judge whether his behavior following the visit results from the stress of the visit or whether it represents his general behavioral pattern. If a child was reacting to the recurrent stress of weekly visits with a week of regression after each one, it would be impossible to make this differentiation. Then, too, visiting begun on a weekly schedule only too frequently has to be limited eventually. It has been found that parents can tolerate restrictions on visiting best at the beginning of their child's placement. They tend to see limitations added later as deprivations meant to punish them for anger and destructive impulses toward the child or as a judgment of their adequacy as parents.

Immediately after admission it is most effective for a child to be visited on grounds, biweekly or monthly, for an hour or two each time. Although visits may be increased to a biweekly or a weekly basis after a year or so (actually, only 2 of the 30 children at Lakeside have weekly visits), some children continue to be visited by their parents on the original, limited schedule for much longer. In such cases, the children may themselves not wish for an increase in visiting, they may need protection from stress for a longer period of time, or their parents may practically or psychically not be able to visit more often. It is rare that visiting is reduced on the treatment center's initiative to less than once a month. Sometimes, irregular and infrequent parental visiting is incorrectly viewed by the child as the center's plan. In such cases it has occasionally been found helpful to place no limitation on visiting, thereby having the child face the reality that it is actually his parents' decision to visit in a limited way.

VISITING ON GROUNDS

When stress reduction for the child is necessary and a stringent visiting schedule (for example, once every three months) meets great resistance from the parents, the treatment center has the alternative of modifying other variables. Restricting visits to the grounds of the institution is one possibility. The solid physical presence of the grounds and buildings can represent to both child and parents the center's protection and authority. Further, the presence of child care counselors nearby tends to inhibit stressful behavior. With on-grounds visiting, the child need not feel the rage of an unpredictable parent to the same extent that he does away from the center. And a mother's wearing two dresses and wondering if it is Easter in June will be more tolerable to her adolescent son if they visit within the confines of the center than it would be if he had to anticipate being seen on the street with her.

It is possible for the counselor, by plan, to sit in on the on-grounds visit discreetly or as an active participant. A psychotic mother with settled convictions about extrasensory perception is less likely to confuse her child when a counselor is there to help change the subject. The mere presence of a counselor can discourage a mother's nagging and depreciating of her daughter while serving to support the mother's own basic wish to do what is most helpful for her child. Restricting a visit to the living room of the cottage in the presence of counselors protected one child from any threat of seduction by a father who had molested her when she was very young. The counselor can also usefully structure a visit by suggesting some game or activity to the parent who finds conversation difficult or cannot easily initiate play with his child.

Visiting on grounds, particularly for the several months following admission, serves additional important purposes. It helps the child to realize that separation from the parents is real. It symbolically affirms that the treatment center is now the responsible decision maker in the child's life and the provider of need gratification on which he must depend. It gives staff ample opportunity to observe the nature of the relationship between the child and his parents. Direct observation of the visits is particularly helpful in work with those children and parents who have much difficulty in talking of the visits and their feelings about them. The child care counselor's comments about the mother who is withdrawn and uninterested in her child, or about the mother who talks of the superior accomplishments of the sibling, can then be used in individual therapy when a child brings in pertinent material. (About half of the children at Lakeside Children's Center invariably remain on grounds with their parents.)

VISITING OFF GROUNDS OR AT HOME

A child should not be considered ready for off-grounds or home visits until the staff judges his ego sufficiently strong to be reasonably adaptive to the anticipated degrees of stress. Off-grounds visits clearly enhance the likelihood of stress; yet they are not all of a piece: for example, visiting a nearby drugstore has a lower probability of generating stress than going home for a full day's visit. Visiting off grounds precludes planned observations by treatment center staff. Therefore, such arrangements imply that the agency expects the child or the parent to be capable of communicating later, in a relatively meaningful way, about both tangible and intangible aspects of the visit.

When the visit is off grounds, it is possible, because of the location of our treatment center, for children to go to a nearby market, beach, park, or restaurant with their parents and yet be within very close range of the center. An adolescent girl whose psychotic mother unexpectedly became involved in a street argument with another woman had only a block to go in fleeing back to her cottage. Parents and children who are better integrated, whose behavior is more rather than less predictable, can venture on longer trips and more distant visits. They can go to the zoo, the museum, or the ball park or window-shop at downtown department stores.

Careful planning with parents about the activities engaged in during off-grounds or at-home visits can forestall difficulty. For instance, it would be unwise for parents to go to the circus with a child who is tormented by fantasies of wild animals and who uses counterphobic defenses. Similarly, a child who is fearful of his father's hostile aggressions could have a fine time fishing with him, but not hunting.

Short, close-by excursions, as well as on-grounds visits, are most typically planned to be an hour or two in duration. Special outings and events can be longer; they vary from an afternoon's trip to the museum to an all-day fishing excursion to a weekend visit home.

Visits to the parental home provide little or no protective control and can generate much stress. Therefore, the children permitted to visit their parents' home are those whose adaptive capabilities have been greatly strengthened and who have feelings of security in their relationship to the center and to home. Home-visit stress can be minimized by short stays of one hour to four hours. Overnight and weekend visits are usually contraindicated unless the child's adaptive capabilities are reasonably able to withstand family pathology, be it gross or subtle. Only five children at Lakeside are currently visiting home with any regularity, though there may be occasional home visits planned for some of the others.

Generally speaking, a child's having ego strength compatible with at-home visiting implies that he is close to the end of his need for residential treatment and for the protective care it exercises. Consequently, overnight visiting tends to have primary value in the course of preparing both child and family for his impending return home, though this may be many months away. Home visits, overnight or less, may also be planned when it is considered therapeutically advisable for the child to be confronted with the reality of his parents' mode of living and family relationships. In other instances, for example, when a family has moved into a new house or a new neighborhood, the counselor or the child therapist may visit the home with the child, particularly if this will help the child to feel part of the family.

THE PEOPLE WHO VISIT

Parents should be the main figures in all visiting plans, since they are usually the most meaningful as well as the most ambivalent figures in the child's life. It is with the parents that the treatment center works most closely in order to help them understand and deal with the behavior of the child. If there have been other people of positive significance to the child, such as grandparents, they also visit on a regular basis. Distant relatives and family friends can visit by arrangement on an infrequent schedule. Siblings may or may not visit, depending on their meaning to the child in placement. Often, the child is under less stress if they visit infrequently and only by plan.

CHANGING PLAN TO REDUCE STRESS

Despite all precautions that may be taken to insure that stress-producing elements of a visit are kept to a minimum, one may often see what is most frequently described as "upset" behavior by a child after a visit. It is highly important that all residential treatment staff be alert to such behavioral patterns, particularly since the child himself may be quite unaware of, or deny their relationship to, affect stirred up by the visit. Staff assessment may help determine whether a change in visiting arrangements is necessary.

The criteria for evaluating visiting stress are the type, the degree, and the length of the child's defensive reactions and ego disintegration. When there is a serious intensification of symptomatic behavior after a visit, it can be assumed that anxiety has been aroused with which the child could not deal in a suitably adaptive fashion, and thus he handles with maladaptive defenses. These defenses, of course, may be present in varying degrees at all times. When they are intensified by visits and persist in aggravated fashion over a long period of time, thereby seriously interfering with growth processes, an effort must be made to reduce the stress caused by the visiting.

A psychotic boy of latency age withdrew into a long fantasy, and his behavior became extremely compulsive for four or five days after each weekly visit with his mother. When visits were reduced to once a month, the regressive behavior reactive to the visits became but a minor portion of his functioning, and he was able to make a steady push toward healthier modes of adaptive behavior.

Another child displayed increased hyperactivity for several hours after weekly visits with parents, and sometimes even prior to each visit. In this instance, however, the child's reaction could be worked with in individual therapy and therefore did not call for a change in the visiting schedule. The child was helped to handle his anxiety by making him aware of its relationship to the impending visit.

Persistently demanding, pestering behavior on the part of another child was noted for several days after each weekly visit. Again, visiting was reduced, and the parents were requested to come without the child's envied sibling. The child care counselors soon noticed a longer span of better-integrated behavior.

Still another psychotic youngster displayed increased head banging and a much lower frustration tolerance after brief off-grounds visits with cooperative parents. A return to on-grounds visiting led to diminution of the regressive behavior.

CHILDREN'S REACTIONS TO VISITING

At times, one notices in reaction to visiting certain behavior that is indicative of guilt in a particular child: for example, being provocative, handling responsibilities so poorly that restrictions on activities must surely follow, or avoiding therapy sessions. In one instance, a parent was stirring up guilt in a child by creating conflict of loyalties, acting out through him, and generally disrupting his treatment. In that situation, the duration rather than the frequency of visits was reduced. The child was told that if he was able to cope with the stress his mother produced, the center would have no objection to the longer visits, but since his behavior showed that they were too much for him, limitations were necessary. Although the problem was by no means promptly resolved, this procedure did help the boy take a major step in understanding how his mother acted out her own problems through him.

Sometimes aggressive, provocative behavior is a child's defense against experiencing the loss of self-esteem that an unhappy visit has stirred up in him. Such loss may be the result of anything from a parent's utter inadequacy in giving psychically to the child to the flaunting of the virtues of a sibling before him. Some children, on the other hand, will be more conforming and isolated after an unhappy visit with the parents, as a result of increased fear of the loss of their love.

There is great variety both in the content of specific conflicts that are triggered in children by parental visits and in the consequent defensive maneuvering in which they engage. Treatment staff must know the defensive patterns of a particular child in order to be able to judge whether a given sequence of behavior, be it greater difficulty in learning or extreme temper tantrums, may have been set off by the visit. Any piece of maladaptive defensive behavior that results from a visit and persists for an extended period of time, so as to interfere with a child's treatment, would certainly indicate the need for a thorough review and possible revision of visiting arrangements. This does not mean that change is initiated suddenly. It sometimes takes a considerable period of time to become aware that the defensive behavior may be connected with the visiting. It may also take some time to test out that hypothesis. When major changes in visiting arrangements have to be made, a thorough understanding of the relationship between the visits and the child's regressive behavior enables staff to meet in a helpful way the parental opposition that can arise.

If a child can express feelings about visits, can use his observations and reactions to further understanding of himself, and can grow from these experiences, the treatment center does not try to protect him from all pain or stress.

> Tom, an adolescent, went home for his first visit in four years. He had not seen his parents in more than three months. He was deeply disappointed at finding his family and home much the same as he had known them. Although he returned proclaiming great pleasure in the visit, within a few days there was return of much earlier symptomatology, deterioration in schoolwork, regressive relationship with peers, and renewed manipulative behavior with adults. As Tom was helped to become aware of his reaction to the visits, he was able to let himself know about the affect involved and the conflicts stirred up.
>
> After several weeks, he did regain a more mature integration. When he was later invited to attend the wedding of an older sister, he expressed the desire to go. After the pros and cons of the matter had been explored with him, he was allowed to attend. This time the way he handled the situation resulted in minimal aftereffects, and he was proud of his heightened capacity to cope with it. Thus, for this boy, at his particular level of integration, the first visit home was a significant learning and mastering experience.

WORK WITH PARENTS

The effectiveness of a visiting arrangement is obviously influenced by the extent to which the parents are able to understand the limitations established by the treatment center and to cooperate in planning. This in turn is made possible by the parents' relationship to, and work with, their therapist. Their cooperation in the visiting arrangements is one important way in which the parents more actively participate in the child's treatment. (Some parents who do not wish to visit frequently find it helpful to have the center relieve them of guilt; the center will "take the blame" when this is in the child's best interests.)

At the center, casework with the parents is usually carried on by the child's therapist. The foundation for cooperation over visiting arrangements is laid, however, at the time of the preadmission study. The reasons for initial visiting arrangements, as well as the inability to know or to promise what future arrangements may be, are thoroughly explained. No encouragement is given to expect frequent visits. It should be noted that these matters are discussed with the parents before they make the final decision to place the child.

In order to maximize the growth-producing potential in the parent-child relationship, parents must also be helped to understand the child's behavior and their own behavior in relation to him. For instance, a mother and father were helped to understand why, in the course of visits, they should discourage their son's apparently self-sufficient behavior, such as treating the family to a soda. The child really needed the constant reassurance that everyone would care for him, even though his defensive pattern was to deny the fear of abandonment by acting more grown-up and independent. Another mother and father were helped to see that their son's request to have them say good-bye to him by shaking hands was not a sign of withdrawal and distancing, but rather of his greater maturity.

When parents, through the casework services given them, have developed a generally positive, cooperative relationship with the agency, they become able to use the examples and guidance of the child care staff to make visiting a more positive experience for them and the child. Thus, a father was receptive and not threatened when a child care counselor provided a ball and bat so that he could play with his son when it was observed that the two were uncomfortable with each other during the visit. Parents may also be helped to learn to play cards or to become acquainted with a new table game that the child enjoys. In another case, a counselor provided the opportunity for a child to show off her increased skill at the piano and guided the parents into appropriately complimenting her when they could not do so on their own. After listening to the meandering tales of a psychotic mother, a counselor provided cookies and milk for her and her child in order to give the two a means for overt relating. A father was able to be more patient with his autistic son, who ignored him, after the counselor had demonstrated a way of attracting his attention. She encouraged the boy to turn his head toward the father, who had a balloon ready to help catch the child's eye. On the whole, unassuming demonstrations of ways of dealing with a child can help parents alter their own methods slightly during a visit, while giving the therapist further opportunity to deal with the underlying attitudes that have made it impossible for the parents to use such methods themselves earlier.

THE DECISION-MAKING PROCESS

At Lakeside, final decisions concerning visiting arrangements rest with the child's therapist. But all staff involved with the child gather information, provide observations, and give opinions before the decision is made. Such mutual cross-checking guards against preconscious and unconscious motivations that may bias a decision. For example, denials of parental requests may arise out of rivalry with the parents, while assents to requests for more liberal visiting arrangements may result from overestimating the child's strengths as an assurance to oneself of the effectiveness of therapy. Further, persistent pressure by parents and children in regard to visiting can push a therapist to make a decision without fully attending to certain facts of the case. The more that staff is aware of the dynamic reasons for, and the principles underlying, visiting arrangements, t e more confidence there will be both in the decisions made about visiting and in the evaluation of the resultant stress.

NOTE

1. Lakeside Children's Center provides residential treatment for seriously disturbed children. It is located in Milwaukee, Wisconsin, on a five-acre plot in a middle-class neighborhood of small homes and businesses. The neighborhood is immediately adjacent to an older, wealthier section. The premises contain three cottages for children with a population of 6 girls and 24 boys. The children, ranging in age from 6 to more than 18, live in five group units containing six children apiece. The child care counselor staff consists of 22 men and women, the majority college educated, who are employed on a 45-hour week. Five psychiatric social workers are responsible for individual psychotherapy, and a child analyst serves as consultant. Most of the children at this treatment center attend special classes of from one to five students in the school building on the grounds, the teachers being employed and assigned to the center by the Milwaukee public schools.

7. Termination of Residential Treatment of Children With Emphasis on the Process with the Parents

J. Cotter Hirschberg

The gains achieved from the residential treatment of an emotionally disturbed child can be viewed from three standpoints: (1) from the assessment of all aspects of the improvement within the child; (2) from the change within the parents; and (3) from the changed that might occur in the interaction between the parents and the child. The purpose of this paper is to examine the process of termination from the standpoint of the parents of the child who is ending treatment.

From the very beginning of a child's residential treatment, the implicit and explicit message to the parents is that there will come a time when the work of the residential placement is over. Regardless of length, residential treatment is viewed by the treatment team and by the parents of the patient as a time-limited process — a meaningful, vital, and important episode in the child's growth and development. Termination is not merely a goal but a continually discussed topic, and the caseworker is consistently identifying and clarifying any comments relative to treatment ending. It is important to keep this focus in working with parents because one of their

Reprinted from the *Bulletin of the Menninger Clinic,* vol. 33, no. 6 (November 1969), pp. 364-69, by permission of the author and the bulletin.

inevitable concerns is whether the treatment team will in some way hold onto their child too tightly or reject their child too easily. The parents' own ambivalence about their relationship with their child is frequently projected onto the process of residential treatment, and it is through the continual awareness of the goal of the child's ending residential care that one continually conveys to the parents that to lose sight of this goal is a reflection of someone's anxiety and the defenses against that anxiousness.

It is difficult for the parents to realize that residential treatment does not have to do the job completely but that something can be left for the positive interplay between the child, the parents, the environment and its resources. The issues of termination also depend upon how much and in what ways the child and his parents are brought together in the treatment process. The parents should be involved in a significant way and the interaction between the child and themselves studied, understood, commented upon, and influenced by the treatment team. Termination problems become clarified as the result of keeping in the forefront the tasks the parents must accomplish.

Residential treatment, like socialization itself, is a process that is accomplished with different degrees of success. The end point is defined in optimal terms, not in terms of the maximum or the ideal. The parents must be helped to direct their attention not only to the problem areas of the patient but to his problem-free areas also. It is important for parents to realize that residential treatment is a means toward helping the child, and not a cure for the child or his problems. The parents' continual awareness that the residential treatment is both temporary and time limited does not lessen their awareness that residential treatment has also enabled their child to achieve a genuine relationship and a corrective experience. The child has been able to achieve a more genuine relationship with them as well as with other love objects. This is a process of differentiation that both the parents and the child must experience.

The questions that Levine states as being in the mind of the therapist during a treatment process are also those questions that are in the minds of the parents when their child or adolescent leaves residential treatment.[1] They wonder, "How would I feel under the same circumstances?" "How does your child feel under these circumstances?" "If I were in his shoes, how might I be feeling?" Levine has stressed that in such an empathic process there is always the danger of excessive identification, and it is this danger that the parents and those who work with them need to resolve.

At the time of discharge of the child from residency, the caseworker helps the parents recognize that it is likely that there will be on their part too great a participation in their child's anxiety, too great an agreement with the child's rationalizations, and too much sympathy with the child's struggle (particularly with his attempts to blame that struggle onto some specific immediacy). The parents are vulnerable to expecting too little from the child and, at this moment, also, they are permissive towards the child's use of regressive gratification to defend against his anxiousness. It is hard for them to side with those feelings of strength on the child's part that are allowing him to free himself and leave the residential care. However, when the parents side with the child's strengths, then the child can move on to a more active form of constructive thinking and planning and will need less to look back upon the past gratifications of residential life. Dicharge from residence usually occurs when the child is not completely well and when the therapy is not completely done, and this fact must be accepted and planned for by the treatment staff and the parents together.

It is certainly true that, in discharging a child from residential care, the treatment team wants to know if the parents can again take on the task of raising their child, and if they are reasonably comfortable with whatever their specific roles in the parent-child relationship may be. The role of the parents is constantly tested throughout the child's treatment and not precipitously measured just at the end. The caseworker must report what shifts have occurred in the adjustment of the parents, from which they find strengths and gratifications. If they have differentiated themselves from the child, and experienced growth in doing so, it is less likely they will return to overidentification with the child. Nonetheless, the decision to end residential care has the primary goal of returning the child to his process of growth and development within a family and within a normal social matrix as soon as possible. Therapy and casework can both continue past the specific end of residential treatment and, consequently, the discharge from residence is not delayed for treatment completion but is predicated on a continued satisfactory developmental process. Therefore, once termination of the residential treatment has been decided upon, then the reality of ending becomes the major focus for the parents as for the child.

The parents' own assessment of the termination will depend upon their dealing adequately with several of the inevitable consequences of the reality of ending:

The *first* of these centers around the parents' ability to recognize and support the child's readiness to leave the residential treatment. One derivative of the child's illness in the past has been his difficulty in bringing things to a successful end. The parents need to know and deal with the realization that the child's anxiety about ending is both inevitable and necessary. He will feel anxious about his ability to make good use of the resources in his coming environment, and he will be anxious out of his awareness that this will require expanding ego functioning and expanding interactional experience.

Second, no matter how successful the residential treatment has been, the child feels on leaving residential treatment that he has been abandoned by the residential staff. Regressive behavior or return of earlier symptoms are consequently frequent on the child's part. The parents must be aware of these inevitable feelings of abandonment, and they can help the child by identifying these feelings as part of the anxiety about leaving residential treatment. The difficulty for the parents (as well as for the child) is to recognize that a part of the regression or the symptom return is the child's unconscious or preconscious repetition of the dilemmas he faced at the beginning of residential treatment that made the residential treatment necessary. He can now be experientially aware that the anxiety aroused by reexperiencing these affects is of a different quality and a different impact and does not carry the potential for disorganization that the earlier anxiety did.

Third, the reality of ending will require of the parents that they accept consciously their awareness of the patient's change. Such awareness and the recognition of change in their child or adolescent is viewed with ambivalence, is painful, and the parents retreat from it. This retreat on the parents' part is very commonly expressed by them in their "doubts about the wisdom of the child's being discharged." The parents will doubt whether the child is truly ready, whether his strengths are hollow rather than genuine, whether his reexperienced symptoms represent new failure, and the parents will wish consciously or unconsciously to extract from the staff a promise for a problem-free future. The parents can intellectually accept the fact that development always involves problem solving, but their anxiety about the child's ending residential treatment is conveyed to the staff in their experiencing new concerns as to whether the child will be able to do the normal problem solving in developmental tasks. The answer is not found in reassurance to the parents; it is more helpful if these doubts can be identified and if the parents can be aided in exploring them fully, rather than minimizing or denying their anxiety. After all, the best reassurance for the parents is the awareness that their doubts do not have to be concealed or hidden from themselves or the staff; rather, the staff is aware of these doubts on the parents' part, and the child's discharge from residential treatment is not interrupted because of them.

A *fourth* aspect of the parents' struggle around the reality of ending is seen in their feelings of anger toward the residential treatment staff. No matter how well the termination has been handled and no matter how successful the child's treatment has been, the parents will, if the process with them has been a meaningful one also, have feelings of abandonment and rejection. To an important degree, many parents struggle with the illogical but deeply felt thought, "If you really liked my child and if you really liked me, you would not be willing to let us go. It makes me angry that you do not insist on holding onto us. I thought we meant more to you than this." These thoughts express their past dependence upon the residential treatment setting. Such a sense of trust is both mature and necessary, but it cannot escape from the earlier meanings of dependency and trust. And it is these earlier affects that temporarily are repeated around the parents' acceptance of the child's leaving residential care.

Fifth, the staff needs to convey to the parents that at the very same time that their child is ending residential treatment, they, too, are ending a process and no such ending is without sadness. No termination is without its feelings of loss. Realistically the parents have invested in and have shared the child's experience of residential treatment. They can be helped to accept this sadness, and even to gain from experiencing it if the sadness is seen as an appropriate response to their participation. It can be further helpful to them if they are aware that the staff, too, feels a sense of normal loss as well as the achievement of a successful discharge. Such sadness is often conveyed in its metaphors: in questions about the possible failure of the child in coping without the security and protection of residential treatment; in the parents' "fears" of assuming greater responsibility in the child's life; in the parents' questions as to whether the child can return if necessary; in the parents' wish to (or denial of their wish to) continue contact, communication, and follow-up. Not only has the child been in treatment, the parents have been in treatment too. There are transference manifestations to work through. There are positive feelings to be controlled and dealt with. The parents, themselves, leave as "good parents" and must go on to their own independent functioning. They raise many questions as to their capacities, their adequacies, and seek reassurance that the treatment team sees them as good and worthwhile and able to assume independent functioning.

Sixth, the parents, as well as the child who is being

discharged, need to have expressed, sometimes in explicit verbal comment and sometimes indirectly through a discussion of the realities of the outside future activities of the child and the parents, the fact that the residential staff accepts that the child is leaving, knows that the child and the parents will be substituting their own relationship as well as other meaningful relationships for the ones that previously existed between child and parents and staff. An important part of the parents' assessment of a successful ending comes out of their feeling that the residential treatment staff not merely "lets go" but expects them to succeed past and beyond the work of the residential treatment center.

The involvement of the family helps the residential treatment team solve the problem of treatment terminable and interminable. The reality of the family, involved significantly in the treatment process to give it a whole aspect, helps with the constant analysis of counter-transference phenomena that becomes an intrinsic part of successful treatment. Then it is that the staff can risk, the child can risk, and the family can risk the return back to an altered social matrix and not the identical one in structure and quality from whence the child originally came.

NOTE

1. Maurice Levine, "Principles of Psychiatric Treatment," in *Dynamic Psychiatry*, ed. Franz Alexander and Helen Ross (Chicago: University of Chicago Press, 1952), pp. 207-66.

Part III
Treatment Approaches

OVERVIEW

The treatment approaches in residential centers are several—education, casework, psychotherapy, group care, occupational therapy, the overall milieu, and so on. Centers plan their activities to offer an overall approach. However, individual centers are likely to emphasize different activities, and in so doing their program may reflect a distinct type. For example, individual psychotherapy may be used as the major thrust of a center's therapeutic program. In this strategy, other activities are adjunctive and provide opportunities for the patients to experiment with and test reality and to "work through" their internalized problems. In addition, the other activities such as recreation, work, and special group living experiences are areas where the patients can gain satisfactions and express their tensions.

In this strategy, the problems experienced by the individual in the adjunctive activities become a part of the grist for the psychotherapy sessions. If the adjunctive staff provide a positive milieu, then the problems experienced by the children may be interpreted as symptomatic of their maladjustment. Such problems may then be reviewed in psychotherapy for their particular significance to the patient's personality dynamics. If the adjunctive staff fail to create a helpful setting, then such difficulties as the patients experience may be viewed as "reality problems" generated by the setting. However, reality problems may still be considered in psychotherapy for their particular relevance to the patients' personalities. Should the adjunctive staff have been inconsistent in their management of the patients, the inconsistency and the patients' reaction might be related, for example, to their inconsistent upbringing.

In contrast to being the major element in residential treatment, psychotherapy may be one among a number of other services available to the children. Such an eclectric approach might accent special group living arrangements, education, recreation, case- and group work along with psychotherapy—all of which are viewed as being equally important.

Centers that carefully organize their milieu into a highly unified treatment approach and emphasize it stand in contrast to the strategy of an eclectic approach and even in greater contrast to the strategy that encourages an individual psychotherapeutic approach. Such a highly organized milieu works through the forces of the environment including its various activities, staff and peer relationships, as well as the overall administration of the program. Within a milieu approach, elements of its psychotherapy techniques may be modified and used through the milieu. Child care workers, for example, may draw ideas and feelings from the children to ease their tension, confront the children with their behavior to sensitize them to themselves, and make suggestions to the children to guide their behavior.

The articles in this section give particular attention to the program activities found in most center programs. Several articles give attention to broader approaches. For example, Redl ("The Concept of a 'Therapeutic Milieu' ") and Lehrer et al. consider operant conditioning. Marshall and Stewart ("Day Treatment as a Complementary Adjunct to Residential Treatment") and Mora et al. ("A Residential Treatment Center Moves toward the Community Mental Health Model") illustrate some innovations in residential treatment.

8. The Concept of a

"Therapeutic Milieu"

Fritz Redl

Speculations about the therapeutic value of the "milieu" in which our patients live are neither as new nor as revolutionary as the enthusiasts, as well as the detractors, of "milieu therapy" occasionally want them to appear. If I may risk shocking you so early in the game, the most extreme degree of "holy respect" for the tremendous impact that even the "little things" in an environment can have is represented in the original description of the conditions for a Freudian psychoanalytic hour. The ritual of interaction between patient and therapist is certainly sharply circumscribed. Even items such as horizontality of body posture and geographical placement of the analyst's chair are considered important conditions. Of course, the "basic rule" must be strictly adhered to, there should be no noises from the analyst's children coming through from the next room, one would worry whether patients might meet each other on the way out or in. The idea that months of solid work even by the greatest genius of transference manipulation might be endangered if doctor and patient should happen to meet at the Austrian equivalent of a cocktail party,

Reprinted from the *American Journal of Ortho-psychiatry*, vol. 29, no. 4 (October 1959), pp. 721-36, by permission of the author and the journal. This paper was read at the 1958 Annual Meeting of the American Orthopsychiatric Association.

instead of in their usual office terrain, is certainly impressive evidence for the great impact classical psychoanalysis has ascribed to factors such as time, space, and other "external givens."

If you now want to argue with me by reminding me that all this is true only for the duration of the 50-minute hour, and that other "milieu" factors in the patient's wider circle of life have not been deemed as relevant, then I might concede that point. But even so, I would like to remind you that we have always had a holy respect for two sets of "milieu" factors, at least in child analysis: (1) we have always lived under the terror that the parents or teachers of our child patients might do things to them that would be so traumatic that we could, of course, not analyze them while all this was going on; and (2) we would insist we couldn't touch a case unless we could get the child out of the terrian of parental sex life and into a bed of his own, or unless the parents stopped some of the more extreme forms of punitive suppressiveness at once. These are only a few of the illustrations we could think of. You will find a much more impressive list of "milieu variables," which certainly need to be influenced by the therapist, in Anna Freud's classic, *Introduction to the Technique of Child Analysis*, though not under that heading, of course.

The other case in point of my argument that even classical psychoanalysis has not neglected concern with "milieu" influences as much as it is supposed to have, relates to our evaluation of failure and success. At least in our informal appraisals I have time and again observed how easily we ascribe the breakdown of a child analysis to the "negative factors in the youngster's environment," and I have found in myself an inclination to do the same with the other fellow's successes. If my colleague seems to have presented an unusual piece of therapeutic "breakthrough," I find the temptation strong to look for the good luck he had with all the supportive factors that were present in his case and which, to my narcissism, seem to explain his success much better than the technical argument he put forth.

Now, seriously, if we secretly allow "milieu particles" to

weigh so strongly that they can make and break even the most skillfully developed emotional therapy bridges between patient and doctor, hadn't we better look into this some more?

The fortunate fact that the answer to this question has, historically, been an enthusiastic yes, however, has started us off in another problem-direction. Since more and more of us got impressed by more and more "factors" which in some way or other could be subsumed under the "milieu" term, the word has assumed such a variety of connotations that scientific communication has been overstimulated, but at the same time blocked in its development toward precision.

Since avoiding the traps of early concept confusion is an important prelude to a more rigid examination of meanings and their appropriate scope, we might allow ourselves the luxury of at least a short list of "dangers we ought to watch out for from now on," provided we keep it telegram-style, so as not to take too much attention from the major theme. Since time and space for argument is dear, I shall be presumptuous enough to confront you simply with my personal conclusions, and offer them as warning posts, without further apology.

TRAPS FOR THE MILIEU CONCEPT

1. The cry for *the* therapeutic milieu as a general slogan is futile, and in this wide formulation the term doesn't mean a thing. No milieu is "good" or "bad" in itself—it all depends. And it depends on more factors than I want to list, though some of them will turn up as we go along.

2. It won't do to use our own philosophical, ethical, political convictions, or our taste buds, in order to find out what really has or has not "therapeutic effect." Even the most respectable clinical discussions around this theme drift all too easily into A's trying to convince B that his setup is too "autocratic," or that what he called "democratic" group management isn't really good for those youngsters. Whether a ward should have rules, how many and which, must not lead to an argument between those

who like rules and those who don't; I have seen many a scientific discussion end up in the same personal taste-bud battle that one otherwise finds acceptable only when people talk about religions or brands of cars.

3. Even a concept of "total milieu therapy" does not imply that all aspects of a given milieu are equally relevant in all moments in clinical life. All games, for instance, have some kind of "social structure" and as part of that, some kind of "pecking order" which determines the power position of the players for the duration of the game. Whether the specific pecking order of the game I let them play today had anything to do with the fact that it blew up in my face after five minutes is a question that can be answered only in empirical terms. I know of cases where the pecking order was clearly it; I have to look no further. I know of others where it was of no *clinical* relevance at the time. The boys blew up because they got too scared playing hide-and-seek with flashlights in the dark. In short, the scientific establishment of a given milieu aspect as a theoretically valid and important one does not substitute for the need for a diagnosis on the spot. It alone can differentiate between potential milieu impacts and actual ones in each case.

4. The idea of the "modern" and therefore social-science-conscious psychiatrist that he has to sell out to the sociologist if he wants to have his "ward milieu" studied properly is the bunk. Of course, any thoughtful appraisal of a hospital milieu will contain many variables that the mother discipline of a given psychiatrist may never have dreamed about. On the other hand, the thing that counts is not only the description of a variable but the assessment of the potential impact on the treatment process of a given group of patients. That is basically a *clinical* matter, and it remains the clinician's task. The discipline that merges social science with clinical criteria in a balanced way still has to be invented. There is no shortcut to it either by psychiatry's stealing particles of social science concepts or by selling out to the social scientist's domain.

5. The frequently voiced expectation that the discovery of what "milieu" one needs would automatically make it

easy to produce that style of milieu in a given place is downright naive. An instrumentology for the creation of "ward atmosphere," of "clinically correct policies of behavioral intervention," and the like has yet to be created, and it will cost blood and sweat to get it. The idea that all it takes to have a "good treatment milieu" is for a milieu-convinced ward boss to make his nurses feel comfortable with him, and to hold a few gripe sessions between patients and staff, is a daydream, the simplicity of which we can no longer afford.

"THERAPEUTIC"—IN WHICH RESPECT?

The worst trap that explorers of the milieu idea sometimes seem to be goaded into is the ubiquitous use of the term "therapeutic," if it is coupled as an adjective, with "milieu" as a noun. I have described the seven most common meanings squeezed into this word in scientific writings and scientific discussions elsewhere,[1] but I must at least point at this possible confusion before we go on. Whenever people demand that a really good "therapeutic milieu" have this or that quality to it, they may refer to any one—or a combination of—the following issues:

1. Therapeutic—meaning: *don't put poison in their soup.*
   Example—Demand for absence of crude forms of punishment in a place that calls itself a "residential treatment center."
2. Therapeutic—meaning: *you still have to feed them,* even though that has little to do directly with a specific operation you are planning to perform.
   Example—Youngsters need an activity program, so if you keep them for a while you'd better see that they get it, even if your specific theory of psychiatry thinks nothing of the direct implication of play life and activity diet in terms of therapy as such.
3. Therapeutic—meaning: *development phase appropriateness and cultural background awareness.*
   Example—It would not be therapeutic to keep adolescents in an infantilizing "little

boy and girl" atmosphere; or: a fine lady fussing over a little boy's hair grooming might convey "warmth" to a neglected middle-class child, but would simply be viewed as a hostile pest by a young toughie from the other side of the tracks.

4. Therapeutic—meaning: *clinically elastic.*

    Example—The fact that rules and regulations were too rigid to fit particular disturbance patterns or needs of patients, I have heard referred to as "untherapeutic," and with all due respect to numbers and group psychology, there is a point where the inability to make exceptions becomes "untherapeutic" too.

5. Therapeutic—meaning: *encompassing fringe-area treatment goals.*

    Example—Johnny is here for treatment of his kleptomania. His therapist works hard on that in individual therapy. Johnny also has a severe deficiency in school learning, and is clumsy in his play life with contemporaries. Even while the therapist is not yet in a position to pull any of these factors in, some other aspect of the milieu to which Johnny is exposed must give him experiences in this direction. Or else, the place is not "therapeutic enough" for him.

6. Therapeutic—in terms of *"the milieu and I."*

    Example—Some types of cases with deficient superego formation can be lured into identification with value issues only through the detour of an identification with the group code within which they live. For those cases the "therapist" is only one of the therapeutic agents. The "institutional atmosphere" that makes the child want to identify with what it stands for is another, *on equal rights.* In this case, this part of the "milieu" is expected to become a direct partner in treatment of the specific disturbance for which the child was brought in.

7. Therapeutic—in terms of *reeducation for life.*

    Example—Especially for larger institutions the demand is often made that the institutions should not only provide people who treat the patient, but that they should also have features in them that come as close to "real life outside" as is possible, or else they wouldn't be "therapeutic enough." Thus, all those

> features that would seem to be needed
> for a very sick person are considered as
> rather countertherapeutic and bad,
> though unfortunately still necessary,
> while all semblance to open community
> life is considered a therapeutic ingred-
> ient in its own right. How far one and
> the same institution can cater to illness
> and at the same time lure into normal-
> ity is then often a case for debate.

Enough of this dissection of an adjective. I hope I am understood correctly: Any one of these meanings of the term "therapeutic" is a justified issue in its own right. Any one of them may, in a given case, assume priority importance or may fade out in relevance to the zero point. All I am trying to convey is the importance of remembering who is talking about what—and about which patients—when we use the term in a scientific free-for-all. So far I haven't been too impressed with our ability to do so.

By the way, even in all those seven cases the term "therapeutic" may still be used in a double frame of reference: (1) Was it therapeutic for a given patient—if so, how do you know? (2) Is this expected to be potentially "therapeutic"—meaning beneficial for the treatment goal—from what I know about the basic nature of the issue under debate? These two frames of reference need to be kept asunder too.

A "MILIEU"—WHAT'S IN IT?

Obviously I am not going to use the term in the nearly global meaning which its theft from the French language originally insinuated. For practical reasons, I am going to talk here only of one sort of milieu concept: of a "milieu" artificially created for the purpose of the treatment of a group of youngsters. Within this confine you can make it somewhat wider if you want, and think of the "Children's Psychiatric Unit" on the fourth, eighth, or ninth floor of a large hospital, or you may hold before your eyes, while I am speaking, a small residential treatment home for children that is not part of a large unit. Of course, I know that the similarity of what I am talking about to other types of setups may be quite great, but I can't cover them all. Hence, anything else you hold before your eyes while I talk, you do strictly at your own risk.

So, here we are on the doorstep of that treatment home or at the keyhole of that hospital ward. And now you ask me: If you could plan things the way you wanted to, which are the most important "items" in your milieu that will sooner or later become terribly relevant for better or for worse? The choice is hard, and only such a tough proposition gets me over the guilt feeling for over-simplifying and listing items out of context.

1. *The social structure.* This is some term, and I have yet to see the psychiatrist that isn't stunned for a moment at its momentum—many would run and hire a sociologist on the spot. Being short on time, I have no choice, but let me hurry and add: this term in itself is as extendible and collapsible as a balloon. It doesn't mean much without specifications. So, let me just list a few of the things I have in mind:

a) A hospital ward is more like a *harem society than a family*, no matter how motherly or fatherly the particular nurses and doctors may feel toward their youngsters. The place I run at the moment is purposely shaped as much as possible after the model of an American camp, which is the only pattern I could find that children would be familiar with, where a lot of adults walk through children's lives in older brother and parentlike roles without pretending it to be an equivalent to family life.

b) The *role distribution* of the adult figures can be of terrific importance for the amount of clarity with which children perceive what it is all about. Outspokenly or not, sooner or later they must become clear about just who can or cannot be expected to decide what; otherwise, how would one know when one is getting the runaround?

c) The *pecking order* of any outfit does not long remain a secret to an open door neighborhood-wise toughie, no matter how dumb he may be otherwise. He also smells the outspoken "pecking order" among the adults who take care of him, no matter how carefully disguised it may be under professional role titles or Civil Service Classification codes.

d) The *communication network* of any given institution is an integral part of its "social structure." Just who can be approached about listening to what, is quite a task to learn; and to figure out the real communication lines that are open and those that are secretly clogged in the adult communication network is usually an insoluble task except for the suspicious outside researcher.

I mentioned only four illustrations of all the things I want included under "social structure." There are many more, and I have no quarrel with the rich inventory many social scientists have invented for this. The quarrel I have goes all against oversimplification, and if you tell me social structure is only what goes into a power line drawing or a sociogram, or that social structure is the only important variable in "milieu" that psychiatrists have neglected in the past, then you have me in a mood to fight. By the way—if I list "social structure" as one of the important milieu variables, I'd better add in a hurry: a mere listing or description of the social structure extant on a given ward is of no interest to me at all if it doesn't go further than that. From a clinical angle, the excitement begins *after* the sociologist tells me what social structure I have before me. Then I really want to know: What does it do to my therapeutic goals? What does it imply for my choice in techniques? In which phase of the therapy of my children is it an, asset, and in which other phase does it turn into a serious block? To use just one example for the clinical question to be added to the social scientist's answer: The kind of ward I run—harem society style—makes individual attachments of child to worker difficult to achieve; on the other hand, it pleasantly dilutes too excited libidinous attachment-needs into more harmless distribution over a larger number of live props. Question: Is that good or bad, and for whom during what phase of their treatment?

2. *The value system that oozes out of our pores.* Some people subsume that under social structure. I think I have reasons to want a separate place for it here, but let's not

waste time on the question why. The fact is, the youngsters not only respond to what we say or put in mimeographed writing; they smell our value-feelings even when we don't notice our own body odor any more. I am not sure how, and I can't wait until I find out. But I do need to find out which value items are there to smell. Does the arrangement of my furniture call me a liar while I make a speech about how much at home I want them to feel, or does that gleam in a counselor's eye tell the child: "You are still wanted," even though he means it if he says he won't let you cut up the tablecloth? By the way, in some value studies I have missed one angle many times: the *clinical convictions* of what is professionally correct handling, which sometimes even questionnaire-clumsy workers on a low salary level may develop, and which become a motivating source for their behavior in its own right, besides their own personal moral convictions or their power drives.

3. *Routines, rituals, and behavioral regulations.* The sequence of events and the conditions under which people undergo certain repetitive maneuvers in their life space can have a strong impact on whether they can keep themselves under control, or whether their impulse-control balance breaks down. Since Bruno Bettelheim's classic description of the events inside a child while he seems engaged in the process of getting up or getting himself to sleep, no more words should have to be said about this. And yet, many "therapeutic milieu" discussions still waste their time on arguments between those who like regularity and those who think the existence of a rule makes life an unimaginative drudge. All groups also have a certain "ritual" by which a member gets back into the graces of the group if he has sinned, and others that the group has to go through when an individual has deviated. Which of those ceremonial rites are going on among my boys, thinly disguised behind squabbles and fights, and which of them do adult staff people indulge in, under the even thinner disguise of a discussion on punishment and on the setting of limits? Again—the mere discovery of phenomena fitting into this category is not what I am after. We are still far from having

good research data on the *clinical relevance* of whatever specific practice may be in vogue in a specific place.

4. *The impact of the group process.* We had better pause after pronouncing this weighty phrase—it is about as heavy and full of dodges as the phrase "social structure," as previously pointed out. And since this one milieu aspect might well keep us here for a week, let me sink as low as simple word listing at this point. Items that I think should go somewhere under this name: overall group atmosphere, processes like scapegoating, mascotcultivation, subclique formation, group psychological role suction,[2] experiences of exposure to group psychological intoxication, dependency on contagion clusters, leadership tensions, and so on. Whatever you have learned from social psychology, group psychology, and group dynamics had better be written in right here. The point of all this: These phenomena are *not* just interesting things that happen among patients or staff, to be viewed with a clinical grin, a sociological hurrah, or with the curiosity stare of an anthropological slumming party. These processes are forces to which my child patient is exposed, as real as the Oedipus complex of his therapist, the food he eats, and the toys he plays with. The forces producing such impacts may be hard to see, or even to make visible through X-ray tricks. They are there and as much of his "surroundings" as the unbreakable room in which he screams off his tantrum.

5. *The trait clusters that other people whirl around within a five-yard stretch.* I first wanted to call this item "the other people as persons," but I know this would only call forth a long harrangue about feelings, attitudes—Isn't it people anyway, who make up a group?—and so fourth. From bitter discussion experience, I am trying to duck these questions by this somewhat off-the-beat phrase. What I have in mind is this: My youngsters live as part of a group, true enough. But they are also individuals. And Bobby who shares a room with John is within striking distance of whatever personal peculiarities John may happen to throw at others. In short, we expect some children to show "shock" at certain colors on a Rorschach card. We expect children to be lured into excited creativity

at the mere vision of some fascinating project outline or plane model seductively placed before their eyes. Well, the boy with whom Bobby shares his room is worse than a Rorschach or a plane model. Not only does his presence and the visualization of his personality do something to Bobby, for John not only *has* character traits and neurotic syndromes, he swings them around his body like a wet bathing towel, and it is going to hit whoever gets in its path, innocent or not. In short, personality traits remain psychological entities for the psychologist who watches them in the youngsters. They are *real things that hit and scratch* if you get in their way, for the roommate and all the other people on the ward.

We have learned to respect the impact of certain extremes in pathologies upon each other, but we are still far from inspecting our milieus carefully enough for what they contain in "trait clusters" that children swing around their heads within a five-yard range. Let me add: not all traits and syndromes are "swung"; some stay put and can only be seen or smelled, so they become visible or a nuisance only to the one who shares the same room. Also: we are far from knowing what this all amounts to clinically. For the question of just what "milieu ingredients" my ward contains, in terms of existent trait clusters of the people who live in it, is still far removed from the question of just which *should* coexist with each other, and which others should be carefully kept asunder.

6. *The staff, their attitudes and feelings—but please let's not call it all "transference."* This one I can be short about, for clinicians all know about it; sociologists will grant it to you, though they may question how heavily it counts. In fact, the attitudes and feelings of staff have been drummed up for so long now as "the" most important aspect of a milieu, often even as the only important one, that I am not afraid this item will be forgotten. No argument needed, it is self-evident. Only two issues I would like to battle around: One, while attitudes and feelings are very important indeed, they are not always all that counts, and sometimes other milieu items may gang up on them so much they may obliterate their

impact. My other battle cry: Attitudes and feelings of staff are manifold, and spring from many different sources. Let's limit the term "transference" to those for which it was originally invented. If Nurse's Aide A gets too hostile to Bob because he bit him too hard, let's not throw all of that into the same terminological pot. By the way, if I grant "attitudes and feelings of staff" a place on my list of "powerful milieu ingredients," I mean the attitudes and feelings that really fill the place, that are lived—not those that are only mentioned in research interviews and on questionnaires.

7. *Behavior received.* I tried many other terms, but it won't work. There just isn't one that fits. In a sentence I would say: what people really *do* to each other counts as much as how they feel. This forces me into a two-hour argument in which I have to justify why it isn't unpsychiatric to say such a thing. For, isn't it the underlying feelings that "really" count? That depends on which side of the fence your "really" is. The very fact that you use such a term already means you know there is another side to it, only you don't want to take it as seriously as yours. In short, there are situations where the "underlying feeling" with which the adult punishes a child counts so much that the rather silly form of punishment that was chosen is negligible. But I could quote you hundreds of other examples where this is not the case. No matter what wonderful motive—if you expose child A to an isolation with more panic in it than he can stand, the effect will be obvious. Your excuse that you "meant well and love the boy" may be as futile as that of the mother who would give the child an overdose of arsenic, not knowing its effect.

This item of *behaviors received in a day's time* by each child should make a really interesting line to assess. We would have to look about as "behaviors received" from other boys as well as from staff, and see what the implications of those behaviors received are, even after deducting from them the mitigating influences of "attitudes that really were aiming at the opposite." The same, by the way, should also be taken into consideration for staff to be hired. I have run into people who really love "crazy youngsters" and are quite willing to sacrifice a lot. Only they simply cannot stand more than half a pound of spittle in their face a day, professional attitude or no.

In order to make such an assessment, the clinician would of course be interested especially in the *forms* that are being used by staff for intervention—limit setting—expression of acceptance and love, and so on. The totality of prevalence of certain forms of "behavior received" is not a negligible characteristic of the milieu in which a child patient has to live.

8. *Activity structure and nature of constituent perform-ances.* Part of the impact a hospital or treatment home has on a child lies in the things he is allowed or requested *to do.* Any given activity that is halfway shapeful enough to be described has a certain amount of structure to it—some games, for instance, have a body of rules; demand the splitting up into two opposing sides or staying in a circle; and have certain assessments of roles for the players, at least for the duration. At the same time, they make youngsters "do certain things" while the game lasts. Paul Gump introduced the term "constituent performances" into our Detroit Game Study, and referred by this term to the performances required within the course of a game as basic. Thus, running and tagging are constituent perform-ances of a tag game, guessing word meanings is a constituent performance in many a charade, and so forth. We have plenty of evidence by now that—other things being equal—the very exposure of children to a given game, with its structure and demand for certain constituent performances, may have terrific clinical impact on the events at least of that day. Wherever we miscalculate the overwhelming effect that the seductive aspect of certain games may have (flashlight hide-and-seek in the dark just before bedtime) we may ask for trouble, while many a seemingly risky game can safely be played if enough ego-supportive controls are built right into it (the safety zone to which you can withdraw without having to admit you get tired or scared, etc.). In short, while I would hardly relegate the total treatment job of severely dis-

turbed children in a mental hospital ward to that factor alone, I certainly would want to figure on it as seriously as I would calculate the mental hygiene aspects of other factors more traditionally envisioned as being of clinical concern. What I say here about games goes for many other activities patients engage in—arts and crafts, woodwork, outings, overnight trips, cookouts, discussion groups, musical evenings. Which of these things takes place, where, with which feeling tone, and with what structural and activity ingredients is as characteristic of a given "milieu" as the staff that is hired.

9. *Space, equipment, time, and props.* What an assortment of names, but I know as yet of no collective noun that would cover them all equally well. Since I have made such a fuss about this for years, I may try to be shorter about it than seems reasonable. Remember what a bunch of boys do when running through a viaduct with an echo effect? Remember what may happen to a small group who are supposed to discuss plans for their next Scout meeting, who have to hold this discussion unexpectedly, in a huge gym with lots of stuff around, instead of in their usual clubroom? Remember what will happen to a baseball that is put on the table prematurely while they are still supposed to sit quietly and listen, and remember what happens to many a well-intended moral lecture to a group of sloppy campers, if you timed it so badly that the swimming bell started ringing before you had finished? Do I still have to prove why I think that what an outfit does with arrangements of time expectations and time distribution, what prop-exposure the youngsters are expected to stand or avoid, what space arrangements are like, and what equipment does to the goals you have set for yourself, should be listed along with the important "properties" of a place where clinical work with children takes place? So far I have found that in hospitals this item tends to be left out of milieu discussions by psychiatrists and sociologists alike; only the nurses and attendants have learned by bitter experience that it may pay to lend an ear to it.

10. *The seepage from the world outside.* One of the hardest "milieu aspects" to assess in a short visit to any

institution is the amount of "impact from the larger universe and the surrounding world" that actually seeps through its walls and finds its way into the lives of the patients. No outfit is airtight, no matter how many keys and taboos are in use. In our own little children's ward-world, for instance, there are the following "seepage ingredients from the world outside" that are as much a part of our "milieu," as it hits the boys, as anything else: Adult visitors and the "past case history" flavor they leave behind. Child visitors and the "sociological body odor" of the old neighborhood, or the new one that they exude. Excursions that we arrange, old haunts from prehospital days, which we happen to drive through unintentionally on our way to our destination. Plenty of purposely pulled-in outside world through movies, television, pictures, and stories we may tell them. And, of course, school is a full-view window hopefully opened wide for many vistas to be seen through it—if we only could get our children to look.

There is the "hospital impact" of the large building that hits them whenever they leave the ward floor in transit, the physically sick patients they meet on the elevator who stir the question up again in their own mind: "Why am I here?" There are the stories other boys tell, the staff tells, the imputed secrets we may by hiding from them whenever we seem eager to divert attention to something else. As soon as the children move into the open cottage, the word "seepage" isn't quite as correct any more. Suffice it to say: the type and amount of "outside world" particles that are allowed in or even eagerly pulled in constitute a most important part of the lives of the captive population of an institutional setting, and want to be given attention to in an appraisal of just what a given "milieu" holds.

11. *The system of umpiring services and traffic regulation between environment and child.* Those among you who have a sharp nose for methodological speculation may want to object and insist that I am jumping category dimensions in tagging on this item and the next one on my list. I don't want to quarrel about this now. For even

though you may be right, it is too late today to start a new chapter, so please let me get away with tagging these two items on here. In some ways they still belong, for whether there are any umpiring services built into an institution, and what they are like, is certainly an important "milieu property" in my estimation.

What I have in mind here has been described in more detail in a previous paper.[3] In short, it runs somewhat like this: Some "milieu impacts" hit the children directly; nobody needs to interpret or translate. Others hit the child all right, but to have their proper impact someone has to do some explaining. It makes a great difference whether a child who is running away unhappy, after a cruel razzing received from a thoughtless group, is left to deal with this all by himself; or whether the institution provides interpretational or first-aid services for the muddled feelings at the time. Some of our children, for instance, might translate such an experience, which was not intended by the institution, into additional resentment against the world. With sympathy in the predicament offered by a friendly adult who tags along and comforts, this same experience may well be decontaminated or even turned into the opposite.

A similar item is the one I had in mind in using the phrase "traffic regulations." Much give-and-take can follow naturally among the inhabitants of a given place. Depending on the amount of their disturbance, though, some social interactions that normal life leaves to the children's own resources require traffic supervision by an adult. I would like to know whether a given milieu has foreseen this and can guarantee the provision of some help in the bartering custom among the youngsters, or whether that new youngster will be mercilessly exposed to the wildest blackmail with no help from anyone, the moment he enters the doors to my ward. In short, it is like asking what medical first-aid facilities are in a town before one moves into it. Whether this belongs to the concept of what makes up a "town," or whether it should be listed under a separate heading I leave for a later chance to thrash out. All I want to point at now is that the nature of and existence or nonexistence of umpiring services and social traffic regulations is as "real" a property of a setup as its walls, kitchen equipment, and clinical beliefs.

12. *The thermostat for the regulation of clinical resilience.* If it is cold in an old cabin somewhere in the midst of "primitive nature," the trouble is obvious: either there isn't any fire going or something is wrong with the stove and the whole heating system, so it doesn't give off enough heat. If I freeze in a building artificially equipped with all the modern conveniences, such a conclusion might be off the beam. The trouble may simply be that the thermostat isn't working right. This, like the previous item, is a property of a given milieu rather than a "milieu ingredient" in the stricter sense of the word. However, it is of such utmost clinical relevance that it has to go in here somewhere. In fact, I have hardly ever participated in a discussion on the milieu concept without having this item come up somehow or other.

The term under which it is more often referred to is actually that of "flexibility," which most milieu therapy enthusiasts praise as "good" while the bad men in the picture are the ones that think "rigidity" is a virtue. I have more reasons to be tired of this either/or issue than I can list in the remaining time. It seems to me that the "resilience" concept fits better what most of us have so long tried to shoot at with the flexibility label. A milieu certainly needs to be sensitive to the changing needs of the patients during different phases of the treatment process. It needs to "tighten up"—lower the behavioral ceiling when impulse-panic looms on the horizon; and it may have to lift it when self-imposed internal pressures mount. Also, it needs to limit spontaneity and autonomy of the individual patient in early phases of intensive disorder and rampant pathology; it needs to throw in a challenge toward autonomy and even the risking of mistakes, when the patient goes through the later phases of recovery. Especially when severely disturbed children are in the process of going through an intensive phase of "improvement," the resilience of a milieu to make way for its implications is as important as its ability to "shrink back" during a regressive phase.

JUST HOW DOES THE MILIEU DO IT?

Listing these 12 variables of important milieu aspects that can be differentiated as explorable issues in their own right is only part of the story. I hold no brief for this list, and I am well aware of its methodological complications and deficiencies. The major value of listing them at all lies in the insistence that *there are so many of them* and that they *can be separately studied and explored.* This should at least help us to secure ourselves against falling in love with any one of them to the exclusion of the others, and of forcing any discipline that wants to tackle the job, whether it be psychiatry, sociology, or what not, to look beyond its traditional scope and directly into the face of uncompromisingly multifaceted facts.

Since the major sense in all this milieu noise is primarily the impact of these variables on the treatment process of the children we are trying to cure, the question of the clinical assessment of the relevance of each of these items is next on the docket of urgent jobs. This one we shall have to skip for today, but time may allow us to point at the other question leading into the most important core of the problem: If we assume that any one of these milieu ingredients, or whatever you want to call them, may have positive or negative impacts on our therapeutic work—how do they do it? Just what goes on when we claim that any one of those milieu givens "did something to our youngsters"? This gets us into one of the most noteworthy gaps in all our theory of personality, and frankly, I don't think even our most up-to-date models are quite up to it. True enough, we have learned a few things about just how pathology is influenced in the process of a specific form of psychiatric interview, and we know a little about influence of human over human, here or there. We are not so well off when we come to the impact of more abstract-sounding entities, such as "group structure." We have even more trouble to figure out just how space, time, and props are supposed to do their job, whenever we claim that they have the power to throw an otherwise well-planned therapeutic experience out of gear.

One phase of this problem sounds familiar—when

psychiatry first began to take the impact of "culture" seriously, we were confronted with a similar puzzler: just where, within the individual, is what going on at the moment when we say a "cultural" factor had some influence on a given behavior of a person?

This problem is far from solved. I think it might help, though, to introduce a thought that might lead to greater specificity in observation and ultimately to more "usable" forms of data collection. Frankly, I have never seen the "milieu" at work. My children are never hit by "the milieu" as such. It always hits them in a specific form and at a given time and place. I think the researchers who play with the concept of a "setting" have a technical advantage over us in this field. Of course, the setting alone doesn't interest me either. For what it all hinges on is just what *experience* a given setting produces or makes possible within my child patient and what this child patient does with it.

Rather than study the "milieu" per se, and then the "reactions of the children," how about making it a four-step plan? Let's keep the "milieu" as the overall concept on the fringe; its basic ingredients come close to my youngsters only insofar as they are contained in a given setting. For example, my children on the ward can be found engaged in getting up, eating a meal or snacks; they can be found roaming around the playroom, or in a station wagon, with all their overnight gear, on the way to their camping site. They can be found in their arts and crafts room, or schoolroom, engaged in very specific activities. Enough of illustrations—the point is, in all those settings the whole assortment of milieu aspects hits them in very *specific forms:* There is an outspoken behavioral expectation floating through that arts and crafts room at any time. There are spatial characteristics, tools, and props. There is the potential reaction of the other child or adult, the feeling tone of the group toward the whole situation as such; there is the impact of people's goal values and attitudes as well as that of the behavior of the child's neighbor who clobbers him right now with his newly made viking sword. In short: *I may be able to isolate observations of milieu ingredients as they "hit" the child in a specific setting during a specific activity.* On such a narrowed-down level of observation, I may also be able to trace the actual *experience* that such a concrete situation in a given setting produced in the child; and if I know what the child *did with the experience*, it may make sense, since I have both ends of the line before me. The youngster's reaction to his experience—the nature of the ingredients of the "setting" on both ends of the line, plus plenty of good hunches on the child's experience while exposed to its impact.

It seems to me that much more work needs to be done with the concept of "setting" so as to make it clinically more meaningful, and that sharper observational techniques, capable of catching "implied milieu impact" as well as "child's coping with" the experience produced by the setting, need to be developed. This, however, leads into a theme to be discussed in other sessions of our Annual Meeting.

One more word before closing. It is time that we take Erik Erikson's warning more seriously than we have done so far—and I mention him as symbolizing a point of view that many of us have been increasingly impressed by. If I may try to say what I think he would warn us about after all this discussion of "milieu impacts" on therapy of children, it would run somewhat like this: Why are you still talking most of the time as though "milieu" or "environment" were some sort of rigid structure, and the individuals were good for nothing but to "react" to it?

How does some of that "environment" you talk about come into being, after all? Couldn't we reverse the story just as well, and ask: "What do your child patients do to their milieu?"—not only: "What does the milieu do to them?" Mine, by the way, are doing plenty to it, and I have little doubt but that many of the items that we describe as though they were fixtures on the environmental scene are actually products of the attitudes and actions of the very people who, after they have produced them, are also exposed to their impact in turn.

I, for one, would want to exclaim loudly what I didn't

dare whisper too much at the start of my paper, or I would have scared you off too soon. I would like to find out not only what milieu is and how it operates but also how we can describe it, how we influence it, and by what actions of all involved it is, in turn, created or molded. At the moment I am convinced of only one thing for sure—we all have quite a way to go to achieve either of those tasks.

NOTES

1. Fritz Redl, "The Meaning of 'Therapeutic Milieu,'" in *Symposium on Preventive and Social Psychiatry, 15-17 April 1957*, Walter Reed Army Institute of Research (Washington, D.C.: U.S. Government Printing Office, 1958).
2. Some more detailed description of this appears in *Group Processes: Transactions of the Fourth (1957) Conference*, ed., Bertram Schaffner (New York: Josiah Macy, Jr. Foundation, 1959).
3. Fritz Redl, "Strategy and Techniques of the Life Space Interview," *American Journal of Orthopsychiatry* 29 (1959): 1-19.

9. The Role of Education in the Treatment of Emotionally Disturbed Children through Planned Ego Development

J. Cotter Hirschberg

In discussing the role of education in the treatment of emotionally disturbed children through planned ego development, I shall consider the following areas: (1) the teacher's need for an accurate, dynamic diagnosis of the child, his learning problems, the total picture of his emotional problems in particular, and the assets or resources he brings that the teacher may use; (2) the evaluation of the school as an educational community and as a social community, including both peers and adults in authority; (3) the *therapeutic* meanings of school as a reality experience to the emotionally disturbed child; (4) the *educational* meanings of school as a reality experience to the emotionally disturbed child; and (5) the parental attitudes to such a school experience and the child's reaction to such parental attitudes.

The school experience can play a major role in the total treatment process with an emotionally disturbed child. It

Reprinted from the *American Journal of Ortho-psychiatry*, vol. 23, no. 44 (October 1953), pp. 684-90, by permission of the author and the journal.

is an experience with great ego-building potentials since it is oriented to reality; it aims toward the development of skill and mastery; it can aid in the development of self-image and even of self-esteem; it can offer a source of gratification at varying levels of ability, of aspiration, and of interests; and it can utilize, in successive stages of development and improvement in the child, varying amounts of group participation and group identification depending on the child's strengths and the needs at the time.

Unfortunately, it is also true that the school experience can be an ego-alien experience for the emotionally disturbed child unless certain factors in the school structure, in the teacher, and in the child himself are carefully evaluated.

To consider the child first, it is obvious that an adequate educational program must be based on an adequate evaluation of the individual child and his total dynamics, not simply in relation to his problems but also in relation to whatever conflict-free areas of response he has, as well as every interest, desire, or need that can motivate a positive, active response in the educational setting. Interests in bugs, worms, food, kittens, radios, television, the planetary spaces — whatever their dynamics — may be used as stepping-stones to satisfying reality and ego-building experiences. One child at the time of his entrance into the educational program was so bound by his own anxiety that he was unable to deal with any teaching material that related to the present in any way whatsoever. The only two available areas for the teacher were in terms of the archaeological past or the far distant space. It was necessary that the teaching material begin with a study of dinosaurs and the earth in the time of their inhabiting it on the one hand, or with the science of astronomy on the other. Through the use of these meaningful but "safe" areas, the teacher gradually constructed stepping-stones on which to bring the child into more presently related educational material.

In careful studies of the severely disturbed child, the child of "atypical development," or the schizophrenic child, it is of great interest that varying degrees of organic brain damage are so frequently found, which different children handle differently — compensating, narrowing the area of response, or retreating deeply. However, even where no question of organic brain damage exists, the need for careful consideration of the total dynamic picture in the child is always paramount, since the rate of growth and development varies in each individual child, and even within the same child, the various aspects of the developmental process do not always proceed at the same rate, and are differently affected by the dynamics of the child. Moreover, since each developmental step is taken tentatively, an emotionally disturbed child may fluctuate even more than normal children do from one level of adjustment to another in the transitional stages, and the educational program must be flexible enough to meet the changing individual needs of each child. In this sense a positive school experience is one that not only meets the particular "educational" need of the child but that serves to improve the child's total functional capacity. The teacher of an emotionally disturbed child is required to teach in the best and broadest sense of that term: that is, to teach in a manner that both imparts knowledge and skill, and also best meets the emotional needs of the child and his individual potentialities for growth in coping constructively with his problems.

This means that we must always conceive of our total dynamic picture of the child as one that sees this child, at least potentially, in his family unit and in his community. We may have to start with a tutor who works with him individually; we hope to end up with his full participation in a normal school group. Before we start we need an evaluation of the school experience, first, as an educational community; and second, as a social community. Considering the school as an educational community first, we have three major possibilities: the ordinary classroom, the special class, and the special school. The emotionally disturbed child will be able to use or will need one or the other of these possibilities depending on several factors:

He can usually adjust to the *ordinary classroom* if: (1)

he is able to respond positively to group pressure and to the direction of an adult who is concerned with the group as a whole, and is not free for intensive attention to him alone; (2) his motivation for cooperation is high; (3) he is able to derive satisfactions from usual classroom activities; (4) his overt behavior is not disrupting to the group; and (5) he requires no special supervision or observation.

A *special classroom* or special school will be necessary depending on the degree of deviation from these. Although these factors have usually been stated so as to imply negative criteria for special schooling. I am sure it is obvious to us all that genuine positive values accrue to the individual child in special schools who has not been able to use constructively the ordinary classroom experience. Special schools provide smaller groups, special motivation, and more attention for each child within the framework of a group situation.

Thinking at this moment of the child only, the following factors play an important role in the decision to place an emotionally disturbed child in a *residential* school:

1. In general, any child under five years of age is so much better dealt with within a family unit (his own home or foster home care) and the role of the parents is so crucial in the younger child that day care is usually preferable to full residential schooling.

2. In general, a child is not brought into residential care unless the home situation is destructive to the child's emotional development or the child has become psychologically intolerable to the home. In general, such residential care must be evaluated not only in terms of the ability of the particular child but also in regard to the family unit and the effect of removal on the child's interaction with other children in the family.

3. When the child's emotional conflict is directly centered about his struggle in his relationships with his parents, one needs to think seriously about the effects of separating the child from his parents and removing him from an active struggle in his attempt to resolve his relationship with them unless, of course, the struggle becomes destructive for the child and his parents. However, in a child in whom the major conflicts are those of

unmet dependency needs or other oral-fixated problems, or in whom the major struggle centers about anal conflict — in such a child the relationship with his parents is so greatly disturbed and the defensive patterns so firmly formed that it may be necessary to separate the child from the parents in order to more adequately treat the illness.

When we think of the educational experience as involving both an educational and a social community, we see that although the relative emphasis placed on individual therapy, group living, and "formal education" will vary according to the diagnosis and the analysis of the dynamic factors entering into the emotional disturbance, we must plan our schooling as a comprehensive approach to the total growth process of the child. This means that we must allow in our structure for the interaction of the individual therapist, the social worker, the group worker, and the teacher.

However, when the reality of the school experience is examined in terms of its *therapeutic meanings* in the planned ego development of an emotionally disturbed child, we have two important aspects to consider:

First, to be part of a total therapeutic experience (or part of planned ego development) the teacher-pupil relationship must offer dependable acceptance of the child and of his dependency strivings, and his need for security, while at the same time the teacher must have insight into her own needs as well as the child's in order to maintain her freedom to give, or to withhold, or to structure the relationship on the basis of the *child* and her understanding. Only in this kind of relationship can the child's ego expand and be strengthened and hence the child gain greater capacity to adapt to life stress. Furthermore, the more insight the teacher has into the teacher-pupil relationship, the greater the relief of the child's anxiety about any such close relationship. Moreover, in those children unable to see problems or causation within themselves, the teacher through her tolerant understanding of motivation can foster through her own attitudes in the relationship the development of a more tolerant superego, with resultant increased ego strength for the child. The achievement of this sort of teacher-pupil relationship depends upon the attitudes of the teacher herself; she must be sufficiently at peace with her own childhood problems to allow a child to struggle with his own solutions and in his own way in the educational process without letting her own conflicts intrude.

Frequently the educational process of an emotionally disturbed child is measured in units that are not used as standards of measurement in the ordinary school experience — such units as the development of less tension within the child, a decrease in testing, demanding behavior so that the learning capacity of the child is freed, and a more comfortable relationship with the teacher. Many times, this sort of progress may have to take place before the child can achieve scholastic progress and before the teacher can observe any increased educational achievement of the child within the school program. In this way the child's educational progress in the school program has to be evaluated in terms of the individual usefulness of the school experience to the child. It requires real maturity within the teacher to accept these units of educational progress while scholastic achievement is being delayed for many months. The teacher-pupil relationship allows the educational process to help the child learn and to help the child grow, but it always remains structured around the purpose of *education*, and not *treatment* of the child. In both teaching and treatment there is the common goal of achieving sufficient emotional growth in the child so that more effective functioning will be possible from the child, but the methods and the structure differ.

This leads us to our second important point regarding the therapeutic meanings of education: namely, that the child's anxiety is dealt with in the educational process through the *use* of reality rather than through the *interpretation* of it. This can be seen in several ways:

1. The relationship between the teacher and the child is seldom if ever interpreted, whereas in psychotherapy the therapist-child relationship is often interpreted.

2. In teaching, the need is to know which defense patterns are healthy for the particular child in his conflicts

and then to attempt to support and strengthen such defenses; whereas in therapy an attempt is made to give the child either verbal or experiential insight into the nature of his defenses, into the ways in which conflict is handled.

3. In teaching, we try to help the child with the reality pressures that have increased his need for the disturbed behavior, and to offer tolerable or attractive reality stimulations at his level or capacity to respond; whereas in therapy the task is to free the child of his own internal needs for disturbed behavior; we are attempting to make certain unconscious material conscious. By and large, educational procedures are aimed to affect consciously available material.

4. The teacher is focused on the "situational present" and offers the child realistic help with difficult patterns of adaptation and learning; whereas the therapist focuses on the "historical present" by offering his help in relationship to the internalized as well as situational conflicts.

5. As a corollary to much of the above, the teacher seeks generally to allay the child's anxiety through the educational process; whereas the therapist often intentionally arouses, for a therapeutic goal, amounts of anxiety that the child can tolerate in order to facilitate the treatment process. Although anxiety may be generated in the child by the teaching process, the teacher frequently uses her relationship with the child for the purpose of absorbing such anxieties; this ability to "feel oneself" into the child's attitudes and yet not lose one's identity is a valuable capacity for both teacher and therapist. Although anxiety may be part of the motivation toward learning, the teacher responds to such anxiety by realistic environmental modification (such as elasticity of the daily program to meet the individual's interest span and ability to interact with others, or the elasticity of the daily program to meet each individual's different levels of ability or each one's specific handicaps) rather than by the interpretive use of such anxiety, as a therapist might.

In regard to the specifically *educational* role of the school experience in planned ego development, the emotionally disturbed child is dependent upon the educator to a far greater degree than is the average child in the classroom, since he is frequently less able to endure the ordinary anxieties aroused in a classroom and is more sensitive to the teacher-pupil relationship.

Likewise the *content* as well as the *process* of the teaching may have particular significance for the emotionally disturbed child. We cannot neglect the "what" in our interest in the "how, when, and why." One of our children was so disturbed by continual sexualized fantasy material that the content of almost all of the ordinary classroom teaching was itself sexualized. With this child considerable time was spent by her teacher, who recognized the great interference of such sexualization with the child's learning process, in helping the child deal with the teaching material in terms of its reality meanings. The more the content can be oriented to the reality of the child and his interests and needs, the greater the likelihood that the learning experience will be integrated into the personality with a decreasing need for maintaining defense patterns that prevent learning. Thus the pedagogical techniques of the teacher become a major tool, and the need for the teacher to uncover conflict in order to teach emotionally disturbed children does not exist. This does not mean that *feelings* of the children about the realities of the learning process and the classroom are to be ignored. Emotionally disturbed children need to learn that, although certain actions can and should be controlled in the classroom, the feelings themselves are not forbidden and need not lead to guilt. If the teacher is willing to let the children be honest about their feelings in the day-to-day realities of the school situation, the children can use this experience to help them face their feelings in therapy about the larger conflicts that lie behind their disturbed behavior. Indeed the child's feeling about the classroom and about the learning process may provide the therapist with vivid and inappropriate reactions to reality that can make his treatment process a more meaningful experience for the child.

In addition to all these values, however, the achievement of mastery and skill through learning provides the child with positive methods for dealing with anxiety, for changing a previously passive role into an active one, and for gratifying needs in accord with their aims through the use of ego mechanisms and skills. The school must provide a well-rounded program in which each child can experience some degree of educational success, however small, and, in time, success in group activity as well. This means that ability in any field of endeavor can have a positive value at first to the emotionally disturbed child—painting, singing, gardening, carpentry, making doll clothes, cooking can all be valued as well as scholastic achievement. Some disturbed children make progress through small doses of formal achievement where others need to start with nonacademic experiences.

When sufficient therapeutic progress has been made, and when the school experience has been sufficiently weighed on the side of successful experiences, then the readiness of the child for a broader educational approach will become apparent. It is evident that the focus in this paper is on the emotional disturbance of the child and on the use of education in relation to it, rather than any emphasis on the training of the child in preparation for a particular potential future. This choice of focus for the teaching program can give rise to concern on the part of parents whose philosophy about the goals of education may differ considerably from this.

Moreover, the child brings into the school experience the many guilts and the many angry feelings that parental attitudes such as these have aroused within him, and the child wishes to discuss not only his feelings about these attitudes of his parents but also his past traumatic events, his past failures, his past anxieties in other school experiences—a remembrance of things past that every emotionally disturbed child carries with him. All such feelings that parents may reveal in discussing the education of their child have to be recognized and dealt with in order that their anxieties within the parent-child relationship can emerge and the parent be helped to see his role in the emotional disturbance and to accept change within the child. I do not wish to discuss any aspects of the casework process with parents that is essential to the treatment of emotionally disturbed children, but rather I wish to stress the continuous communication between the parents and the school that is necessary in order to make possible a worthwhile educational program for emotionally disturbed children. The need to integrate the total process of treatment of the child with the attitudes of the parents is as important in the education of the emotionally disturbed child as in any other aspect of the treatment program.

There are many provocative areas that cannot be discussed in this brief presentation: the necessary inter-action of teacher, therapist, caseworker, and residential staff; the dynamics of the interaction of the children themselves within the educational setting; the multiple aspects of group dynamics with emotionally disturbed children in the classroom; such ego-alien educational experiences as "slack time" in the classroom, punitive behavior of teachers, and social stress; the ways in which motivation toward learning can be cultivated; the point at which in a total therapeutic program "schoolwork" should be attempted; the flexible use of community resources to enrich the educational program; the preparation of the child to enter public school; the operation of mental hygiene principles in the traditional teaching program and in relation to the overall school administration; modifica-tion of curricula and of environmental facilities for emotionally disturbed children; and a whole host of issues that will undoubtedly occur to others.

10. Social Casework Service

By training and experience the social caseworker is basically concerned with the individual in the situation, ever sensitive and mindful of the individual needs of the child, and alert to opportunities during case conferences and in private consultations to interpret these personality needs and the corresponding treatment program to other staff members.

There are other important functions for the social caseworker, too: (1) He should gather and evaluate significant material from appropriate sources to be used as a basis for the initial (or intake) case conference and, as a member of the treatment planning committee, aid in planning the treatment program for the individual. (2) He should discuss such material at the conference and share it with other staff members who will be working with the child. (3) He should maintain a continuing relationship with the child, keeping alert to, and calling attention to, imminent or changing needs, and interpreting these to other staff members. (4) He is responsible for recording the student's progress reports, case conference summaries, reports from various staff members, reports from the community, and, in general, maintaining the individual record of the student. (5) He should maintain a continuing relationship with the families of the children, geared toward better understanding of the student's problems and improvement of the family relationships, by serving as the

Reprinted from *Institutions Serving Delinquent Children: Guides and Goals,* Children's Bureau Publication no. 360, Washington, D.C.: U.S. Government Printing Office, revised 1962, pp. 59-60.

liaison between the child and all contacts he has with the outside community, including visits from relatives, emergency home visits, vacation visits, and contacts with other social agencies concerned with the child or his family. (6) He should assist the staff and the local community in becoming more aware of the needs of children as individuals by active participation in the inservice training, staff development, and public relations program.

Every student should be specifically assigned to a social caseworker. This, of course, does not mean that every child will have a sustained contact with the worker on an intensive, frequent interview basis. In many cases, it simply means that the social caseworker will be available to the child and to the staff members who are in contact with that child, and will take a continuing interest in the execution of the treatment plans for the individual child as long as he remains in residence. The way the social caseworker may discharge his functions may vary from case to case and depends on an analysis of the situations in which a student may need interview service.

11. Some Aspects of Psychotherapy in a Residential Treatment Center

Richard D. Brodie

It is the thesis of this paper that individual psychotherapy in a residential setting differs sufficiently from outpatient psychotherapy to justify an effort to outline some dimensions of the problem. The problems the child brings into therapy, especially in the early phases, are determined not only by his psychopathology but also by specific conflicts that are aroused by his removal from the home and by the nature of his peer group. The therapist's relationship with the patient shifts from the more traditional office-centered neutral role to that of a more active participant in the child's daily life. Certain functions normally performed by parents, such as visiting the schoolteacher, accompanying a frightened child to a medical exam, or attending Boy Scout functions, are more or less regularly done by the child's therapist. Informal contacts outside the office, frequent conferences with residence personnel, and participation in decisions about numerous aspects of the patient's life become a part of the therapist's activity to a degree that cannot happen in

Reprinted from the *American Journal of Orthopsychiatry*, vol. 36, no. 4 (July 1966), pp. 712-19, by permission of the author and the journal. The author wishes to thank Dr. Robert A. Young for his assistance in the cases described here and for his help in clarifying issues in residential treatment.

outpatient therapy. Finally, the therapist gears his efforts initially toward encouraging the patient to interact with his milieu which is intended to be therapeutic and growth fostering and which is much more predictable than the environment of an outpatient about which we usually know very little.

While these variations make the psychotherapy a more complex process to understand, particularly in sorting out transference reactions from the child's reaction to one as a real person, they also permit a more effective and comprehensive effort toward the final goal which is defined here, as it was by Bettelheim, as "the mastery over inner and outer forces."[1]

The degree to which the therapist involves himself in the child's daily life varies according to the child's involvement with the milieu. Four phases of attitudes and behavior are postulated. They represent the stages of evolution of the child's relationship to the residential treatment center. The major foci of this paper are on the second and third of the following phases: (1) a "honeymoon period" characterized by total compliance to the perceived demands of the residence; (2) a period of intense rejection; (3) a period of (ambivalent) dependence; and (4) a period of increasing independence during which the child becomes involved in preparing to return to the community.

In the first phase, which is often of very short duration, the child's behavior is scrupulously conforming. This appears to be accomplished by inhibition of impulses based on an externalized superego that is perceived as unduly severe. This perception may be due to the child's having experienced placement as a drastic form of punishment.[2]

The second phase is characterized by the active or passive rejection of the residence, sometimes alternated with excessive demands impossible of fulfillment. Derogation of the residence and its personnel and practices is paramount and, to the degree the child is able, he joins with his peers in establishing the validity of his notions regarding the negative or ineffectual efforts of the staff. In many ways, this phenomenon resembles the early phase of group therapy[3] when, after an initial period of breast beating and attention to the task at hand, the group bands together against the leader. In so doing, they avoid recognition of their dependency upon the adults. By banding together for the purpose of expressing hostility, they achieve a degree of closeness without experiencing the anxiety that is aroused by the tender feelings associated with closeness.

Whether the child in an inpatient setting manifests his rejection by running away, withdrawal, depression, or aggression against the environment, he appears to be expressing two facets of his concern. First is his denial of his feelings of abdication by his parents, frequently expressed as recurring strong wishes to go home, combined with the expression of varied ingenious notions as to how the residence staff or the therapists were to blame for the child being in "this lousy place." Second is his profound mistrust of establishing another relationship in which he is dependent and therefore vulnerable.

The principal differences in conducting psychotherapy occur during phase 2, and the main body of this text will be devoted to that phase.

> Larry, an 11-year-old borderline psychotic boy, had been in the residence for a year when I began to see him. He had spent a good part of the previous year requesting to go home and refusing to participate actively in the residential program including therapy. In school, he did no work other than silent reading. He was negatively regarded by most of the residence personnel. When I entered his room, not without trepidation, to introduce myself to him on the day the residence opened, he turned his back and refused to speak with me. I left a slip of paper on his desk which contained his therapy schedule and informed him of this, to which he replied that he would have no therapy.
>
> When he arrived the next day, bolstered by a decision he and some of his peers had made to "get $5.00 models out of their therapists," he launched into a tirade about my cheapness, the lack of supplies in my office, which was accompanied by swearing, spitting on the floor, and threats to destroy me as he thought he had his previous therapist. Over the next several weeks there evolved a sequence of behavior and thought, which focused on the negatives of his environment as contrasted with the

fancied positives of his home, and finally culminated in the notion that I was the cause of his being in the residence and therefore the proper object for his intense rage. When I commented that I must indeed be very powerful since at the time of his entrance I knew neither him nor anything about the residence, he grinned and conceded that perhaps there were a few people around who were not totally bad. This signaled a beginning shift in Larry from total rejection to ambivalent dependency characterized by splitting residence personnel into good and bad. He was still a year away from being able to focus his rage and feelings of abandonment onto his parents. Only when he became somewhat secure in the residence could he evaluate the destructive aspects of his own home.

The transition into phase 3 occurs gradually and evokes a variety of countertransference problems. Although it is generally agreed that the child's relationship to his therapist is less intense than that of an adult,[4] due to his natural dependence on his parents, the entrance of a child into a residence, which is often located far from his home, alters the usual paradigm in therapy and places the child in a position where he needs to find a central object for his dependency. It is not surprising that the therapist becomes invested with this role. The intense ambivalent expression of the child's most primitive needs places a considerable amount of stress on the therapist's energy and on his capacity to manage anxiety and anger without interfering with the therapeutic process.[5] It also provides him with more therapeutic leverage than is possible in outpatient treatment.

A part of the general problem of dealing with intensified dependency demands is the therapist's real function in the life of the child[6] and especially his possession of both power and information. Although administrator-therapist splits[7] exist in principle, they frequently are inseparable in practice. To expect the patient to be unaware of this is naive and destructive of the patient's trust. In fact, the taking over by the therapist of certain administrative functions seems to be indicated in some cases, particularly those in which anxiety is avoided by marked behavioral construction which is difficult to alter by verbal interchange. These children, probably originally phobic, have substituted behavioral avoidance accompanied by experiential dislike and apathy. They resemble some of the children described in the literature of school phobia[8] whose original panic and dread gives way over time to marked ego constriction and blunting of affect.

> One such patient is David who, compared to most of the boys, was a model of decorum and stability. He rarely became upset, was nearly always on the "honor list," and was involved only superficially with the staff and most patients. He did a minimum of schoolwork and avoided most physical activity, such as basketball and Scout overnights. In the first month of treatment with me, he indicated that he had "slid by" his previous year of therapy and intended to do the same with me. All of his avoidance of interaction was well rationalized by derogation of both the residence and such "kid stuff" as basketball and Boy Scouts. I told him that I did not know him well enough to be certain of what anxieties he was covering up by avoiding these activities, but that we would find out during the year as his participation in Boy Scouts and basketball was to become a mandatory part of his treatment. In disbelief, he told me that these programs were optional and that anyway he went home every three weeks, and his mother would brook no interference with these plans. I told him that the director of the residence and I had agreed that the plan I outlined would be best for his treatment and that I would deal with his mother if this became necessary. In the ensuing year, David's fear of injury and related inability to become aggressive in other than a passive way were demonstrated again and again on the basketball court. Parts of many of our therapy hours were spent in the gym playing basketball, which turned out to be an excellent vehicle for eliciting and dealing with fears of hurting me and himself. My assumption of an active fatherly role enhanced the development of a strong, albeit ambivalent, dependency relationship, and led David to a discussion of feelings of vulnerability and inadequacy in an affectively meaningful context.

By assuming a parental role, the therapist further complicates the technical problems involved in using information obtained outside the therapy hour with the child in a constructive manner. Even in outpatient therapy, the use of information obtained from parents and teachers and others is a controversial issue.[9] Weiss recently stated that in child analysis no outside information need be obtained or used.[10] His arguments do not appear to be valid for residential treatment, especially when the communicative patterns of the residential therapist are aimed at increasing trust and enhancing learning.

The importance of communication in the etiology and treatment of childhood disorders has been stressed by Reusch, Goldfarb, and Anthony, among others.[11] All of the children in the Manville School suffer from learning disorders whatever their primary diagnosis. The presence of family secrets,[12] and more recently the existence of a pattern of secrecy in communication,[13] has been found to be a significant factor in the mothers of children with learning disorders. For the therapist to be secretive and withholding with the patient may reproduce and perpetuate certain crucial aspects of the environment in which the patient's difficulties originated and place undue strain on the relationship to the detriment of the mutual respect necessary for successful therapy. For all patients communication or lack of communication has a special meaning correlating to some degree with social class and with parental use of language.[14] In a residence, it is further complicated by the abundance of information that is available to the therapist. The use of the information with the patient can have an accusatory or feeding quality dependent on the patient's history. When the patient has experienced much secrecy, withholding, and behind-the-back maneuvers by his parents, an open approach is indicated.

> David's parents had been in severe marital discord for years. Very little communication occurred between each other or between them and the children. While proper social decorum in the form of an armed truce existed, David was bewildered by the absence of explanations from his parents. Early memories revolved around being told not to see or hear what was going on. His placement in the residence had been sudden, and the reasons for it obscure to him. In treatment he was eager for information about what the counselors knew and said about him, what teachers said, what was in the counselor's notes, and how and what had led me to say or do a certain thing. Each question was answered fully and

directly and led to an increase in trust and in material relative to his own life. His curiosity, long inhibited, became alive again, and he engaged in long discussions with certain counselors and teachers. His hunger for information began to encompass things of a more objective and less personal nature. In short, one major aspect of his learning problem, that related to the acquisition of knowledge, became accessible to the milieu.

Larry, on the other hand, had been barraged by stimuli that his young mind had lacked the capacity to assimilate. In his first 18 months, he witnessed from his crib frequent sexual behavior on the part of his natural mother, culminating in her running off with another man. From then, through his sixth year, he witnessed frequent arguments, was alternately indulged and punished, and slept with his father, who was in a profound depression over the loss of his wife. When his father remarried, his new stepmother, an ambulatory paranoid schizophrenic, engaged in a three-year running battle with him, aimed at proving that he was crazy so that she could feel that she was not. When he entered the residence, his experience with the receipt of environment stimuli in general and words in particular had been largely in an ego-assaultive context. He showed no interest in the notes for more than a year, and would tolerate no communication from me of information obtained from counselors (phase 2). In his second year of treatment with me he allowed me to comment on what he said to me, but did not want me to tell him about the observations of the residence staff (entering phase 3). In his third year, he eagerly sought information from the counselor's notes (phase 3).

David avoided peer relations just as he avoided interaction with other aspects of his environment.

In therapy, David's references to peers were disparaging, and he held himself aloof from them. Historically, he had experienced no close peer relationships. In his family, which was characterized by aloofness, his guarded relationship with his parents was reflected in his lack of closeness with his two younger sisters whom he regarded as the personification of ego-alien primitive impulses. In line with the therapeutic program outline with David (above), his disparaging contempt of peers and aloofness from them was challenged by me, the defensive character of his behavior and his underlying loneliness were emphasized. The constant challenge by me in the context of our fairly close relationship set him to increased involvement with his peers, which provided more material for therapy and (to his surprise) provided gratification for him.

The advantage of treating a patient in a residence is clear both in terms of the pressure one can put on the patient once a therapeutic alliance is established and in terms of the feedback available from the therapeutic milieu.

Prior to the pressure in treatment David had rarely presented difficulties to the childcare staff.

After he had been in residence for a little over one year, the counselor's monthly notes read as follows:

> "David still seems to be the same quiet, cooperative boy of the past months. . . . he often seems uninterested in or unaware of activities going on about him." Later in the year the following description was recorded: "For the last few weeks, he has spent very little time in his room. Tommy has been the object of scapegoating, led by David. Recently David has been in an argumentative mood. He has continued to set the group against the counselors. He himself has been revolting against the rules and the attitudes of the counselors." At the end of a year, the counselor's summary noted: "Until March, 1963, David was obeying rules without incident, but since March he has rebelled against the rules and has had a difficult time accepting any explanations. David's peer group has increased during the year. Some of the changes noted from one year ago are that David appears to use scapegoating of others less, does more acting out against counselors and has more and closer ties with his peers."

PEER GROUP ACCEPTANCE

When the child begins to use mastery of school material and Boy Scout achievements as a source of peer group acceptance, the therapist has a golden opportunity to enter the picture and enhance the emergence of socially rewarding autonomous ego functions as well as to improve peer group acceptance. While it may be argued that such aspects of the child's development should be handled by others, so that the therapy should not be contaminated, it is often the case that the child must test out his approach to learning in the relative comfort of the therapy hour. As Ekstein pointed out, learning to love precedes loving to learn, and learning in a love relationship precedes learning in a neutral relationship.[15]

Larry's maneuvers around math were extremely phobic. He floundered upon presentation of the simplest addition problem and refused to take the annual achievement test in arithmetic. Given the WISC by a female staff psychologist with a small scar on her leg, he reacted to the arithmetic subtest by asking her what happened to her leg, and then fleeing the office. For two years he was terrified of engaging himself in arithmetic. In his third year of residential treatment, he arrived carrying an arithmetic book and asking me for help. When I set up a problem for him, he headed out the door, announcing that I was a mental nut. I called him back and told him that calling his therapist a mental nut had become a religion with him. He returned to his seat and confronted the problem. Several weeks of calling himself stupid, referring to his sister's good arithmetic skills, the cost of his residential treatment, and his parent's financial difficulties ensued. The comfortable therapeutic relationship was used to encourage skills in their nascent phase. After these few sessions, I rarely saw Larry in the context of math tutoring. His teacher reported erratic work, but steady progress in math. His peers ceased teasing him about his stupidity in math.

SIBLING RIVALRY

The occurence of sibling rivalry is a common characteristic of both adult and child therapy.

A college student with achievement difficulties is seen in the same office as the children who are patients of the author. Following an hour with a child patient in which there was arithmetic material scattered on my desk, the adult patient arrived for his next appointment with his college statistics book and demanded tutoring. On another occasion, the same patient, after viewing a plastic model built by an outpatient, spent his whole weekend compulsively building models.

Sibling rivalry in a residence is more intense due to the physical closeness of the patients and their constant contact with each other. The patients of the same therapist compete for him, and all of the patients compete among themselves as to who has the best therapist.

Severely traumatic experiences with siblings emerge with striking clarity in a residence, and are acted out with the other patients.

When Larry was in his third year of residence, a new patient was assigned to me. Larry regressed dramatically and, shortly thereafter, as he was leaving on an afternoon trip, he spied me sitting outside the clinic with two social workers. Repetitively, at the top of his voice, he yelled, "You already have a wife; why are you f——ing aroung with them." For several weeks he acted out his terror at my taking on a new patient while at the same time he denied it in therapy. The blending, in his mind, of his father's remarriage with my taking on another patient was condensed in his expletives toward me and his subsequent behavior in the residence.

SCAPEGOATING

Probably the most difficult and heartrending problem of residential therapy is that of scapegoating. The closeness of the peer group situation, the terror of the children, their intense sadomasochistic fixations, and a history of having been the scapegoat in the family—all contribute to the difficulty. These pathologic phenomena are superimposed on the developmental phenomenon of scapegoating, which occurs in late latency and adolescence.[16] In addition, the scapegoating and sibling rivalry that occur among the staff also contribute to the complexities of the problem.[17]

The therapist in a residential setting is likely to encounter both the scapegoat and the scapegoater. While the group issue of scapegoating must be handled by the childcare counselors, teachers, and administrative personnel, the feelings and masochistically provocative behavior of the patient need to be handled in therapy. The general aim is to increase the thickness of the patient's skin while maintaining some balance between avoiding overprotection and standing idly by while your patient is destroyed. The overprotective therapist not only irritates the childcare staff but also, by infantilization, increases the negative stereotyping and scapegoating of the patient. The therapist who remains aloof leaves his patient unprotected. The therapist's task with the patient is to explore the reasons in the patient that provoke the scapegoating and to enhance his development in the direction of peer group respect.

Larry was both a scapegoat and a scapegoater from the time he entered the residence. Isolated from his peers he attempted to provoke attacks on other children in order to circumvent attacks on himself. Therapeutic endeavors began to diminish his scapegoating, which had all of the characteristics of an identification with the aggressor even to the point where this sensitive Jewish boy glorified Nazis and drew the swastika everywhere. However, he remained without positive peer relations. Toward the end of his second year in the residence, Larry was invited to spend the weekend with Mike, a quiet but fairly popular boy on his floor. Suddenly Mike withdrew his invitation. Consultation with Mike's therapist, who is a close friend of the author's, revealed that an older and bigger boy had devaluated Mike by constantly saying that if Mike brought Larry home, Mike would be the laughingstock of the residence. Mike's therapist was reluctant to push Mike. I did not want to see Larry's defensive hostility heightened by the rejection of friendly overtures. We decided to see if we could help the two boys work it out. Two joint meetings were held. In the first session, the boys joined together in an attack on the residence and their therapists. In the beginning of the second joint interview, Mike and Larry competed with each other to see who had the worst home and the most miserable siblings. Finally, Mike stated that he feared Larry's devaluation of his home in the residence while Larry was anxious about his bed-wetting. The boys agreed to tell Mike's parents about Larry's bed-wetting, and Larry agreed not to devaluate Mike's home. The weekend was pleasant for the boys, and they both achieved an increment in peer group esteem and self-esteem.

PSYCHOTHERAPY AND MILIEU THERAPY

Lourie has described residential treatment as follows:

We would define residential treatment as therapeutically directed institutional or group care for emotionally disturbed children in which all possible ways of helping—casework, education, recreation, planned group life, and psychotherapy—are utilized and integrated into a clinically oriented and directed treatment plan for the individual child. It is not merely the removal of the child to benign environment where he is available for psychotherapeutic interviews. The essence of residential treatment lies in the milieu—in the complement of adult-child relationships and experiences which can be clinically manipulated and controlled in the interests of therapy.[18]

The integration of psychotherapy and milieu therapy is most important during the time the child is actively rejecting the residence, in order to facilitate positive views toward the child and avoid the calcification of negative stereotyping.

> In my first year of working with Larry, I observed that he was generally negatively regarded by residence personnel. He had been in the residence for one year and in treatment camp for two years when I began to work with him. The head teacher upon inquiry informed me that he did nothing in school. Counselors regarded him as an extremely difficult boy who caused constant frustration by his ambivalent response to all things offered. In the early phases of Larry's treatment, the therapist's role in the residence was aimed at dissipating the stereotype[19] and thus encouraging a benign and even benevolent attitude toward Larry.

In the third phase, the manipulations of the environment are less crucial. Here the conjoint therapeutic efforts of the therapist and other residence personnel are geared more toward the patients' unaddressed difficulties, that is, less toward pervasive problems and more toward identifiable specific conflicts.

In the fourth phase the milieu is accepted as representative of the outside world and therefore nontherapeutic or at least nonidiosyncratically adaptive.

> In his last year in residence, David complained incessantly about the rules. Although I could have ameliorated their effect on him, I refrained. Finally, he asked me what I thought of his being kept off the honor list for having taken only one shower in the last week rather than two. I told him that I thought that it was ridiculous for a residential treatment center for sick boys, but that it was not an unusual rule for a boarding school. He replied that he was in a residential treatment center and therefore he was not going to take a shower. I replied that this seemed reasonable to me if that was the way he saw himself, but that he would have to decide whether or not he felt 10 minutes of avoiding a shower was worth a week's restriction.

On another occasion he was given a room restriction for a very minor offense by a counselor. He asked me what I thought of it. I replied that I thought it was unfair but I could understand the stress the counselor was under at the time. He asked me to rectify the error. I said that I probably could, but that it would be at his expense since it would be hard for the counseling staff not to react on him for my interference with their efforts. He chose to serve the restriction.

In his most recent follow-up interview, David told me that his after-school employer sometimes landed on him, according to his mood, about various things in the store, but that David could see that he had troubles with his wife and daughter, and that things blew over the next day.

SUMMARY

Some aspects of psychotherapy in a residential setting have been presented. Intensification of peer group difficulties and dependency conflicts are described as they emerge in the various phases of milieu therapy that are postulated. Alterations in therapeutic strategy are discussed relative to the therapist's greater responsibility for the patient's overall life, the increased amount of information available to him, and the potential for integrating psychotherapy and milieu therapy.

NOTES

1. B. Bettelheim, *Love Is Not Enough* (Glencoe, Ill.: Free Press, 1950).
2. S. Ginandes, "Children Who Are Sent Away," *Journal of the American Academy of Child Psychiatry* 3, no. 1 (1964): 68-88.
3. J. Mann, "Some Theoretic Concepts of the Group Process," *International Journal of Group Psychotherapy* 12, no. 1 (1955): 3-13.
4. S. Brody, "Aims and Methods in Child Psychotherapy," *Journal of the American Academy of Child Psychiatry* 3, no. 3 (1964): 385-411; E. Buxbaum, "Technique of Child Therapy, in *The Psychoanalytic Study of the Child*, vol. 16 (New York: International Universities Press, 1954), pp. 251-74; S. Kramer and C. Settlage, "Concepts and Techniques of Child Analysis," *Journal of the American Academy of Child Psychiatry* 1, no. 4 (1962): 509-36.
5. B. Bettelheim, *Truants from Life* (Glencoe, Ill.: Free Press, 1955); R. Ekstein, J. Wallerstein, and A. Mandelbaum, "Counter-Transference Problems in the Residential Treatment of Children:

Treatment Failure in a Child with a Symbiotic Psychosis," in *The Psychoanalytic Study of the Child,* vol. 14 (New York: International Universities Press, 1959), pp. 186-218.

6. R. L. Cohen, "The Influence of Child Guidance Practices on Children's In-patient Units," *Journal of the American Academy of Child Psychiatry* 3, no. 1 (1964): 151-61.

7. A. H. Stanton and M. Schwartz, *The Mental Hospital* (New York: Basic Books, 1954).

8. Ekstein, Wallerstein, and Mandlebaum, op. cit.

9. Buxbaum, op. cit.

10. S. Weiss, "Parameters in Child Analysis," *Journal of the American Psychoanalytic Association* 12, no. 3 (1964): 587-99.

11. J. Reusch, "The Therapeutic Process from the Point of View of Communication Theory," *American Journal of Orthopsychiatry* 22, no. 3 (1952): 690-700; W. Goldfarb, et al., "Parental Perplexity and Childhood Confusion," in *New Frontiers in Child Guidance,* ed. Aaron H. Esman (New York: International Universities Press, 1958), pp. 157-70; E. J. Anthony, "Communicating Therapeutically with the Child," *Journal of the American Academy of Child Psychiatry* 3, no. 1 (1964): 106-26.

12. N. Staver, "The Child's Learning Difficulty as Related to the Emotional Problem of the Mother," *American Journal of Orthopsychiatry* 23, no. 1 (1953): 131-41.

13. "Symbolic Processes in Learning Inhibition," NIMH Progress Report, grant no. MH 06335-03, 1964, pp. 18-41.

14. B. Bernstein, "Social Class, Speech Systems, and Psychotherapy," *British Journal of Sociology* 15, no. 1 (1964): 54-64; R. D. Brodie and M. R. Winterbottom, "Some Observations on the Learning Environment of Children Growing Up in the South End of Boston," *Project Literacy Report* 3 (1964): 17-22.

15. R. Ekstein, "From Learning to Love to Loving to Learn," *Bulletin of the Reiss-Davis Clinic* 1, no. 3 (1964): 1-21.

16. P. Blos, Adolescence, a *Psychoanalytic Interpretation* (Glencoe, Ill.: Free Press, 1962).

17. Ekstein, Wallerstein, and Mandelbaum, op. cit.

18. N. V. Lourie and R. Schulman, "The Role of the Residential Staff in Residential Treatment," *American Journal of Orthopsychiatry* 22, no. 4 (1952): 798-809.

19. G. Caplan, "Types of Mental Health Consultation," *American Journal of Orthopsychiatry* 33, no. 3 (1963): 470-81.

12. Group Work with Emotionally Disturbed Children in Residential Treatment

John Matsushima

The group work method in most institutional settings is a relatively recent development. As such, its shape and rationale have been dependent to a large extent on the convictions of the individual group worker. In some instances the program has been of a social experiential nature with a recreational emphasis; in other instances it has stressed discussion techniques that tended to minimize the influence potential in group activity. Underlying these variations has been the ferment in group work as a whole regarding method refinement based on growing knowledge of individual, group, and societal processes.

In seeking direction from theory, group workers have sometimes tended to identify with one scientific discipline or another, possibly as an escape from a seemingly less illustrious background in recreation and informal education. But, inevitably, group work knowledge must be an integration of a multiplicity of processes, and its major tools must include informal social activity as well as verbal communication. Eclecticism is in the nature of group work and must be reflected usefully in practice. Regardless of the varying points of view offering insights to group

Reprinted from *Social Work*, vol. 7, no. 2 (April 1962), pp. 62-70, by permission of the author and the journal.

workers, it is acknowledged that group work theory necessarily embraces elements of individual dynamics and the social sciences. The specifics of this integration, however, present the current challenge.

The residential treatment center affords an ideal laboratory for the investigation of group work concerns, for it is here that one finds the confluence of individual, group, and societal processes. As might be anticipated, the theory of individual behavior underlying the treatment efforts of the institution is generally clear. Such clarity is not apparent, however, with respect to recognizing and using group phenomena in the service of total treatment. Thus, some institutions emphasize interview types of individual treatment while regarding the group living experience as a necessary inconvenience. Others tend to minimize the individual treatment relationship in favor of strategic interviews-on-the-spot by any of several personnel who are in quasi-parental roles. And still others model their program as a school where corrective living experiences and vocational training are emphasized at the expense of more introspective treatment techniques.

The fact remains that any collection of individuals living together develops relationships of influence toward one another, especially in a residential treatment setting where placement involves separation from family relationships. Cliques spring into being, unstated expectations of sanctioned and nonsanctioned behavior arise, subtle power relationships become apparent—all quite apart from the formal institutional organization, functioning for or against its treatment purposes. The staff itself is part of this network of relationships, so that tensions in one element inevitably affect the others.[1] Institutional planning must take into account the useful harnessing of group phenomena toward support of treatment goals.

This paper pictures the group worker functioning in an institutional milieu and attempts to outline his major responsibilities and contributions consistent with the agency treatment philosophy. Implicit is the conviction as to the basic soundness of current group work methodology; equally emphasized, however, is the need to incorporate more recent knowledge from the sciences that are the foundation of the group work method. Attention is focused on the worker's responsibilities and contributions in three areas: (1) the institution as a whole; (2) development of a purposeful recreation program; and (3) direct leadership of treatment groups.

THE INSTITUTION

It is the group worker's responsibility to communicate what he knows and what he has learned about group phenomena, for it is the person specializing in this area who must identify, for example, the significance of informal influence structures, the relationship of individual behavior to a cohesive social environment, and the causes of group resistances among staff and children. The group worker should be perceptive in such areas, and, most important, must then take concrete steps to implement this knowledge in the design of institutional organization and program.

The current program at the Children's Aid Society in Cleveland, Ohio, was introduced six years ago following a total administrative reorganization. The society is a private agency serving local children between ages 6 and 14. Treatment extends over a period of several years in residence, exclusive of follow-up contacts. Referrals come from both public and private sources. Common symptoms include wetting, soiling, running away, fire setting, and instances of impulsivity, unmanageability, and destructiveness that necessitate residential treatment. Regular professional contacts with the families are maintained. The major services include individual psychotherapy, group work and recreation, special education, and cottage group living. These services are centralized under the authority of the medical director, a psychoanalyst specializing in child psychiatry. Inservice training is stressed for all the disciplines under the auspices of the medical director or one of several consulting psychoanalysts or psychologists.

It was inevitable that drastic changes in the institutional social structure at the time of the administrative reorganization would strain individual and group controls among children and staff alike. Cottage parents in particular were temporarily immobilized by divisions of loyalty to the old and new administrations, negation of former means of disciplining children, and a marked change in staff composition. The coherent pattern of role expectations, social attitudes, and behavioral standards that are characteristic of an ongoing institutional structure disappeared. The institution resembled a community where all social controls had disintegrated—and this unpredictability panicked the children.

Runaways, fire setting, excitement, and destructiveness seriously threatened the survival of the new program. Authoritative steps were taken by the administration to retain staff who were in harmony with the goals of the institution. Difficult decisions were made as to the transfer of children who demonstrated serious danger to themselves and to others. Intensive inservice training was begun for cottage parents, not only to provide them with knowledge but to strive toward a consistency of handling that would withstand repeated testing by the children as they desperately searched for organization in the environment. In response to the crisis situation, the professional staff, all experienced in their respective specialties, drew together in a pooling of knowledge that laid the foundation for the unified program that was to result.

In retrospect, the many reasons for the disruption in the institution are quite apparent. In his contribution toward helping to restore control, the group worker cannot claim always to have acted from clearly reasoned theoretical bases, but the group phenomena were identified and responded to with a rough degree of predictability. Group runaways and defiance, along with persistent flashes of behavioral contagion, pointed to flaws in institutional coherence and controls which, in turn, strained the children's tenuous inner controls on both an individual and a group basis.

Identifying the collective causes of unrest and taking active remedial measures was possible in most cases, for example, supporting the effective design of formal channels of communication in the staff hierarchy, pointing up intrastaff tensions as they were subtly transmitted to the children, and reducing the operation of subgroup schisms among children and staff alike. The unstated social sanctions used by some of the cottage parents in reinforcing resistance to the new program among their associates were clearly seen; recognizing their confusion and desperation as causative factors, education in the means to cottage control via the group worker's example was much more helpful than any stated or implied criticism from him ever could have been.

Institutional controls were restored after a brief but trying period. However, the long-term task of engineering a wholesale change in the social climate remained. The new administration had inherited a treatment milieu where raw physical power, manipulative skill, and defiance of societal values permeated peer relationships. It was important to specify the causes of low morale among the cottage parents and the subsequent power of the boys' peer group structure in enforcing standards of delinquency. *The coercive power of peer group controls in an institution is inversely related to the effectiveness of consistent group controls as exercised by the staff.*

At this time, in the absence of consistent controls by cottage parents, a clear power structure and scale of behavioral standards among the older boys' group set the total institutional climate. Completely independent of adult influences, the power of this peer group structure was recognized by every child in the setting, and was sometimes influential in prompting some of the cottage parents to seek status within it!

In the position of indigenous leadership was the tough, demanding, predatory "king" whose followers idealized and imitated him in every way. Fearing his liberal use of physical intimidation, they identified with him, literally giving up their own integrity to a reflected self-esteem. [2] The "king" could administer secret beatings while his victim silently cowered under the threat of even more severe beatings if he screamed for help; more frequently, the "king" would give a whispered command to his followers who would then administer the beating while simultaneously taking the risk of punishment if discovered.

Lower in status were the manipulators—the "idea men"—who organized allowance "payoffs" for protection, coerced other boys into sexual submission, or thought of other forbidden, exciting activities for the amusement of the "in-group." Still lower in the hierarchy were those who had little interest or capacity to become active participants in aggressive relationships, while at the bottom of the ladder were the frightened, passive, smaller-statured boys who needed to be the victims. In enforced seclusion was the boy considered by the indigenous leader as his closest competitor; this boy was shunned by all and sometimes appeared to escape into respectability in order to find acceptance among the adults.

As is true of most organized structures of relationship, this particular hierarchy of power continued to exist irrespective of the movement of individuals in or out of the institution; from the children's standpoint, it was the most reliable, consistent, and permanent form of social organization in the setting.

DEVELOPMENT OF A PURPOSEFUL RECREATION PROGRAM

During the institutional emergency necessity determined the role and function of the group worker, as well as the rest of the staff. Assistant cottage parent, group dynamics resource, tracker of runaway children—all were tasks requiring fulfillment, graduate degrees and professional training notwithstanding. Thus, once order was restored, a recreation program was initiated in a large-scale attempt to influence peer group values and structure. The program was oriented toward the children's impoverished social needs and the standards of the community as represented by the new administration. For those whose relationships were based on coercive power and/or collective excitement, a controlling, protected medium was sorely needed as a social educational device; it was anticipated, of course, that the children would tend to operate in recreational activities, too, according to the primitive rules of relationship that were characteristic of their group living experience.

Resistances were encountered in the form of destruction of equipment, "clowning," and near-riots around game results. Even under liberally revised rules that minimized frustration, the boys often could not bear the humiliation of losing or their lack of athletic prowess. Everyone keenly observed that he was accepted by personnel and that their strength was used in a protective context. Through constant support, instruction, encouragement, and the imposition of unswerving behavioral controls, the boys slowly moved to the point where swimming, gym and canteen activities, and sports were usable as a road to self-mastery.

Participation was encouraged but not forced; temporary exclusion was always followed with an invitation to return; intimidation was penalized by ejection or a team penalty. Team play avoided individual competition, and games were terminated if the children edged toward loss of self-control. Crafts, dramatics, games, outings—all were directed toward creative satisfaction, the acquisition of new skills, and exposure to new experiences. Permeating these experiences were the strengthening relationships with the staff and the boys' confidence in staff consistency, as well as their realization of appropriate use of limits. Progress was not without great difficulty, of course, and many games were interrupted by fighting, cursing, defiance, and tears. But the children invariably returned to the game and found repetitive comfort in the simple but rigid rules.

Team sports became more common, athletic ability competed with raw strength as a desirable quality to imitate, and the use of prestige to insure justice rather than to exploit the weak became increasingly evident. Mutuality of interest moved the children toward social behavior, while the satisfactions inherent in the activities exerted a powerful control over antagonistic actions. For the frightened, confused children in the institutional population these experiences were often the first in which they could venture cautious participation. Encouragement rather than derision, restraint rather than attack, skill rather than violence became more prominent as tentative new social values evolved.

With increasing self-control and a growing ability to enter into the compromise, conflict, and postponement of gratification attendant upon more intensive social relationships, the children were ready to move on to small group experiences. The purposefully planned recreational activities not only had innate value but also served as a useful first step toward involvement in small group treatment.

DIRECT LEADERSHIP OF
TREATMENT GROUPS

Direct leadership of treatment groups varies according to specific objectives. The technique described in this paper was utilized because of the institutional circumstances. Other adaptations of work with small groups are being investigated at present, with variations in composition, membership, treatment technique, and goals. For the purposes of maximum impact on the social climate, however, by enabling value shifts on the part of the older boys, this particular means was most effective.

The formed group was composed of five boys, ages 12 through 14, each from a different layer of the status hierarchy. It was an attempt to create in small group form the major subgroup elements operative in the older boys' cottage. Attendance was required at the two meetings every week. The major program media during the year the group was in existence included sports, table games, outings, and snacks at every meeting. The food was particularly important to the members as one of the few individually satisfying and socially acceptable needs they could agree on. As far as other activity ideas, the worker had to be most active in furnishing suggestions from which the boys could choose, for they soon demonstrated that they had no prior group experience remotely related to this. Decision making was always fraught with fears of status loss or a clash of separate needs for uncompromising personal gratification, and the worker had to be the *group control* until the members could restrain their impulsivity. At times the worker would make a compromise suggestion and the group would accept, but more often there would be an impasse. This was pointed out to the members as a practical problem that often terminated a meeting, thus resulting in dissatisfaction for everyone concerned. The boys saw the common sense in this, and fighting was eventually replaced by shouted arguments, then by beginning attempts at compromise.

The individual relationships with the worker provided the major tie to the group; this held true throughout the experience. In limited but definite ways, however, the group moved toward increasing self-sufficiency, partially because control over impulses was approved by the worker, but also because such behavior resulted in a more satisfying experience for everyone.

At the time of the group's inception, the boys were seen individually on several occasions about tentative membership. The social activity program in order to "learn how to get along better with the others," was accepted by them cautiously:

"I want to get along better with the other guys and get help with my problems, but Sammy better not be there because he's my worst enemy and my biggest problem!"

"Sure, okay, I'll join, but you better have all us 'cats' in there. . . . No 'squares'!"

"I'll come if we can eat and go out."

All agreed to come on a trail basis. Most recognized that animosity was interfering with their group living situation, although the strength of motivations to change varied. They enjoyed the attention and soon embarked on testing attempts to see what the group was really about.

The first meeting was characterized by the two oldest boys staging an orgy of excitement while the other three huddled together at one end of the room. Exposure, feigned masturbation, inviting sexual assault by positioning themselves on a table, grabbing for other members' genitals—all accompanied by raucous laughter and mounting excitement—paralyzed the meeting. They ignored the worker's shouted commands to control themselves until he rose from his chair, at which point one of them collapsed on the floor, fear written on his face, and screamed, "I knew it! Now you're mad! Now you're gonna get drunk and beat us!"

"Damned right I'm mad!" the worker answered angrily. "But I'm not going to hurt you. Now sit down and stop acting silly because the other guys want to get on with the meeting."

Puzzled by the worker's nonviolent reaction, the boys returned to their places and continued the meeting. In a situation like this, suppressive techniques, reassurance about the absence of violence from the worker, and centering on self-control for the sake of the group seemed more appropriate than any extended discussion of the particular means by which fears and anxieties were demonstrated. The social inappropriateness of the immediate behavior rather than its pathological implications was the central focus.

There were constant attempts to repeat the intimidation practiced in the cottage. From direct attacks to veiled threats every such instance was stopped, with physical restraint when necessary but more often with a flat statement that such behavior would not be tolerated. "Why not?" the strongest would shout. "If I want to go to the show but the other guys want to go to the gym, they should do what I want to do. They can't even beat me. That's the way it is. Tough for them. . . . No, there ain't anything wrong with it."

Often the exploited members would support their own domination with a loyal fervor that was expressed as anger toward the worker. In these instances the worker's decision was final even against such group unanimity, and an explanation was made to them that a coincidence of problem behavior did not justify action. In individual and group contacts, technique was always on the present, realistic consequences of their acts rather than the moral implications.

Look what happens when you start pushing the other guys around. They end up hating your guts even if they're scared to tell you. I guess you get pushed around, too, in the cottage; some guys think that's being tough, but nobody likes it, and sometimes the tough guy has to take on everybody. . . . I know you care, because you act like you care a lot. . . . Why not try asking them sometime what they want to do, then back them up. You're strong and you're the boss, but with a few changes the guys will listen to you because they like you, and not just because they're scared.

To the lowest-status members who were discouraged in their efforts to gain respect from the others, the worker was sympathetic.

Sure, I know it's rough. But you've come to every meeting so far, and that alone takes a lot of nerve; I know how hard you must have tried just to sit in the meetings sometimes. But you have to learn to live with these guys, and you're always going to run into this kind of trouble unless you learn to do something about it. I won't let you get hurt, and I can find ways to help you without getting into fights, if you really want to.

At times when the most passive members would provoke attack by screaming and feigning injury in the midst of a game, the worker would point this out to them as problem behavior—just as much so as attacking others directly. Oftentimes the games were called to a halt so that the group could talk over these crises together.

There were frequent occasions when behavioral contagion swept the members into orgies of pool ball-throwing, equipment dismantling, and excited, exuberant leaping and climbing on the furniture. And there were times when a pseudodemocracy would be demonstrated, as in the following instance when the group was deciding what to do for a club meeting.

"Okay now, you want to go for a ride, don't you, Sammy! You want to, don't you, Len! Paul? Jack? Okay, everybody wants to go," Luke smilingly threatened, supported by Sammy, while the others looked down at the floor and nodded; Luke said to the worker, "Everybody decided, and you can't go against the decision."

The group did go for a ride, and it was characterized by Sammy repeatedly climbing on Luke's lap and kissing him "Smack on the lips, man!" and others joining in by playing "grabs" in the back seat while the worker frantically tried to restore order. Later, the boys prevented serious discussion of the incident, but it was all too obvious that the worker's tacit approval of such decision-making methods in the meeting unwittingly gave permission to the boys for a much freer demonstration of impulse-expression. They dramatically made the point that they desperately needed controls, and any concession to their primitive relationship expectations was equivalent to seduction into acting up in this way.

GRADUAL CHANGES

Gradually there were changes. The dominators would try out new techniques with a great show of generosity, only to be surprised at the favorable reaction of the group, and even the more passive members began to assert themselves more openly.

> Y'know, in the cottage whenever I walked past Sammy I'd smile like I wasn't worried and kind of cross my arms in front of me because he might take a sneak punch at my stomach just for the hell of it. Sometimes he would and sometimes he wouldn't, and I worried each time. But he just never lets you alone; all of them laugh if you're sucker enough to pay them off or don't tell staff. Then they keep doing it to you, anyway. You gotta stand up for yourself, and even if you can't beat 'em, they'll sooner or later leave you alone.

All parties concerned were warned that though the spirit was admirable they might not always be successful in their efforts at self-protection. But changes did continue to take place, certainly within the group; and with the efforts throughout the group work and recreation program toward identical goals, the social climate in the institution as a whole became more favorable to the success of such change efforts.

Internalized struggles became more prominent as these values came to be more accepted by the members.

After a particularly destructive meeting when Sammy and Len had taunted the worker by breaking some furniture, Len dashed outside to the top of the jungle gym and tearfully shouted down his curses at the worker. After listening quietly for a while, and making no attempt to chase Len, the worker said: "Man, you're sure mad at me! It seems so hard for you to keep your temper in the meeting. How come? Seemed like you came in today just aching for trouble."

"Because you're a blankety-blank so-and-so, that's why," cried Len. "Why do you have us in the club? If we start acting up why don't you hit us? I used to get clobbered all the time at home and it didn't bother me none. In the club you're always telling us to control ourselves!"

The worker talked with him, then, acknowledging that it was difficult and maybe did not make much sense to him, but that the staff was not going to hurt him and that the only way really to manage to stay out of trouble at C.A.S. or any place was to have him learn to control himself. He could do it, and most of the time nowadays he was doing so much better. Nobody expected him to understand all the time, though, and sometimes he must feel as if he just had to bust loose.

While they talked, Len slowly climbed down until he was quietly sitting next to the worker. They walked silently back to the cottage where Len left, still obviously lost in thought.

Throughout the life of this group, the principle expounded by Wilson and Ryland in which the extent of the worker's activity varies with the degree of group organization was clearly demonstrated,[3] as were Coyle's basic ideas regarding group structure, avowed and unavowed goals, and the importance of the worker's being aware of unconscious as well as conscious streams of group process.[4] As fascinated with aggression and panicked by passivity as these boys were, the primitive peer group structure had been their most reliable means of group control. It was extremely difficult to try anything else, although most of the boys in the group eventually established strong subgroup relationships based on athletic interests and were then able to move on to other group experiences. The central relationship throughout was the one with the worker. After successfully emerging from the frantic testing, the boys were able to identify much more closely with the worker's values.[5]

By the time the group terminated, there were substantial beginnings toward the notion of social justice, moves toward acceptance by adults, and control over immediate personal gratification in favor of eventual group satisfactions. The standards that had evolved were crucial in every decision ranging from choice of activity to the outbreak of exciting and/or aggressive behavior. Many decisions, particularly those closer to the expression of impulses, were not made consciously, of course; but as the group became less receptive to such outbreaks, many of the members mobilized their energies toward maintaining self-control in the most trying situations. In short, the more direct instinctual satisfactions in property destruction, fighting, and sex play became subservient to less direct but more acceptable expressions. Most significant, the ground rules for peer relationships and the social structure of the institutional community moved in a simultaneous change that supported the establishment of each. All institutional services worked toward these ends from a variety of directions, so that the durability of individual gains was assured following the limited-goal group experience that has been described.

As stated earlier, this group was designed to meet the priorities existent in the institution at the time. The group worker, through his participation in revising the institutional framework, initation and coordination of the recreation program, and direct leadership of small groups, was instrumental in effecting the following changes:

1. Closer coincidence between adult-sanctioned and peer group relationship patterns, which in turn helped to improve the total institutional climate. Preceding this, of course, were contributions toward administrative recognition of group phenomena as related to institutional stresses.

2. Control based on the needs of the children (in harmony with the administrative effort to emphasize discipline as an educative rather than a punitive device).

3. Children's involvement in relationships based on voluntary interactions rather than coercion, exploitation, or the threat of bodily injury.

4. Changing expectations on the part of the children

regarding the institution; in contrast to a setting favoring the growth of antisoical power relationships and activities, usable channels were provided to move toward more socially acceptable means of gratification and self-mastery.

CONCLUSIONS

This paper is intended to indicate those practice areas toward which the group worker's efforts might be organized in order to utilitze his skills in making a maximal contribution to the institution. Of great importance in broadening total treatment skills is the opportunity for the group worker to receive supervision in doing individual psychotherapy with other children who are not members of his group. Such experience results in a more sensitive use of technique as related to a variety of treatment group goals. Essential to the effectiveness of any single element in the total program is the continual collaboration among the various disciplines. At Children's Aid Society, emergence from the common crisis of the recent past has provided a tradition of professional integration that promises to endure.

If there is any one aspect of the group worker's direct practice that can be specified as most important, it would be his work with treatment groups. For as useful as the group worker's training may be to administration, cottage parent consultation, or recreation, the unique area in which methodology must be developed and can find general application in the other areas is in direct work with treatment groups. The concern most strategic to group work theory development and which insures its place in the total range of services is obviously that in which knowledge is available from psychiatry and the social sciences to be combined with the essence of practice experience peculiar to group work.

NOTES

1. For a few representative references, *see* Norman A. Polansky, "Determinants of the Role-Image of the Patient in a Psychiatric Hospital," in *The Patient and the Mental Hospital*, ed. Milton

Greenblatt (Glencoe, Ill.: Free Press, 1957); Howard W. Polsky, "Changing Delinquent Subcultures: A Social-Psychological Approach," *Social Work*, vol. 4, no. 4 (October 1959): 3-15; Fritz Redl and David Wineman, *The Agressive Child* (Glencoe, Ill.: Free Press, 1952); Alfred H. Stanton and Morris S. Schwartz, *The Mental Hospital* (New York: Basic Books, 1954).
2. Theoretical exposition of Sigmund Freud, *Group Psychology and Analysis of the Ego* (1921), trans., James Strachey (London: Hogarth Press, 1948).
3. Gertrude Wilson and Gladys Ryland, *Social Group Work Practice* (Boston: Houghton Mifflin Co., 1947).
4. Grace L. Coyle, *Group Work with American Youth* (New York: Harper & Bros., 1948).
5. *See* Saul Scheidlinger, *Psychoanalysis and Group Behavior* (New York: W. W. Norton & Co., 1952), and S. R. Slavson, *Analytic Group Psychotherapy* (New York: Columbia University Press, 1951).

13. Occupational Therapy in Children's Residential Treatment

Phyllis Doyle

We in occupational therapy must learn to recognize the heightened anxiety, the lability and intensification of mood, and the state of flux that are signs of the child in psychiatric treatment. We are prepared to support him through the inevitable upheavals that mark progress in psychotherapy, but we are not permissive of acting-out or talking-out of those problems with which the child must come to grips in his psychotherapy hours. This does not mean that the child must leave his symptoms outside the shop. It does mean that realistic demands are made of him in terms of performance and behavior because he is a patient and not in spite of it. As occupational therapists we may properly clarify for the child the facts of his behavior in the light of the immediate reality.

Since each child's use of the occupational therapy situation is uniquely his own, we will examine in this paper the O.T. records of one patient who was in treatment at the hospital for over a year. Melvin was chosen because through him we can demonstrate social isolation, defensive use of fantasy, and an attempt early in treatment to solve

Reprinted from "A Commentary on the Behavior in Occupational Therapy of Two Emotionally Disturbed Early Adolescent Boys," paper presented at the 1961 Annual Conference of the American Occupational Therapy Association, by permission of the author and the association.

conflicts at a symbolic level. We will trace his movement from fantasy orientation toward reality orientation. We will note his growing capacity to relate both to adults and to peers, the growth of ego skills, and the building of a more flexible defensive system.

Melvin was a stocky, muscular lad of 13. He spoke in clipped phrases and laughed in an abrupt, harsh chortle. There was an air of tension and brooding about him.

From psychological tests and from the psychiatric examination we learned that Melvin scored well above average in intelligence with indications of a superior potential. Projective tests indicated a diagnosis of schizoid personality pattern disturbance with passive-dependent features.

A summary of the problem on admission included violent temper, poor school adjustment, stealing, jealousy of mother's attention to siblings, and no friends. Melvin's therapeutic tasks included gaining control of his instinctual impulses and learning to relate. His acting out was, in part, a denial of his passive-dependent needs.

Even before Melvin came to O.T. he had inquired about the possibility of making gun stocks in the shops and almost immediately on starting O.T. he began to construct a gadget that seemed already to exist in his fantasy — a cigarette lighter made in the shape of a gun. For five months, with two interruptions of several weeks' duration each, Melvin wrestled with the construction of this gadget. He seemed to know exactly how the gun-cigarette lighter was to work but was vague in his explanation of how he was going to construct it. The occupational therapist's attitude toward the improbable task was that she did not see how it could be done but that she would help Melvin in every way she could. Her goal, at this point, was to establish a relationship at the only level Melvin could tolerate, one of support and acceptance.

In the ensuing weeks he pursued his task with single-minded intensity. He referred to the gadget variously as his invention, his experiment, his dickie-gun. At times he cradled it tenderly and protectively in his hand. Later it was to be used as a prop for aggressive fantasy play as he stood holding the partially completed gun menacingly and swept it in an arc around the shop as if holding an enemy at bay. An admiring young peer told the O.T. that Melvin had talked about using the gadget in a fantasied escape from the hospital, imagining the police broadcasting this warning: "Watch out for Melvin ——. He is armed with a cigarette lighter."

Our young inventor was not to be permitted to work in peace, however. He was subjected to persistent, noisy, provocative intrusions into his obsessive task by one peer in particular. Irritated, hostile rebuffs only incited his tormentor to more and more brazen affronts. Melvin's anxiety mounted to unbearable intensity. Since he was incapable of dealing with Conrad's aggressiveness directly, he was permitted to withdraw into an adjoining work area when possible, and the occupational therapist worked with him. He could not, at this time, ask for help nor could he formulate his wants. He could only indicate by frantic, futile activity that something needed doing. The O.T. had to sense what was needed and provide a ready-made solution. "Look, Melvin, will this metal strip hold the barrel upright?"

Eventually Conrad dared "accidentally" to knock Melvin's highly invested gun out of a vise in which Melvin had clamped it. An outraged Melvin cursed Conrad roundly, turned on his heels, and fled. Melvin was quite incapable of settling the score, and on the ward, immediately after the incident, he and Conrad were more friendly than ever. Because Melvin could not be safely and appropriately angry he had to defend himself by an excessive show of forbearance toward Conrad.

The gun-cigarette lighter which Melvin used initially to keep people away from him became, in time, an object through which he began to form relationships. Ward staff took Melvin on errands downtown to shop for parts. The maintenance man's help was enlisted when some work involving a blowtorch was required. Peers, instead of regarding the project and its perpetrator with awe, began to give Melvin advice and even began to predict that the lighter would never work.

On the day when all parts were in place, the culmination of five months of effort, Melvin was able to concede with annoyance and irritation that the lighter indeed would not work. He could accept this bit of reality and was able to face in this instance his own limitations. He quickly undid weeks of work, commenting that he was wrecking hell out of it. The O.T.'s role was to support him in this acceptance of reality. Even so, Melvin was reluctant to be done with the task, and for two weeks more he painted and embellished what was just a toy gun after all. Quite appropriately, in the light of Melvin's relationship with his mother, and of the symbolic meaning of the object, the gadget was sent home with her for safekeeping.

This was not the last of Melvin's weapons, however. During periods of stress in his treatment he returned, again and again, to their production but never for long and never with the intensity that had marked this early phase in his treatment.

It was mentioned earlier that Melvin interrupted his work on the cigarette lighter only twice during five months. The second of these interludes coincided with a two-week absence of his doctor in the third month of treatment. Melvin did not mention that his doctor was away but came to the shop in a quiet, dejected mood. He stood with his back to the group looking bleakly out of the window, furtively wiping away his tears. He could not acknowledge that anything was wrong but got out his work, examined it briefly, then slipped the project sadly into the O.T.'s smock pocket, murmuring that it was no use, he couldn't get the parts he needed to finish it. For the first time Melvin was accessible to the O.T. and seemed to be silently asking for suggestion and attention. A leather wallet was drawn out, and Melvin compliantly cut and glued the parts as directed saying only that he didn't need a wallet. The next day when the O.T. entered the shop Melvin greeted her brightly with, "I've been waiting for you to show me what to do next." Before his doctor's return Melvin had made two wallets and many, many trips to the O.T. office for additional instruction, extra materials, and, more important, for much personal attention from the O.T. He had been able to accept, briefly, a warm, dependent relationship.

During the gun-cigarette lighter phase Melvin had accomplished several things. He had become more realistic, less withdrawn, and less absorbed in fantasy. He had begun to relate both to peers and to adults.

The next phase might properly be called "getting actively involved in talking therapy" with his doctor and was heralded by many and varied somatic complaints. Toward the O.T. he assumed a hypercritical, irritated bossiness, and with peers Melvin needed to set the conditions on which he could relate to them, be it bully, buddy, or clown. There was a sense of unrest and an ever present depression.

Melvin indicated the content of his brooding when he asked about another of his doctor's patients who had improved markedly and had been discharged after a brief admission, "Does that mean he had a good doctor?" He seemed to be asking if it was safe to form a closer relationship with this doctor. "Will he help me to get well, too?"

Two projects occupied Melvin during this time, each representing a distinct and characteristic mood. The first was a mosaic tile picture executed in black and white of an ambiguous, silhouetted figure that appeared to be standing in a clump of trees. We speculated that this probably represented both Melvin and his father who had committed suicide when Melvin was seven years old. This was his thoughtful, pensive project which he ruminated over, put together bit by bit. Sometimes he praised it extravagantly, at other times threatened to smash it. "What damned good is it if I can't sell it," seemed to be his way of devaluing it. By noisily proclaiming his destructive intentions Melvin seemed to be asking that the picture be spared, and it was repeatedly put aside by the O.T. for another time. Eventually, he stopped working on the mosaic, like the earlier gun-cigarette lighter project, though he never completed it. It seemed at the end no longer to serve any useful purpose for him. When he returned it to our office for the last time he remarked that he couldn't work on it, "I'm too sick. . . . I mean I'm sick of this place." By this slip of the tongue Melvin seemed to indicate recognition on his part that he needed help in putting the pieces of his life together.

Melvin's other project of this period was produced in a burst of hyperactivity and expansiveness in the midst of construction of the mosaic puzzle. It was a large, wooden storage box, a popular project among the children. It seemed to indicate the strengthening of his identification with peers. It also indicated the surrender of some of his omnipotent and magic qualities. Melvin could maintain the fiction of superiority only so long as his projects were unique and mysterious. Melvin's pathology was, however, reflected in his various associations to the box project. It could be a retreat — "It would be nice to make a box big enough to put a chair, a lamp, and book in, and then I could read in peace." A "coffin" association was too threatening, and Melvin quickly revised it to a "playpen": "The staff treats us like babies, and now they have us making our own playpens." These comments were directed toward peers whom Melvin had enlisted in a patients versus staff campaign.

Another and more trying phase of Melvin's therapy followed and involved an initial probing with his doctor of his feelings about significant people in his life and a laying of the groundwork for permanent separation from his mother and eventual emotional autonomy. Now Melvin was talking — talking about his feelings and about people. He was no more the isolated genius. The bad people, he said, were in the hospital and the good people were at home. His true feelings were revealed, however, when he began a flurry of gift making for his mother. His ambivalence was reflected in his inability to get these gifts completed in time for a special occasion. Should they be completed, the gifts were misplaced until the occasion had passed. During this period Melvin began relating to the O.T. in a dependent, little boy fashion. He would appeal to her trustingly with, "You've just got to help me."

During the latter part of Melvin's hospitalization he was

involved in establishing his identity, his independence, his maleness, his right and ability to be aggressive.

Some nine months earlier Melvin, in the face of severe provocation from a peer, Conrad, could only run away when to retaliate would have been more appropriate. He now obsessively licked old wounds by recalling humiliating defeats at the hands of skinnier but tougher adversaries both at home and in the early weeks of his hospitalization. He seemed, at this point, to be facing his own inadequacies and to be revealing a devalued self. He constantly measured himself against peers, which one was taller, which one smarter, which one a better craftsman.

An incident occurred at this time that is indicative of the change in Melvin's mode of behavior. It also illustrates how the roles of psychotherapist and of occupational therapist complemented each other in this case.

The O.T. had left the group, five patients and an occupational therapy student, to go into an adjoining room. On her return moments later she found a circle of patients, Melvin included, standing around the crumpled figure of one of the boys. When asked what had happened all eyes turned toward Melvin. He muttered that Ted must have had one of his seizures. Ted whispered that Melvin had hit him, and the other boys concurred. Confronted with this evidence Melvin turned away abruptly and in a distraught tone said, "Damn it, I can't say anything. Can't you see I'm too scared?" After making certain that Ted was not hurt, everyone was told to get back to work with a stern reminder that this sort of behavior was not allowed in shop.

The occupational therapist, however, found occasion to leave the shop shortly thereafter and took the still panicky Melvin with her. As they went on their errand Melvin was asked if he would like to explain what had happened. Using the O.T. as his "victim," Melvin reenacted the incident. He showed how he had approached Ted and spanned his throat in a "playfully" menacing gesture with his hands. Ted had reacted by pushing Melvin's arms away sharply. Then it was that Melvin lashed out, landing a fist on Ted's jaw. The first time, Ted fell to the floor. In the reenactment, the O.T. was the surprised recipient of a controlled blow on the jaw. It was indicative of the trusting nature of his relationship with the O.T. that he could repeat the act of aggression, confident that there would be no retaliation and that he could control his aggression.

The incident was recounted to Melvin's doctor, and in the next psychotherapy hour Melvin reported this dream: the *doctor* was lying on the floor of the O.T. shop, and Melvin was standing over him, hammer in hand. Melvin's association to the dream was that he was angry at his doctor because the doctor had been talking to him about placement in a boarding school.

When asked what connection there might be between the dream and the events of the previous day in the shop, Melvin became incoherent but in essence said he just couldn't apologize to Ted in front of the other boys or the O.T. because they would think he was a sissy.

It is interesting to note Melvin's utilization of the different roles of the O.T. and the doctor. With the O.T. he could recapitulate the events as he perceived them and used the O.T. to clarify for himself what had happened. With the doctor he recalled aggressive fantasies and related these to his anxieties about his masculine identification and about his separation from the hospital.

Melvin thus experimented with his newfound capacity to express aggression directly. He had at the same time established a somewhat shaky leadership in the group. Much of his behavior could be classified as adolescence, acute. He could be high-handed and rejecting of the O.T. in the presence of the group — "*We* don't need *you*" — but pleasant and respectful when alone.

He cultivated a "hoodish" look and in shop constructed masculine props — a cigarette holder, a pipe, a tobacco pouch, a cigarette case — all more conventional versions of his original phallic gun-cigarette lighter. He remarked half-seriously to a peer, "I've got to get started on my career of smoking."

Many of Melvin's problems during this period were peer-related. His ego boundaries were not so firmly fixed, nor was his identity well established. He tended to become caught up in the pathology of peers and to act out their fantasies as his own. During this time he was frequently excluded from shop for part or all of an hour because of his aggressive, uncontrolled behavior.

One of his last pseudoscientific projects was a compressed air tank made from a large tin can, a project suggested to him by and lifted out of the fantasy life of his tormentor of nine months ago, Conrad. The two boys had, at this time, a sticky, sexualized relationship. The compressed air tank was made as a conciliatory gesture to Conrad, who partly due to their mutual difficulties was at the time excluded from O.T.

As time approached for him to leave the hospital Melvin directly indicated apprehension of the future and an honest recognition that he had still a long struggle to health. He returned briefly, for part of one hour, to the construction of a weapon but quickly rejected it.

Melvin, when he first came to the hospital, had lived essentially within himself. He could then in his omnipotent fantasy be scientist, inventor, genius. However, his magic worked only if he shared his secrets with no one. Upon attempting to make his fantasy real, as when he attempted to construct the gun-cigarette lighter, Melvin opened that inner door a crack and reality began to impinge upon him. Still far from well, Melvin had taken great strides toward reality and relatedness and had established a tentative adolescent identity.

14. Operant Conditioning in a Comprehensive Treatment Program for Adolescents

Paul Lehrer, Lawrence Schiff, and Anton Kris

Operant techniques, based upon the results of laboratory experimentation on the systematic application of reward and punishment,[1] have been gaining increasingly wider application in psychiatric settings during the past decade.[2] Most of the studies thus far reported have focused on the effectiveness of specific techniques on specific behaviors, often in research settings where no other treatment was available to patients. In this paper we describe the clinical use of these techniques in a comprehensive treatment program for severely disturbed adolescents in a state mental hospital. Operant conditioning was used in conjunction with psychoanalytically oriented psychotherapy, and practitioners of behavioral and psychoanalytic persuasions collaborated in structuring a 24-hour per day milieu program. More specifically, psychoanalysis provided us with a theory of the motivation of behavior and of the development and integration of

Printed by permission of the authors and *Archives of General Psychiatry*. Article is in press with the Archives. This study was supported by Public Health Service Grant MH 14861-04 from the National Institute of Mental Health. The authors are indebted to Dr. Harry MacKay, who aided them in establishing their token economy and collaborated in leading the parents' course in operant conditioning.

personality and was thus helpful in deciding what behaviors to modify in what sequence and in evaluating the appropriateness of particular rewards and punishments. The psychoanalytic perspective also led us to emphasize the importance of "real life" goals and rewards and the personal relevance of treatment to patients' verbalized and unverbalized needs and goals.

Operant techniques were first introduced in order to overcome the apathy and behavioral disorganization that prevented many patients from becoming involved in an active treatment program, but were later used much more widely. In this paper we describe our uses of these techniques and present the hypothesis we have developed regarding conditions for successful treatment in our setting. We also address the issue of the compatibility of operant conditioning with psychoanalytically oriented insight therapy with severely disturbed adolescents.

DESCRIPTION OF THE ADOLESCENT SERVICE

Setting

The Adolescent Service of Boston State Hospital was initiated in 1965 as a "participatory consultation" service,[3] involved in every phase of the patient's treatment. It provides central daytime facilities for education and recreation and offers consultation to the primary caretakers of adolescents in the hospital's basic inpatient and outpatient services, who retain responsibility for treatment planning and decision making.

The program at the Adolescent Service's central facilities includes four schools (a high school, a remedial classroom, a vocational training program, and a class for the severely retarded), a library, an occupational therapy shop, a social lounge, and a variety of trips, games, and social activities. The Adolescent Service's programs operate seven days a week from 9 A.M. to 9 P.M. and thus provide the bulk of the daily experience of those involved with them.

Patients

About 60 patients, aged 14 to 22, are involved in the treatment program at any one time. Although the full spectrum of major psychiatric problems occurring in adolescence is represented, the modal patient tends to be chronically ill. Approximately 50 percent at any one time are outpatients, but almost all are seen on an inpatient basis at some point in their treatment.

THE USE OF OPERANT CONDITIONING

Throughout the treatment program an emphasis is placed on the use of rewards that occur naturally in the patient's world outside the hospital and that are related to realistic, often long-term goals rather than special rewards that are contrived within the hospital setting. We assume that the more similar our treatment program is to the contingencies in the real world, the more easily will patients be able to transfer what they have learned in the hospital to life outside. Thus in the high school patients receive a diploma through the Boston public schools that is indistinguishable from the one they would have earned if they had continued their education in the school at which they were registered before they came to the hospital. In the remedial school, where programmed materials, supplemented by tutoring, are used in sequence to teach arithmetic,[4] reading,[5] spelling,[6] writing,[7] and high school subjects,[8] students can see their progress at each step as they advance in preparation for the General Education Development Test, for a high school equivalency certificate.

Another important guideline in selecting reinforcers has been their personal relevance to the patient. School materials are chosen to be inherently of interest to students of this age group. Similarly, patients play an important role in deciding what extracurricular activities are made available. Whenever attendance or enthusiasm fails in an activity this is taken as a signal to reevaluate it and to change or discontinue it, if called for. At a weekly community meeting patients are encouraged to give suggestions for new activities as well as to make complaints about ones already in progress.

Nevertheless, because of the feelings of hopelessness, apathy, and fear of involvement that characterize the severely disturbed adolescent, these measures often, by themselves, are not sufficient to motivate the patients to participate actively in treatment. External incentives are often required to supplement the more natural reinforcers in order to overcome inertia and to involve patients in activities and personal relationships that may later become reinforcing in themselves. It was for this reason, for example, that a token economy was instituted in the Adolescent Service's milieu program.

In practice, treatment programs at home, on the ward, and at the Adolescent Service's central facilities are integrated, and programs for individual patients are decided upon in consultation with family members and hospital personnel serving in all locations. For the purposes of exposition, however, the use of operant techniques in each of these geographic areas will be discussed separately.

Operant conditioning at the Adolescent Service's central facilities

One of the most visible uses of operant conditioning at the Adolescent Service is the token economy. As we employ it, the token economy is a highly individualized system. Although there are many "standard" things for which all patients are charged or paid, most patients are on individualized programs in which special charges or payments are tailored to individual needs or problems. Patients are routinely paid for attendance and productivity in school and for participation in various extracurricular activities. The medium of exchange is "points," which may be redeemed at one penny per point for up to five dollars a week. In order to encourage saving and to teach delay of gratification, however, patients are not permitted to deplete their points balance to below 500 points by withdrawal of money. Patients can spend the balance of their points directly in a social lounge designed as a typical teen-age hangout, with a soda fountain and grill. Points are used to buy food, such as pizza, hot dogs, hamburgers, cans of soda, ice cream, milk shakes, and, occasionally, complete meals, and to play the jukebox and various games, such as pinball, Ping-Pong, and board games. A continual effort is made to find additional activities and goods that can be offered to back the points system. Special events during the past year for which patients paid points included parties, dances, and trips to local attractions, as well as several more ambitious expeditions, including a trip to Montreal, camping trips on Cape Cod, and mountain-climbing trips in New Hampshire.

Points are taken away from patients as punishment only for minor infractions of the rules, such as failing to pay for an item at the social lounge. Serious violations, however, such as physical abuse of property, other patients, or staff, lead to automatic restriction from participation in all activities until the patient, with one of the Adolescent Service psychologists, has worked out a strategy for controlling his behavior and for undoing whatever damage he may have done. Although points fines and payment in points for repair or replacement of property are often imposed for these more serious infractions, they are not used alone because we have found, as others have,[9] that points fines alone are ineffective and that their use only stimulates unproductive struggles that may injure positive personal relationships.

All transactions take place through a credit card system, rather than through the traditional medium of tangible tokens. This system has been described elsewhere in detail.[10] One important effect of the points system that was unexpected by some Adolescent Service staff members unfamiliar with the potential of token economies was the increase of communication between staff and patients that followed introduction of the system in our program. Discussion of points provided valuable structure to the weekly community meeting. These patients find it easier to talk about things that they are going to get or are required to pay for than about less tangible, often affectively charged community issues. Such issues, it was found, could often be approached through discussions about the points system. Further, brief weekly individual meetings of the patient with his Adolescent Service nurse to evaluate his program through the concrete matter of his earning and spending often became important opportunities for personal exchange.

Several case examples of operant conditioning programs at the Adolescent Service central facilities will be offered here. Some of the interplay between these programs and a psychodynamic approach to pinpointing patients' problem areas is illustrated.

> Peter B., a compulsive points earner, was known informally as the "Rockefeller" of the Adolescent Service, since he amassed huge sums of points, rarely spent any, and *never* missed any opportunities to earn. This was an extremely obsessional psychotic boy, who had previously done so poorly in school at another hospital and been made so anxious by it that he was referred to Boston State Hospital with the recommendation that he not attend school. In fact he had responded well to the structure of the remedial school, had completed the sequence of material designed to bring his reading and mathematical skills to a sixth-grade level, and was beginning work on materials designed to prepare him for the high school equivalency certificate. His hoarding of points appeared to be helpful at first in increasing his self-esteem. Later, however, when it appeared that Peter never allowed himself to have fun, his hoarding was seen as another symptom.
>
> After he demonstrated his ability to succeed in school and in the Adolescent Service's points system, a program was instituted to teach Peter to spend just for the fun of it. Initially, he was paid for playing games with other patients in the lounge. (Ordinarily patients must *pay* for the privilege.) He was required to play a specified minimum number of games in order to be paid by any points for playing, and gradually this requirement was increased. Never before had Peter been observed to initiate games with other patients. Throughout the first few weeks of this program, however, Peter often invited other patients to play and regularly played more games than was required for him to earn points for playing. Then the program was changed so that Peter was no longer paid for playing games but was required to pay for playing. He was also now required to play a specified minimum number of games per week in order to earn

anything for the week. Peter's game-playing behavior continued on a level well *above* the required minimum. He began to have fun.

Lester J. was a 15-year-old nonpsychotic, school-phobic patient who came from a broken home. His father had been severely alcoholic, had had a violent temper, and had been unable to take a role in the discipline of his children. Lester's mother had attempted to enforce his going to school, but his hypochondriacal symptoms and, eventually, his drinking kerosene, stabbing himself, and taking an overdose of aspirin, all in his battle to avoid school, led to his hospitalization on a stubborn child charge. His affect was angry and depressed, and, in an interview, he acknowledged strong feelings of having been abandoned by his parents and feelings of guilt over his violent outbursts. He was accident prone and frequently got into various kinds of mischief. It was felt that he needed long-term treatment to reverse the dangerous, self-destructive path he was following. Major elements in the problem were thought to be his marked dependency and low self-esteem, intimately connected with inadequate development of self-discipline.

At the hospital Lester was provided with the strong controls he needed and was able to confide in a therapist and to attend school on a fairly regular basis. Occasionally his temper led him to violate some of the rules of deportment at the Adolescent Service, and this led to his restriction to the ward; but generally his behavior was entirely appropriate. Perfect school attendance was not required, initially, to avoid premature confrontation. In the summer of his second year of hospitalization, however, the coordinator of special education of the Boston public schools, in reviewing Lester's school attendance, ruled that he must not miss any days of school during the summer session if he was to pass the ninth grade. Lester responded to this by dropping out of school and taking a job at a butcher shop without permission or approval. In view of the good relationship he now had with the hospital personnel and in view of his increased self-esteem, it was felt that he was now ready for confrontation. He was required to leave his job and return to summer school.

A program was instituted whereby Lester was paid a bonus of 100 points for each perfect day of school. Any day on which he failed to come to school, either in the morning or in the afternoon, an attendant who had a good relationship with him was to be sent to look for him and to take him back to school. Whenever this was necessary, Lester was to be charged 100 points for "services rendered." On the first day of the program Lester frequently excused himself from the classroom, became nauseated, and fainted three times, behaviors that, in milder form, had previously excused him from school. (This may be considered a typical example of the intensification of a previously enforced response that often occurs during the early states of extinction.)[11] Limits were put on Lester's permission to leave the classroom, and within a week he was attending regularly, paying attention, and making satisfactory academic progress. Although he was usually tardy and rarely earned his bonus, he needed to be brought by the attendant only on four occasions during the summer. Lester passed the ninth grade.

Irving S., a 17-year-old boy with the diagnosis of autism, benefited demonstrably from the remedial school, which was organized as a programmed classroom, modeled after the CASE program at the National Training School for Boys in Washington, D.C.[12] For years Irving could not function in the ordinary classroom. He was barely verbal, and he seemed completely unable to work independently on any prolonged task. He had been taught only on an individual tutorial basis. In the classroom, however, he was expected to do independent work. Although his subsequent course in school was stormy, he nevertheless made steady progress.

One of the problems that interfered with Irving's work was his tendency to give wrong answers deliberately. A teacher's attempts to correct his work and to tutor him generally led to an argument that resulted in both parties becoming angry and confused. This appeared to be a repetition of events at home, where his father would severely reprimand him for giving misinformation. Irving appeared to seek the confusion as a way of avoiding serious work on which he might be taken to task for his answers. A program combining reward with "time-out from reinforcement"[13] was used in order to modify this behavior. Whenever his errors appeared to be deliberate his work was taken away from him and he was asked to sit in his seat without work or to leave the classroom until he was ready to work properly. During this time he could not earn any points. Also, since he liked to play with blocks, he was allowed to play with them for one half hour each time he correctly completed a specified minimum number of pages of work. Whenever he made an "honest" error in his work he was not reprimanded but was shown the proper way to answer the problem. Appropriate materials were chosen so that he could learn while making a minimum of such mistakes. This program markedly reduced Irving's tendency to make deliberate mistakes.

Irving's progress in the remedial classroom was dramatic. In arithmetic, where his work was initially evaluated in small units (by the page or by the individual problem), he successfully completed books on addition, subtraction, multiplication, and division and proceeded to fractions and decimals. He became able to work on this material independently for up to an hour at a time. In reading he began in a teacher-administered program taught in a small class and gradually advanced to books in which he was required to read independently and to retain several paragraphs at a time.

Operant conditioning on the wards

We have already indicated that the ward staff are the primary treaters of adolescent inpatients at our hospital and that they supervise and sponsor all the activities in the hospital in which patients engage, including those at the Adolescent Service. The ward is the one place in the hospital where violent and potentially violent behavior can be handled and is the place where patients feel safest when they are unsure of how well they can control themselves. Thus patients ordinarily return to the ward voluntarily (and are encouraged to do so) when they get upset, and they generally stay there until they feel more comfortable.

With the ward as a firm home base, the privilege of coming to the Adolescent Service can function as a strong and important reinforcer. Admission to the Adolescent Service's activities, however, is not unconditional. When a patient's behavior cannot be controlled at the Adolescent Service, he is excluded from its activities and is required to earn his way back by good behavior on his ward and by demonstrating his readiness to make proper use of the activities in which he chooses to engage. Only the physical security and 24-hour control available on a hospital ward can insure the effectiveness of a time-out program; for only on the ward can such powerful basic reinforcers as visiting privileges, grounds privileges, sleeping arrangements, or even the "privilege" of remaining out of a seclusion room be controlled and used systematically.

The case of Herman I. illustrates how reinforcement contingencies on the ward were used, in conjunction with those in the remedial classroom, to treat a case of severe school phobia in a moderately retarded psychotic boy.

Herman's experiences with school had been uniformly ones of complete failure. Eventually he sustained a series of losses that made him unable to tolerate the stress of school. These losses included his therapist, his ward administrator, and his nurse at the Adolescent Service, who all left the hospital at about the same time. He stopped attending school and remained out for two months, making only two brief visits to school during this time. Numerous attempts at positive reinforcement met with failure. We supposed that this was related to the intense, self-punitive attitude that characterized his depressive reaction to loss.

To deal with this a program was implemented in which Herman was required to work for one half hour each day in the ward's occupational therapy shop in order to avoid having to spend the evening in a seclusion room. When Herman first learned of the program he appeared greatly relieved, and he dramatically thanked us for proposing it. He attended occupational therapy faithfully every day and remained out of seclusion. After approximately one month he was also required to spend some time in the Adolescent Service's occupational therapy shop, and, thereafter, some time in the classroom. Special programs were written for him to help him learn multiplication. His work was evaluated by a tutor after every arithmetic problem, and Herman was paid generously for his work. The seclusion provisions in the program were gradually eliminated. Within a month Herman was attending school for 1½ hours each day. The rest of his day was progressively filled with work assignments and other activities. Despite several severe stresses, including the admission of his mother to the hospital and several changes in ward administrator, Herman continued attending school regularly.

Operant conditioning in the home

Parents are encouraged to join one or more of several groups conducted by the Adolescent Service soon after the patient's initial hospital contact. Some of these groups focus on orientation to the hospital, others on the experience of having a sick child and on more personal insight. In addition there is a group called "Friends of the Adolescent Service" that plans social activities for the patients and hears invited speakers on topics relevant to the children's treatment. The general orientation has been to treat parents as co-workers in the treatment of their children.

A 10-week course in operant conditioning was offered to parents, irrespective of their participation in other groups. The parents of 15 patients volunteered to participate. Although there was reluctance on the part of some parents to see their children's problems as being treatable behavior problems (rather than problems of innate badness or physical illness), parents were nevertheless enthusiastic about receiving concrete help with handling their children's behavior at home. The course was modeled after ones given by Walder and by Patterson for parents of younger children.[14] Parents met once weekly in a two-hour session. The first hour of each session consisted of a lecture on the basic principles of operant conditioning. Lecture topics included methods of observation, record taking, schedules of reinforcement, extinction, punishment, shaping, and programming. The second hour consisted of individual meetings with a staff member in which the parents were trained and supervised in systematic observation of the behavior of their children and in the design of programs to modify it.

In the individual meetings, parents were first helped to isolate a behavioral problem that was important, that occurred frequently, and that was sufficiently well specified to be countable. It was thought that involvement in the course would be most helpful and appealing to the parents if they were given their initial choice of what behavior to work on. Thus, although the staff felt free to suggest important behaviors, the final choice was left to the parents. Choices included teaching new behaviors as well as eliminating bad ones. Frequently both were done at once. After selecting a behavior, the parents were asked to take a baseline count on the frequency of occurrence of the target behaviors (or, in the case of behaviors not yet learned, to record the elements or approximations of the target behaviors that the patient was able to perform) and to record the antecedents and consequences of the behaviors. Considerable effort was invested in taking these preliminary steps with care. Only then was attention turned to modifying the behavior. The target behaviors chosen by parents included teaching cleanliness and self-care (shaving, washing, care of hair), conversational abilities, getting up in the morning, doing chores at home, behaviors associated with independence (shopping, traveling by public transportation), talking to self, asking repetitive and annoying questions, bizarre gesturing, and aggressive behaviors.

After the formal course was over, monthly follow-up meetings were held for a year in order to help parents continue working behaviorally with their children. Most of the parents were, in fact, able to modify significant behaviors in their children during the course. These led to important therapeutic advances, and, often, to a "snowballing" of other, more global changes in the behavior of the patient and his family. Even in cases where parents were unable to carry out programs successfully with their children, they almost universally reported a new appreciation of the extent to which they punish their children for bad behavior while ignoring good behavior. They saw the effectiveness of positive reinforcement and of teaching important behaviors in small steps. In several cases significant changes occurred in the *parents'* behavior, which were necessary in order to modify the behavior of their children, and which altered the general pattern of communication in the family.

> The mother of Christopher S. chose to work on his talking to himself which she saw as the hallmark of his chronic psychosis. When she observed the antecedents and consequences of this behavior she noted that it tended to occur when he was not doing anything in particular and that one of the consequences of the behavior generally would be her nagging him to stop. This seemed to be a general pattern for the interaction between Christopher and his mother. She would nag him about not doing the right things or about doing the wrong things, and generally she would overlook times when he did things on his own initiative. (Her capacity to face so squarely her own behavior was characteristic of parents in this group. The potential for relevant action offered by the course appeared to facilitate such insight.)
>
> The effective program for eliminating Christopher's talking to himself involved his mother's counting the times he did it and taking him out to dinner at the end of each week in which he did not talk to himself for a specified number of evenings. She also established her own points system at home and paid him points for helpful things he did around the house without being

asked, such as putting away his clothes and taking out the garbage. The points could be exchanged for gifts. In addition she made concerted attempts to engage him in conversation, especially about things he would read in the newspaper, as an incentive for him to spend time reading rather than talking to himself. After two months he stopped talking to himself, and this behavior has not recurred in more than a year since then.

The parents of Irving S. (described above) decided initially to work on his repetitive questions. After observing the consequences of this behavior which usually occurred at home, they realized that they generally answered all of Irving's questions and that eventually they became angry. The program consisted of their counting the number of times that he asked a question, and refusing to answer it after he repeated it four times. Irving became visibly upset when this program started and frequently asked whether his behavior was being counted. The repetitive questions disappeared within two weeks. He still tended to use language in a babyish way, however, generally with the effect of producing anger and confusion in his parents. Thus it was decided to teach the S. family to talk together.

The best site for this training seemed to be at the dinner table, where Irving and his parents were together every evening. Initially it was found that no communication ever took place at this time. Rather, Mrs. S. would read a book while eating, and Mr. S. would watch the news. Irving would receive attention only if he did something wrong. At first the program consisted of tape-recording the dinner table conversation and bringing the tape to the operant conditioning course for feedback. Some of these early conversations sounded like Irving's father's giving him the third degree about school. Mr. S. asked pointed factual questions. The atmosphere was tense, and periodically Irving would give some wrong information, confuse the issues being discussed, and get his parents angry with him. It was suggested that the parents ignore instances of misinformation, that they bring more of their own daily experiences into the conversations, and that they expand on any topics Irving brought up that were interesting. This program continued for about five months, during which Irving's conversational ability markedly improved both at home and at the Adolescent Service, with a host of associated changes in social behaviors.

Several parents in the course were not successful in modifying their children's behavior. In three cases, violence on the patient's part required ward treatment to provide effective reinforcers and behavioral control. In another three cases, the parents could not see the relevance to themselves (for example, one mother was preoccupied with her marital difficulties and had no motivation to pursue the course), although one of these couples was later able to participate successfully in a conditioning program at home, after subsequent events had demonstrated to them the importance of working on their child's behavior. In one instance a staff member's difficulty in setting limits with his patients made it impossible for him to help the parents, since no other approach was equally relevant in the case of this assaultive patient.

BEHAVIOR MODIFICATION AND PSYCHOTHERAPY

For the majority of our patients individual psychotherapy has been an important component of the treatment program. In our setting, with its wide range of diagnostic differences among patients and its considerable variation in aptitude, experience, and theoretical persuasion among therapists, psychotherapy is not closely definable as one kind of procedure. All versions share, however, the relative intimacy of private conversation, directed to an examination of the patient's personal experience, his hopes and fears, and, particularly, his feelings about the people close to him. No other setting offers the patient a comparable opportunity. For some patients psychotherapy becomes the central focus of treatment, while for others it appears never to achieve such intensity, although even in the latter it may be of great importance to the patient. In this paper, however, we are not so much concerned with psychotherapy itself as with simultaneous use of psychotherapy and behavior modification techniques in the various forms described earlier.

In the past several years we have seen many cases in which behavior modification has facilitated psychotherapy but no cases in which the two have interfered with each other. Interference is, of course, often a matter of individual interpretation. Psychotherapists, ward administrators, and various members of the Adolescent Service have often disagreed over diagnosis or specific aspects of treatment planning, but these disagreements have not as yet revealed areas of incompatibility between behavior modification and psychotherapy as we have employed them.

The case of Peter B. (described above) illustrates how involvement with the behavioral program in the Adolescent Service enabled a seemingly unreachable patient to take advantage of psychotherapy.

> At the time of his admission Peter was extremely anxious, and although he was obsessively attempting to obey all the rules and to be approved of by everyone, he avoided close relationships with staff memebers and with other patients. At times his anxiety made it impossible for him to carry on a conversation, for he could not concentrate on what anyone else was saying. He adamantly denied that he was a patient, and preferred to think of himself just as a student in the school. For these reasons, use of psychotherapy, in our setting, at this time, would have been ill advised, and we made use of operant conditioning programs such as the one described earlier. After approximately a year's involvement in the Adolescent Service, however, during which Peter demonstrated, for the first time, that he could succeed in school, he began to admit that he did, in fact, have some problems, and he asked to have psychotherapy.

> During the 10 months since therapy began, Peter has been able to speak to his therapist about his feelings of loneliness, his intense rage at people who are even slightly critical of him (including his parents), and his fear of becoming overtly psychotic again and becoming chronically hospitalized. Peter has markedly loosened up during this period, his anxiety has diminished, and he has begun, very tentatively, to express some of his anger and depression more openly and to show a capacity for warmth and understanding both in his relationships with staff members and with other patients.

DISCUSSION

We have described the clinical use of operant conditioning for behavior modification in a comprehensive treatment program for a diverse population of disturbed adolescents. It will be evident to those familiar with inpatient treatment that proper administration (that is, case management by the patients' ward administrator) employs a similar behavioral frame of reference.[15] For example, demands are regularly made on patients, requiring at least a minimal degree of behavioral organization, before the patient is allowed to leave the ward. Programs for adolescent inpatients have generally recognized, in addition, the need for developmentally relevant activities (for example, school and recreation) as integral parts of hospital treatment.[16] Our report has, therefore, been concerned less with these principles of treatment than with ways in which operant techniques can be used to systematize these aspects of treatment and to apply them in various settings where treatment takes place.

Operant techniques and more traditional methods have been integrated into a consistent approach to treatment that has drawn from several bodies of psychiatric experience. A psychodynamic approach is taken to interviewing, to diagnosis, and to psychotherapy, and psychoanalysts and behaviorists cooperate in planning treatment programs. Choice of reinforcers and areas of reinforcement are influenced and directed by psycho-dynamic considerations. The decision to gratify Peter B.'s need to hoard and, later, to challenge it and the decision to avoid an early confrontation with Lester J. but to insist upon one later were determined by assessments of many factors affecting their capacity to tolerate the new demands and to respond with benefit.

Operant techniques have been especially useful where other methods are least effective. Where words fail, these not-necessarily verbal methods are powerful alternatives. Their emphasis on learning in a continuum of small, definable steps, with provision for recording of progress, their use of immediate, usually positive contingencies, and their attention to behavior and its consequences make them especially suitable for work with very sick adolescents, for whom action and nonverbal communication play such an important role. An indirect but nonetheless important aspect of operant techniques is inherent in their clarity and simplicity: they require that the goals of treatment be accurately specified. They can therefore be used to coordinate the efforts of a diverse staff scattered throughout a large hospital. As in every other aspect of treatment, however, proper diagnosis and timing are required in the use of operant conditioning. Further, these techniques do not obviate the need for personal investment in the patient, nor is operant conditioning a substitute for the painful process of making life's decisions. Also, patients develop deep emotional attachment to staff members who apply contingencies to their behavior, and the importance of these attachments must be considered in treatment planning.

The question is sometimes raised: Does operant conditioning deal only with the surface, leaving the underlying problem untouched? The behaviorist argues that there is no "underlying" problem but that the behavior *is* the problem.[17] Neither the question nor the answer adequately represents our experience with operant techniques. Like the psychoanalytic approach to treatment,[18] operant techniques must *start* from the "surface," that is, where problems are readily identifiable. In our experience, when we modify behaviors that most obviously interfere with a patient's academic and social adjustment and most directly contribute to his low self-esteem, we also often make the patient (for example, Peter B.) more capable of fruitful self-examination. Similar observations have been made by others.[19] Finally, as in the case of Irving S., long-term sequential operant conditioning programs in various settings have, in fact, been found to deal effectively with the complexities of human behavior.

NOTES

1. W. B. Honig, *Operant Behavior: Areas of Research and Application* (New York: Appleton-Century-Crofts, 1966).
2. C. M. Franks, *Behavior Therapy: Appraisal and Status* (New York: Appleton-Century-Crofts, 1969); L. Krasner, "Assessment of Token Economy Programmes in Psychiatric Hosptials," in *CIBA Foundation Symposium: The Role of Learning in Psychotherapy* (London: Churchill, 1968); R. Ulrich, T. Stachnick, and J. Mabry, eds., *Control of Human Behavior: From Cure to Prevention*, vol. 2 (New York: Scott, Foresman & Co., 1970); C. Nueringer and J. L. Michael, eds., *Behavior Modification in Clinical Psychology* (New York: Appleton-Century-Crofts, 1970).

3. A. O. Kris and L. F. Schiff, "An Adolescent Consultation Service in a State Mental Hospital: Maintaining Treatment Motivation," *Seminars in Psychiatry* 1 (1969): 15-23; A. O. Kris, L. F. Schiff, and M. J. Kelly, "Participatory Consultation: A New Approach to Organizing a Comprehensive Treatment Service for Adolescents" (manuscript submitted for publication); M. J. Kelly, "Comprehensive Long Term Treatment of a Schizophrenic Adolescent," *Psychiatric Opinion:* 7 (1970): 36-41.
4. *M. Sullivan, Programmed Math,* books 1-15 (New York: McGraw-Hill, 1968).
5. C. Buchanen, *Programmed Reading for Adults,* books 1-8 (New York: McGraw-Hill, 1968); Science Research Associates, *Job Corps Graded Reading Program* (Washington, D.C.: Office of Economic Opportunity, 1967).
6. C. Buchanen, *Spelling,* books 1-6 (Palo Alto, Calif.: Behavioral Research Laboratories, 1967).
7. B. F. Skinner and S. Krakower, *Handwriting with Write and See,* books 1-6 (Chicago: Lyons & Carnahan, 1968).
8. Performance Systems, Inc., *Advanced General Education Program* (Washington, D.C.: Office of Economic Opportunity, 1968).
9. Krasner, op. cit.
10. P. Lehrer, L. Schiff, and A. Kris, "The Use of a Credit Card in a Token Economy," *Journal of Applied Behavior Analysis,* in press.
11. J. M. Notterman, *Behavior: A Systematic Approach* (New York: Random House, 1970).
12. H. Cohen, "Educational Therapy: The Design of Learning Environments," in *Research in Psychotherapy,* vol. 3, ed. J. Shlien (Washington, D.C.: American Psychological Association, 1968).
13. C. Ferster and B. F. Skinner, *Schedules of Reinforcement* (New York: Appleton-Century-Crofts, 1957).
14. L. O. Walder, "Teaching Parents to Modify the Behaviors of Their Autistic Children," (paper read before the American Psychological Association convention, New York, 1966); G. R. Patterson, R. S. Ray, and D. A. Shaw, "Direct Intervention in Families of Deviant Children," *Oregon Research Institute Research Bulletin* 8, no. 9 (1969).
15. L. Linn, "Hospital Psychiatry," in *American Handbook of Psychiatry,* vol. 2, ed. S. Arieti (New York: Basic Books, 1959).
16. P. G. S. Beckett, *Adolescents Out of Step: Their Treatment in a Psychiatric Hospital* (Detroit: Wayne State University Press, 1965); H. Beskind, "Psychiatric Inpatient Treatment of Adolescents: A Review of Clinical experience," *Comprehensive Psychiatry* 3 (1962): 354-69; E. L. Hartmann, et al., *Adolescents in a Mental Hospital* (New York: Grune & Stratton, 1968); Council of the American Psychiatric Association, "Position Statement on Psychiatry of Adolescence," *American Journal of Psychiatry* 123 (1967): 1031; W. Schonfeld, "The Adolescent in Contemporary American Psychiatry," *Archives of General Psychiatry* 16 (1967): 713-19.

17. B. F. Skinner, *Cumulative Record* (New York: Appleton-Century-Crofts, 1961); J. Wolpe, *Psychotherapy by Reciprocal Inhibition* (Stanford: Stanford University Press, 1958).

18. S. Freud, "Fragment of an Analysis of a Case of Hysteria" (1905), in *Standard Edition*, vol. 7 (London: Hogarth Press, 1953), pp. 1-122.

19. B. Weitzman, "Behavior Therapy and Psychotherapy," *Psychology Review* 74 (1967): 300-317.

15. Day Treatment as a Complementary Adjunct to Residential Treatment

Karl A. Marshall and Malcolm F. Stewart

The Eastfield Children's Center in Campbell, California, has provided residential treatment, along with outpatient, foster care, and group home services, for several years. In 1966, a day treatment service was added to the existing program. The service is from 8:30 A.M. to 5:00 P.M., Monday through Friday. In the morning, children attend public school either in regular classes or in classes for the educationally handicapped or in the school on the center grounds. In the afternoon, the program includes individual recreational activity, discussion group therapy, field trips, and supervised free play. It is compulsory that parents become involved in family therapy. Parents retain nurturing responsibility for the child, providing clothing, medical and dental needs, transportation to and from the agency, and so forth. Payment for service is on a sliding scale. Case direction is under a psychiatrist, with caseworkers and a child care supervisor having day-by-day planning responsibility.

The staff at Eastfield viewed the addition of day treatment as a step broadening the spectrum of services within the program and offering a wider choice of treatment possibilities for the child and his family.[1]

We think day treatment differs from residential

Reprinted from *Child Welfare*, vol. 48, no. 1 (January 1969), pp. 40-44, by permission of the authors and the journal.

treatment in both degree and kind. When we accept a child into residential treatment, we accept total responsibility for the child—his nurturing needs as well as treatment needs relating to his pathology. In day treatment, with nurturing needs remaining largely with the parents, the therapeutic intervention is directed to a more specific goal and is more limited in scope. It may actually involve a contractual agreement. One agency, Miramonte Day Treatment Center in Palo Alto, California, draws up a treatment contract between the patient and the agency. The contract is posted in the day treatment headquarters, and all the patients assume responsibility to help one another fulfill their contracts. Our contract in residential treatment is generally very broad. The contract in day treatment is usually focused on specific symptoms, the problems they reflect, and the responsibilities of all parties.

When it has been established that a child needs help, a decision to use day treatment implies that the problem has not infected the child's psychosocial environment to the degree that total separation from his family and community is indicated. This implies that there are some strengths in the child and his environment, and these are to be built upon in the plan for treatment. There are three potential sources of strength—the child, the family, and the community. If we assigned a numerical value to each source, the total would indicate the treatment of choice: a high total would suggest outpatient; a lesser total, day treatment; and a low total, residential.

RATIONALE FOR NEW SERVICE

Factors in the rationale for adding day treatment to our services included:

1. *There are some parents who can continue to have their disturbed child live with them if they are relieved of the total burden of responsibility for him.* Most children with problems come from families with problems. Some parents, because of great anxiety and lack of ego strength, have all they can do to cope with the demands of the day themselves, and they are totally unable to handle problems

of a disturbed child. Other parents, however, given the relief and support of a day treatment program, have the energy to meet most of the child's nurturing needs while involving themselves with the child in a treatment program designed to alleviate family problems.

> Brian, age 10, was referred for residential treatment by the local school principal because of school problems—inattention, truancy, defiance of teachers and principal, failure to work up to capacity—and the inability of his parents either to cooperate with the school or to control the child during periods of suspension. At intake, it was learned that Brian had been "a behavior problem most of his life." The parents were overwhelmed by the child, confused by their anger and guilt around Brian's not meeting their achievement goals, and, after several weeks of school suspension, afraid of their own homicidal wishes.
>
> A program of day treatment was undertaken that included on-grounds schooling, nine hours a day relief for the mother, tight structure and strict limits on Brian while in the program, and weekly family therapy. At first the change was "miraculous"; then a plateau was reached, and only as the parents were able to clear up communications, meet the child's need for parental control, and also allow the child to gain successes did real change take place. Thus residential placement was not necessary; on the contrary, change and growth were facilitated by the family's remaining intact.

2. *The trauma associated with separation of child and family should be avoided where possible.* Freud and Rank are among the many who have spoken to the deep psychological significance of separation.[2] Separation too often confirms the child's (and the parent's) feelings of guilt and lack of self-worth. The child separated from the parent frequently engages in fantasy about the "all-good parent" coming to spirit him away from these "bad people" who steal children from their parents.[3]

3. *The day treatment program provides care for the child who needs more than outpatient therapy, without filling up beds needed for children requiring 24-hour care.* For some children nine hours a day of therapeutic intervention, utilizing the resources of the agency while the family continues to meet nurturing needs, may effect growth and change. Such children include those for whom

a suitable school plan cannot be made, and whose environment is not meeting their needs for social interaction. The presenting symptoms may be extreme acting-out behavior or withdrawn or bizarre behavior.

> Artie, age seven, and the oldest of four siblings in a fatherless home, was a depressed child. The mother placed the children in nursery and extended day schools while she worked. Artie was a nonachiever in school, isolated, pathetic looking. His mother demanded that he supervise his siblings and blamed him for their negative behavior.
>
> Artie was referred by a school psychologist to the child guidance clinic which, after 17 weeks of therapy, referred him to Eastfield for residential treatment. During the intake study, it was determined that day treatment was the treatment of choice. He was so placed, and the contract included on-grounds schooling, two activity therapy groups, and the mother's weekly involvement with the caseworker around her handling of Artie and the feelings she had about trying to work and care for four small children.
>
> Without "responsibility," Artie blossomed in day treatment through the first four months. Then a gradual return to severe depression was observed. This coincided with the mother's discussing with Artie plans to move from the community and to remarry. These plans did not relate to a realistic situation, but rather to mother's attempt to escape from "her problem." A change to residential treatment was recommended, unless there was reversal of Artie's move toward depression. The caseworker was able to help mother see the connection between Artie's downswing and her talk of plans. Mother canceled both plans and Artie improved. Subsequent situations indicate that mother was talking to Artie in a more appropriate parent-child manner, [4] resulting in no depressive relapses.

4. *Day treatment offers opportunity for better observation and diagnosis of children whose pathology cannot, in outpatient treatment, be untangled from that of other family members.* Prior to the development of our intensive day treatment program, it would have been necessary to use residential facilities in such cases.

> Buddy, age seven, was referred to us by his mother on the recommendation of his psychiatrist. On the phone the mother tended to minimize the problem, but the psychiatrist knew our problem and we guessed there

were factors she was not stating. Buddy's symptoms included extreme acting-out and aggressive behavior in school (he had been excluded by public school and was in a day nursery that offered little more than baby-sitting service), vomiting at will, and temper tantrums. At times of stress he would sit and stare off into space, "being out of touch." He had many imaginary friends and no real friends.

Buddy had been given a neurological workup which indicated "abnormal, diffuse E.E.G. [electroencephalogram]." He was accepted into the program for extended diagnosis and treatment. The pediatric neurologist used the controlled milieu to manipulate medication for Buddy and get observational feedback. In work with the mother and the child separately, it became obvious that the primary problem lay in their relationship. An important aspect of treatment was both the relief the mother got by having the child out of the home for the day and the casework help she received that made it possible for her to continue in the role of the nurturing parent to the child. Buddy also had his first good school experience through the class for the educationally handicapped on the Eastfield campus.

5. *The day treatment meets the need for expanded resources for treatment of emotionally disturbed children, and obviates the need for expansion of residential facilities.* There was a rapid, progressive increase in demand for Eastfield treatment facilities, with a slower growth in funding for the services. Therefore, we searched for a method of increasing the number of children and families who could be served on the residential treatment campus, without increasing cost for facilities.

INTEGRATION VERSUS SEGREGATION

Because the day treatment program was carried out on the institution campus, we discussed at length the question of integration versus segregation of the patients. (In the beginning the discussion was purely academic, since we had no specified quarters to house the new program, and integration was our only possibility.)

Arguments for integration were as follows:

1. Since a primary placement factor is the ego strength

of the parents, the symptoms of children in the two groups might be similar. Integration would provide a larger population from which to select therapy and activity groups. It also would give residential children a chance for broader peer interaction.

2. Initially, the funding source of the day treatment program required short-term, intensive treatment of child and family (limited to nine months). We determined to work with symptom alleviation or symptom substitution. We anticipated that integration would make possible more rapid turnover among residential placements.

3. Integration might serve to (1) assure residential patients that the step from group to family care need not be so abrupt or frightening as it generally is (even with planned increase in both frequency and length of home visits during discharge preparation in our agency); (2) assure residential children through their own observation that they need not be perfect to return to the natural community; and (3) encourage residential children to work toward a return home, avoiding the depression many long-term residential patients have. Point (3) was contradicted in the early months as day treatment youngsters, on hearing about trips, allowances, clothes, purchases, and the like, asked staff how to get into the residential program. This behavior, happily, is now reversed.

4. A quickly discarded argument for integration was that the "weaker" residential patients could gain from association with the "stronger" day treatment children. The day treatment children did not prove to be necessarily healthier than residents; and when they were, we could not help residents if it were to the detriment of those in day treatment.

Arguments in favor of separation of the two programs emphasized "cleaner programming." They included:

1. Since in residential programming staff provides the nurturing needs, and since in day treatment parents are expected to meet these needs, there were two quite different foci and goals. Symptoms of day treatment children could be attacked more readily and effectively if the programs were segregated. For residential children, the

program centers primarily on treatment in the milieu. This involves a "treatment day" different from that in the day treatment program. In residential treatment there are times that are highly significant in the general interaction. Important periods include when the child gets up, when he goes to bed, when he is ill, and so on.[5] In day treatment the milieu is more contrived, more highly structured, and more easily manipulated to concentrate on specific symptoms. The two "treatment days" do not mix well.

2. If the programs were separate, the staff members in each would have fewer children to handle, and could focus on treatment needs more clearly than they could with the larger group in an integrated program.

3. The children in residence do not have to face up to the knowledge that other youngsters are going back to families every night and every weekend. Conversely, the day treatment youngsters do not have a constant fear that some action by them or their parents will separate them from the family.

4. Integration might foster a negative tendency to pace day treatment as though the child were to be a patient for a long time, and all his needs should be met in day treatment. Historically, residential treatment has had a long-term approach. (When the new program was introduced and integrated, the staff tended to operate from the existing pattern in treatment. Theoretically, staff members could differentiate goals and the time factor in the two programs. In practice this proved to be most difficult, and we believe it would be a problem for other agencies adding day treatment to existing residential treatment.)

Our resolution of the question of integration or segregation was a compromise. Lunchtime, all off-grounds trips, and after-school recreation are programmed separately for residential and day treatment. Schooling, both on-grounds and in the public schools, and including transportation, is not separated. Some activity and some discussion groupings purposely include children who would gain from them or need the experience, regardless of their program affiliation. For example, a play therapy group led by two of our caseworkers has children from both programs who can and need to learn to share, to wait their turns, and to handle aggression and withdrawal at the discussion level. A visual-motor coordination weekly workshop for four brain-damaged children has representation from both programs.

Thus, since neither forced integration nor contrived, artificial separation is always effective or efficient, we have attempted to integrate where this is therapeutic, and separate elsewhere.

CONCLUSION

Day treatment has proved to be an exciting adjunct to residential treatment. This addition to the spectrum of services has demonstrated itself to be both therapeutically and economically sound. We have been learning from our experiences and our mistakes. We hope this paper will stimulate discussion in other agencies so that all might learn more about this rather new service.

NOTES

1. Beryl C. Kester, "Indications for Residential Treatment of Children," *Child Welfare* 45, no. 6 (1966): 338 ff.
2. Sigmund Freud, *The Problem of Anxiety*, trans. H. A. Bunker (New York: W. W. Norton & Co., 1936); O. Rank, *The Trauma of Birth* (New York: Robert Brunner, 1952).
3. Almeda R. Jolowicz, "The Hidden Parent" (paper read at the New York State Conference of Social Welfare, New York City, November 1946).
4. Eric Berne, *Games People Play* (New York: Grove Press, 1964).
5. Bruno Bettelheim, *Love Is Not Enough* (New York: Free Press, 1950).

16. A Residential Treatment Center Moves toward the Commuity Mental Health Model

George Mora, Max Talmadge,
Francis T. Bryant, and Benjamin S. Hayden

The Astor Home for Children was established on a nonsectarian basis in 1953 as a pilot project of the New York State Mental Health Commission in cooperation with Catholic Charities of the Archdiocese of New York, to determine the effectiveness of residential treatment of emotionally disturbed children who could no longer be maintained in home, school, or community, but who were not so severly impaired as to warrant hospitalization. Astor Home is in Rhinebeck, New York, 90 miles north of New York City, in the Hudson Valley. It is administered by the Daughters of Charity of St. Vincent de Paul. The staff consists of 59 professional personnel, representing the fields of psychiatry, psychology, casework, group work, nursing, and education, as well as maintenance, domestic, and secretarial personnel. The 14 highly trained sisters play important roles, the principal one that of group mother, providing a 24-hour-a-day interpersonal experience for the children. The school program represents an extension of the special education system of the New York City Board of Education, and is known as PS 203.

Reprinted from *Child Welfare*, vol. 48, no. 10 (December 1969), pp. 585-90, continued on 628-29, by permission of the authors and the journal.

The children admitted suffer mainly from severe personality disorders of the neurotic and acting-out type. Occasionally children with borderline psychotic disorders are admitted. They must be residents of New York State; the majority are from New York City's most disadvantaged group. Age at admission ranges from 6 to 11 years; the children are of average intellectual potential. The children are assigned into groups, each group under supervision of a sister. Since the goal frequently is to return the child to his family, casework with the family is vital to the program. The average length of treatment is 30 months, with some children being discharged at the onset of adolescence.

The treatment plan integrates the small group approach with individual psychotherapy and specialized education. This is accomplished through a close interaction among professional, educational, and child care staff.

THE EARLY RESIDENTIAL PROGRAM

During the first few years of operation little was known concerning the types of children who would best respond to such a program. Similarly, little was known about the influence of different aspects of the program on various types of children. Also, there was little awareness of the need for postresidential treatment services. The treatment approach at that time was limited to isolating the child from his pathological environment and offering him a program of intensive treatment.

It was difficult to conduct traditional casework with families because of the pathology and resistance of the parents, due to their primitive way of functioning and to the disorganization of their environment. Individual psychotherapy had to be limited, and was not well integrated into the total therapeutic program.

From the beginning, the institution had two strong assets: (1) a child care program of sisters and counselors characterized by close integration and high consistency, and (2) a school program of five hours a day, conducted by competent and dedicated teachers.

The need for postresidential services became apparent

after children began to be discharged. Originally the only alternatives were return to natural families, even when casework had not been successful, or transfer to other institutions or state hospitals. Occasionally a child was readmitted to Astor when he failed to adjust to his own home and community. In general, reinstatement in school and his own community presented a great problem, since special educational facilities were limited.[1]

Children at intake were, on the average, at least two years retarded academically. They gradually began to make up the deficiency, although at discharge they were not always up to age level.[2] Although a theroretical framework concerning the functions and relations of the residential treatment center to the community was lacking, it was believed that the main reasons for the child's failure to adjust to his own environment were: (1) the onset of adolescence at the time of discharge; (2) pathology in the families, in spite of the casework; and (3) limitations in the environment for reabsorbing the child, especially in terms of schools.

Because of these difficulties, in 1954 the Astor Home initiated a foster care program by recruiting foster homes where children could be under close supervision of caseworkers. For the selection of foster homes, a "foster parent attitude test" was developed by Dr. Ralph W. Colvin, then chief psychologist. This research was described in several papers,[3] as well as in the master's theses of social work students.[4] The theory was that, potentially, there is a home for each child, regardless of his individual problems. Therefore, the research concerned itself with identification of factors in the child and in the family that would match.

PROGRAM EVALUATION

At the end of the five-year pilot project, the need for continuation and expansion of services was obvious, even on the basis of the limited data available. More detailed data were gathered in a 10-year follow-up study and a study by McKenna.[5] A total of 126 children who had been discharged for at least six months were rated independently by at least two staff members on a seven-point scale in the areas of home, school or employment, and community. The ratings were based upon information and questionnaire material obtained by social workers directly from children, parents, and agencies such as schools, employers, and institutions. More than half the youngsters were rated as making a good adjustment, and less than 20 percent as making a poor adjustment.

Analysis revealed that the age of the child at the time of follow-up seemed to be significant. The youngest group, those under 13, had the highest adjustment rating. The ratings went progressively downward until age 19, where there was a small, but significant, rise. The findings also revealed that the most difficult period began about two years after discharge from Astor, and the situation did not improve until the sixth and seventh year after discharge. These years coincide with the onset and duration of adolescence. In this same group, a significant correlation was found between adjustment ratings and intelligence. A correlation between severity of diagnosis and poor adjustment was also determined.

The findings in regard to destination at discharge revealed that 60 percent went to their own homes, 24 percent to foster homes, 7 percent to childcare institutions, and 9 percent to state hospitals. For those boys who returned to their own homes, a major hazard to a good adjustment was parental pathology, as measured by the Bloch-Behrens Scale.[6] There was a high correlation between poor adjustment and presence of mental illness in the family. There was also a high relationship between poor adjustment and seriously disturbed parent-child relationship. A bad prognosis was apparent for a child returning to a family in which little change had occurred in the parent-child relationship. No significant relationship was found between adjustment on the child's part and indices of marital and financial problems in the home.

CHANGES DUE TO EXPANSION

The program of expansion resulted in: (1) a marked

increase in the ratio of professional to child care staff; (2) provision of intensive psychotherapy for each child by members of the three orthopsychiatric disciplines, under overall psychiatric supervision; (3) an increased focus on neurological aspects and psychopharmacological treatment; and (4) the development of more aggressive and concrete techniques in working with families, which was facilitated by increased services in a New York City office, and the provision of transportation to Astor for New York City families on a monthly basis. With initiation of the bus service, contacts increased from less than 30 percent to over 85 percent of family visitings. This contact between the child and his family helped staff in maintaining awareness of the reality of the home situation, and in reevaluating the child's potential for return to his own family.

As a result of the difficulties encountered in the transition of the child to a new environment, attention was focused on planning for his discharge. A preplacement period of five days was initiated for each child being considered for admission. In addition to psychological and psychiatric evaluation, this allowed an estimation of his potential for interpersonal relations with peers and adults in different settings (classroom, dormitory, recreational area, and so forth), and also made it possible to plan better for aftercare. The preplacement evaluation included a visit to the institution by the parents. They were seen by a caseworker, who assessed the family potential and the need for casework.

The system did not yield full knowledge of the types of children who respond better to the program, nor show the influence of different aspects of the program on various types of children. However, it did direct the focus of the staff on the alternatives available at the time of discharge, and on the limitations that foster homes have for many children at the onset of adolescence — for example, inability to establish meaningful relationships.

RESULTS OF EARLY PLANNING

The emphasis, at admission, on tentative planning for

discharge effected some changes: (1) Children tended to be admitted with the same degree of pathology as previously, but to remain in the institution for less time, since plans for discharge, determined at the onset of treatment and constantly kept in focus, were completed as soon as feasible. (2) The foster home program was strengthened, since a more thorough knowledge of the child's potential and the family's potential resulted in more successful foster parent-child matching. (3) There was an early identification of the educational facilities available to the child during the aftercare period. (4) The problem of eventual separation of the child from the institution was kept constantly in mind, and separation anxiety, fear of returning to an impoverished community, and so forth were handled in therapy.

The emphasis on early tentative planning for discharge also affected the staff work: (1) The clinical conference on each child had a more concrete character, since persons working with the child were aware of the goals. (2) The staff was more willing to revise plans when an original goal could not be achieved, and felt less guilty about it. (3) The importance of social and cultural factors was stressed, especially in the return of children to deprived environments after exposure to middle-class values while in residence. (4) The presence of trainees in psychiatry, psychology, and social work each year brought out new ideas and opened new perspectives for aftercare. (5) Research projects continued to focus on evaluation of the child's progress and planning for his return to the community.

THE GROUP HOME PROGRAM

The experience in the first decade of the program, supported by data from the 10-year follow-up study, pointed to the need to develop other types of aftercare facilities for children accepted for treatment at Astor. It was the consensus that group facilities should be established for youngsters approaching adolescence, and in need of a group program designed to minimize parental conflicts and to buttress identification with healthy forces in the community. Since most of the children come from New York, that city was considered the best location. A low-middle-class area, culturally integrated, was viewed as ideal. In 1964 a group home for eight boys was opened in the Bronx, in a rented two-story duplex. The first floor was devoted to recreation space, and the second floor to living and sleeping quarters for the children and a middle-aged couple who were houseparents. In 1965 a second similar group home for eight girls was opened, also in the Bronx. A group worker (in addition to relief personnel) divided his time between the two homes. The children attended the local high school and became involved in community programs. Contact between the group homes and Astor was maintained through weekly staff conferences, held alternately in Rhinebeck and New York City, under psychiatric supervision. The children were not seen regularly in psychotherapy, but a worker was assigned for individual counseling whenever necessary.

PLACEMENTS AFTER DISCHARGE FROM THE INSTITUTION

Placements over a one-year period, September 1965 to August 1966, illustrated the extent of postresidential treatment possible for the children. The period was one of unusually high turnover. There were 41 discharged children, 23 boys and 18 girls, representing two-thirds of the boy population (35), and the entire girl population. Although the children all had been "treated," most required postresidential treatment, whatever their destination. The children were all relatively young, still highly dependent on adults for support.

Of the 41, 12 boys and 2 girls were returned to their own homes, 4 boys and 7 girls were placed in foster homes, 1 boy (who came from an institution) was returned to an institution, 1 boy and 1 girl were placed in a state hospital, and 5 boys and 8 girls were placed in Astor group homes. The discharged boys averaged 9 years of age on admission, and remained for 2.7 years in residence. Girls averaged 8.4 years of age on admission, and remained 2 years.

Repeated attempts were made to involve other agencies in postresidential treatment, but the efforts usually were unsuccessful. The agencies prefer to accept children who are considered as less "sick" and, therefore, have a better prognosis. Children who have been in residence continue to be viewed as being disturbed, although in many cases they have a better prognosis than children in outpatient facilities.

The addition of the group homes permitted increased flexibility in planning for the children. The staff became involved in a variety of new functions: (1) direct work with adolescent youngsters in the group homes, both at the individual and group level; (2) supervision of and cooperation with houseparents, foster parents, and other child care staff working in settings separate from the institution; and (3) involvement with schools, other agencies, and organizations in the community in which patients resided. In time, the children also became more aware of the various types of placement available at discharge. The families of the children in most cases cooperated on placement of their children in group homes, as they had done in the past for the foster homes.

FOSTER HOME PROGRAM

Astor now has 14 licensed foster homes in operation, caring for 17 children. The homes have been operating for periods ranging from 1 to 12 years and have cared for a total of 27 children. The overall number placed in foster homes so far is 52. With only two current exceptions, there is only one child in each foster home. In most cases, maintenance in the home has required intensive professional help, including casework contact with the child and foster parents. In several situations, the child has been brought to Astor Home regularly for therapy and special education.

Following is a summary of the foster home program during the last year:

Nine children from families with chronic pathology

were placed for long-term care, according to the concept of "matching." Of these placements, six are working out and three have failed. One failed because the child's family did not really free him for placement. A second was unsuccessful largely because of lack of special school facilities in the area. A third failed because the foster parents were insecure and tended to compete with the child's natural parents. Usually, contact of the child with his own family while he is in a foster home has been continued. In this case the contact was arranged at Astor, to avoid foster parents' meeting the natural parents. This was done to prevent criticism of the foster home by the natural parents, and to minimize conflicting loyalties in the child.

Recently, foster parents have attended group meetings at Astor, to exchange views and air their feelings. It is expected that the meetings will help foster parents acquire a better image of themselves as foster parents, and identify more closely with the total Astor program.

CHILDREN WHO RETURN HOME

Children who returned to their own homes have been assisted through social work contact. In addition, group therapy was initiated but then was changed to a community-oriented group work approach as more suitable to children's interests. Attempts were made to utilize state and federal programs, but since many of these programs (for example, the Job Corps) have a starting age of 16, the children were not eligible. The year between 15 and 16 appears to be the most devastating period. The children who are discharged from the program already identify themselves as adolescents but, because of their age, cannot earn money legally. They also view themselves as being independent, and, therefore, adult authority becomes objectionable.

COMMUNITY SERVICES

As the Astor program expanded, the professional staff became involved with the local community in a variety of ways, from regular teaching to occasional lecturing and part-time consultation. It was no longer possible to ignore increasingly evident new needs for mental health services. After long preparatory work with Catholic Charities, with the state, and with community representatives, the Astor Child Guidance Center, staffed by Astor Home personnel, was opened in Rhinebeck in 1966.

With this new center, Astor Home is committed to the whole spectrum of mental health services for children, from treatment and rehabilitation of individualized psychiatric casualties to attempts to modify pathogenic factors in the environment. Although the original program was concerned exclusively with treatment and rehabilitation of children so seriously disturbed that separation from a pathological family was necessary, work is now being done with children who remain in and are treated with their families. In addition, Astor has joined with the local schools in a study of environmental factors that affect ego functioning and development.

The services provided by the Astor Home — inpatient services, group homes, foster homes, and child guidance center — constitute a continuum of integrated services rather than separate entities — a continuum, however, in which each has special characteristics and emphases.

From this broad perspective, the Astor range of services is similar to the range of services being offered in community mental health centers. Indeed, a community mental health center being built in Poughkeepsie, 15 miles from the Astor Home, will include a branch of our child guidance center. The Astor Home is the only child psychiatric facility in the mid-Hudson area, a fact that may have contributed to pressure toward filling gaps in community services.

Involvement of Astor Home staff members in diagnosis and treatment of children belonging to the greater variety of groups typical of child guidance seems to have fostered a more optimistic outlook for all those connected with child psychotherapy. Similarly, the opening of foster homes and group homes has contributed to flexibility of approach and sensitivity to educational and community issues. Awareness of family and group dynamics has been heightened, and this may influence the entire philosophy of treatment in the residential setting.

While these developments are taking place, other aspects and goals are becoming evident. Although activities are limited by present staff and facilities, considerations include:

1. Because most of the children in residence tend to be discharged around the same time (in summer), we are interested in the possibility of working with them through group activities or group psychotherapy, depending on their pathology and developmental level. In this way, it would be possible to focus separation anxiety and community readjustment.

2. The need for more individual contact — at the psychotherapeutic or at the counseling level — with children placed in foster homes or in group homes is evident. Wider knowledge of the interaction between this individual contact and the ongoing group approach is needed. The life-space interview might be useful in this context.

3. Further activity in the New York City office is planned. Group meetings, such as with children in group homes, or former patients, can be used to develop projects.

4. Ways to utilize state and federal programs in the area of education and rehabilitation should be found. It will be necessary to develop programs to bridge the gap between the age of discharge of our children, 12 to 13, and the age at which they are eligible for these programs, 16.

5. The research on the selection of foster parents is being continued. It should be extended to include evaluation of foster parents in their work with children.

6. It is necessary to learn more about the selection of houseparents for group homes, for example, their motivation, their role as semiprofessional workers, and ways of evaluating their work. One view is that older couples entering this field have little potential for learning and, therefore, it is better to staff group homes with young group workers in three shifts daily. Another plan is to test the motivation and learning capacity of potential child

care personnel through courses in child care, such as the one at the Dutchess Community College in Poughkeepsie, in which some staff members of the Astor Home participate. The idea of offering training courses in residential centers for prospective houseparents has also been advanced.

SUMMARY

When Astor Home was founded in 1953, it was involved in only one aspect of treatment, the curative process. With experience, it became apparent that this was only one part of the total ecological picture of the child's life, represented by the family, the school, the community, and the social agencies. From this point of view, the areas of ego strength in the child became paramount, and school was seen as a stabilizing force. The movement of Astor toward the community, which has been described in this paper, is an attempt to integrate the intensive therapeutic approach with the positive aspects of community life.

The residential treatment center offers a specific kind of community. Originally, it was conceived of as a social environment isolated from its community and from the pathological community in which the child lived previous to placement. In time, it was found that improvement in the child means not only adjustment to his present living environment but also an ability to maintain himself in communities with certain pathological aspects. As the focus has changed from isolation to total community involvement, we have become increasingly aware of the importance of strengths in the patient and community, and of the value of harmonizing them. As has been pointed out, the aim is to provide primary, secondary, and tertiary prevention. Involvement in all aspects of mental health has provided a total perspective, so that the various parts of the ecological picture are considered in the pursuit of community adjustment.

NOTES

1. Bernard McKenna, "Postdischarge School Achievement of

Institutionalized Children" (unpublished master's dissertation, Fordham University, New York, 1962).
2. Max Talmadge and Benjamin Hayden, "IQ and Achievement Changes Associated with the Effects of Residential Treatment on the Intellectual and Achievement Functioning of Culturally Deprived, Emotionally Disturbed, Preadolescent Boys" (paper read at the Eastern Psychological Association annual meeting, Boston, 1967).
3. Ralph W. Colvin, "Toward the Development of a Foster Parent Attitude Test," in *Quantitative Approaches to Parent Selection* (New York: Child Welfare League of America, 1961); idem, "Foster Parent Attitudes Related to Placement Success" (progress report, Research Grant M-5884, National Institute of Mental Health, U.S. Public Health Service, 1963).
4. Gloria Etri, "Motivation and Foster Parenthood" (unpublished master's dissertation, Fordham University School of Social Service, New York, 1959); Marian T. Schwagerl, "Foster Parent for Emotionally Disturbed Children" (unpublished master's dissertation, Fordham University School of Social Service, New York, 1964).
5. *What We Have Learned: A Report on the First 10 Years of the Astor Home, a Residential Treatment Center for Emotionally Disturbed Children* (New York: Astor Home for Children, 1963); McKenna, op. cit.
6. Donald Bloch and Marjorie L. Behrens, "A Study of Children Referred for Residential Treatment in New York State" (unpublished report, New York, 1959).

Part IV
Training and Manpower

OVERVIEW

The quality of a center's treatment is closely related to the character of its staff — that is, the level of their skill, how they relate to each other, and their consistency with the children. The number of staff, of course, is also important.

Regretfully, child care workers and other paraprofessionals usually enter residential work without training specifically for it. Even teachers, social workers, psychologists, and psychiatrists, while having training in their respective specialties, usually have not been prepared for work in residential treatment. This means that carefully planned and creative programs of inservice education must be developed.

The interpersonal relations among the staff ought to be amiable and cooperative. However, such may not be the case as individuals with various perspectives about children's problems and how they ought to be handled come to work at centers. The resulting frictions will disrupt treatment and even damage the children. Consequently, the administrator, as well as the groups involved, must be especially sensitive to these problems and correct them when they occur.

Consistency in working with emotionally disturbed children includes not only a coordinated staff effort and individual worker stability but also low turnover in a center's personnel. Many of the children have been plagued by disrupted and broken relationships in their pasts. So, centers must avoid exposing the children to the type of experiences that brought them to the center for help.

Two articles in this section focus on developing staff, particularly child care staff: Mayer ("Differential Education and Inservice Training for Child Care Workers") and Bettelheim and Wright ("Staff Development in a Treatment Institution"). One article, Weber ("Conflicts between Professional and Nonprofessional Personnel in Institutional Treatment"), reflects the devastating effects of staff conflict on children. Schrager ("Observations on the Loss of a Housemother") illustrates the importance of child care staff for children.

17. Differential Education and Inservice Training for Child Care Workers

Morris Fritz Mayer

A few years ago, Susanne Schulze, Eva Burmeister, and others campaigned for the recognition of the nonprofessional child care worker. Their campaign has been successful in that we have become aware of the central function of the child care worker. We have also recognized the lack of professional status and education of the child care worker. At this time, when the need for semiprofessional auxiliary workers is apparent in many branches of social work, it is necessary for us to examine the role that the nonprofessional has, for a long time, played in the institution.

In a previous paper we reported on a study that showed that the staff at Bellefaire Residential Treatment and Child Care Center, Cleveland, Ohio, could be divided into five categories of child care workers, classified by their degree of professional orientation.[1] The study also showed that inservice training and professional education had to be adjusted for each of these categories and that the training of child care workers should not be considered as one uniform task, but as a number of differentiated tasks.

Reprinted from *Child Welfare*, vol. 44, no. 5 (May 1965), pp. 252-61, by permission of the author and the journal.

FIVE CATEGORIES

The five categories of child care workers included:

The *cottage parents*, whose parental instincts and qualifications outweighed all other qualifications. They were foster parents in an institution setting. Training of this group had to be focused on the utilization and specification of their personal qualities, particularly their interest in being parents, and on the recognition and utilization of their social values.

The *people in search of a calling.* Forty-two percent of child care workers in the institution came not only to find jobs but also to find a profession. This group consisted largely of younger people whose education did not qualify them for a regular profession, but who were searching for a worthwhile occupation in the service of mankind. Often the search was also for an understanding of themselves.

The *professional child care workers*, who, although they were not professionals in an academic sense, could function on a quasi-professional level. They could readily modify the role they played and the methods they used according to the needs of the child. These people represented the most flexible, the most versatile, and the least subjective of all the child care workers. Training and education were oriented not only toward helping them develop an understanding of the child and his psychosocial situation but also toward the development of a conceptualization of their work. We found that in a successful inservice training program a considerable number of persons in search of a calling could be moved into the category of the "professional" child care worker.

The other two categories, *people between jobs* and the *professional social worker as a child care worker*, do not need to be discussed for our purpose here. At this time we want to look at the first three of these categories in the light of other variables in training, namely, the methods of training, content of training, and the difficulties encountered in a training program.

DIFFERENTIAL TRAINING METHODS

We see staff development as a combination of three methods:[2]

Individual supervision. This we see as the most important part of staff training. Conferences between the supervisor and the child care worker should be held for the purpose of preparing and reviewing specific parts of the work, clarifying and interpreting this work, as well as noting the worker's reaction to it.

Intra-agency courses. We are most interested in those various group meetings geared primarily to the learning process of the staff rather than to the immediate implementation of theory. These courses may consist of lectures with discussions, or they may be workshops in which the Socratic method is used. They provide a general framework in which the worker can see himself function and be able then to see his work as a part of a total structure and his present contribution as a part of an ongoing process. In addition to these courses, there are other forms of operational group meetings that play a part in the training of the child care worker.

Interagency courses. These are regular courses connected with universities, welfare federations, or other organizations that exceed the boundaries of any single agency. This enables the worker to view child care away from the practices and limitations of his own agency. It also allows the worker to examine underlying principles and concepts.

In addition to these regular courses there are lectures and institutes given by guest speakers.

When we apply the differential methods of teaching to the categories of child care workers, it becomes clear that each group of staff makes its own use of these methods. The three categories of child care workers — the cottage parents, the people in search of a calling, and the professional child care workers — all require specific attention in their training. Yet, often writers on an institution staff have addressed themselves only to the cottage parent rather than to the total group of child care workers.[3]

Supervision

All three categories respond well to supervision, especially since this method can easily be adapted to the individual needs of each worker. This method deals as much with the objective tasks that confront each worker as with the anxiety he experiences about his task.

Supervision of cottage parents. Supervision is the method through which cottage parents learn most effectively. It would be frustrating to the supervisor and to the cottage parents to expect that the cottage parents will understand complex methods of treatment, differential treatment goals, and defense mechanisms. The very value of the cottage parents consists in the directness of their approach to the child and in an ability to function naturally. Their greatest assets are their realization of the ups and downs of everyday life, their value consciousness, and the natural strength of their ego. To help them express these strengths in their everyday activities and convey them to the child is the major goal of supervision. We should expect these people to have a certain flexibility and tolerance. Yet, it would be too much to expect Mrs. Jones to change her attitude toward the fire setter or the bully. The goal often has to be limited to the development of sympathy for the unhappy child in trouble rather than an empathy with the disturbed child in therapy. One may have to settle for acceptance of the child rather than understanding, but this is a great deal. Supervision helps the cottage parents give of themselves to the child in a disciplined way and can help them accept the treatment center's system of controls.

Over many years, the cottage parents may have developed their own practices of discipline which may differ considerably from the ones established at the institution. Only when these differences become unbridgeable is there real cause for concern. The supervisor can help find the many similarities between the cottage parents' own practices and those of the institution in order to help them accept the areas of difference. Above all, he has to help the cottage parents see that their self-esteem and moral concepts are not threatened by the institution's clinically determined approach and that they can retain their own ideas even while adopting some of the institution's practices and principles. If one discovers that a cottage parent does not have the quality of goodness — a discovery that should have been made before he was hired — there is little hope that he can be trained.

Supervision of the person in search of a calling. Supervision of the person in search of a calling is quite different. Although he, too, needs to have positive personality traits, his trainability is far less confined. Usually his age and his desire to find a direction make him respond to supervision more definitely. His desire to find out about the child and the treatment plan may be greater and more subjectively determined. Whatever he does not know he wants to learn, sometimes naively assuming that personal values and strength can be learned along with the methods of discipline or the techniques of play.

Since this group is much less secure than their colleagues, the cottage parents, they need more support. The analytical and critical review of their work can often be accompanied by the question of why they have done what they have. Sometimes this question can lead to a greater awareness of how their own psychological defenses enhance or interfere with their work. Their awareness then may lead them to an ability to utilize themselves more flexibly.

> At one of the conferences, a 28-year-old child care worker with a great interest in social work reported an incident in which a child made reference to his color and speech and also to his supposed lack of masculinity. He rebuffed the child's provocative behavior rather sharply — too sharply, he thought after some discussion. He related his own reactions to events in his background. At a later date, when a similar incident had happened, he could report his more relaxed way of handling the situation because of his realization that he might become just "a little too subjective."

Sometimes child care workers of this group have a

particular strength or weakness in some specific skill. Through knowledge of this, they may become able, for example, to ask that someone else supervise the homework while they supervise the gardening project or the basketball game. Grossbard has stressed that self-awareness is needed by child care staff.[4] Although the cottage parent can achieve this to a limited degree, the person in search of a calling can bring forth a greater amount of insight and change. He can often be encouraged to find the role for which he is most gifted and through this to gain greater awareness of his own abilities. A number of these people in search of a calling will find out — or it will be discovered for them — that child care work is not their calling, and they will be advised to leave the field. A greater number, however, can be helped to reach their goal and to find fulfillment. At Bellefaire we have found that more than half the people in search of a calling become professional child care workers.[5]

Supervision of the professional child care workers. Again, I should like to refer to Grossbard's article on self-awareness. He indicates that "unlike the social worker's role and function, which are expressed through certain well-structured and identified activities, the cottage parent's role is diffuse and all-pervasive."[6] The job of supervision of the professional child care worker can be defined as helping the worker to develop order and system out of diffusion. A basic identification with the professional philosophy of the institution and an understanding of the methods of its implementation are necessary in order to achieve this goal. The distinction between the essential and the nonessential, the primary tasks and the secondary ones, the generic and the specific, can then be taught. The child care worker then does not have to be constantly concerned with the approval or disapproval of any particular part of his work by the supervisor, the caseworker, or the psychiatrist. He sees that his work in its totality is approved because it is in general harmony with the whole. Through supervision he can learn to relate the many activities of every day not only to the total job he has to do but also to the treatment goal for each of his charges. He will then be able to adapt his functions to the demands of the job and to the needs of the child. This is what makes him a "professional."

The supervisor can help him recognize when he has achieved and when he has failed in his task, and how to use his own particular personality and professional versatility to succeed where he has failed. This learning process goes on for many years and is furthered when the professional child care worker enlarges his knowledge by acquainting himself with the theories and literature of the field and, on occasion, by moving on to more formal professional training.

Intra-agency Courses

Each institution must decide on the method of staff training it will use. It is advisable to augment supervision with courses or group discussions of a more theoretical nature. This is necessary for the persons in search of a calling and is mandatory for the professional child care worker. Some group sessions are needed for operational purposes, others for training purposes.

Group supervision. Part of this group training may be some form of group supervision, such as discussion of children in one cottage with all the staff in the unit or discussion of maintenance, household, and managerial problems with all the people concerned. Particular problems and reactions of the staff can best be handled through group discussions. Other problems arising during group supervision may be referred to the individual supervisory session. These group supervisory sessions can also be very efficient devices for economizing time. Often, too great a part of the individual supervisory time is spent discussing details such as the use of the sewing room, food problems, handling of new requisition blanks, or the preparation for semiannual dental examinations. Questions such as these can be discussed in group supervision.

Case conferences. In most institutions child care workers participate in some form of periodic evaluation conferences on the children. These case conferences are effective learning methods. The thorough understanding of one child is the best way to understand the total institution operation. The child care worker's awareness of the role of the therapist and the influence of the therapeutic consideration on the total organization is of great importance.

Nevertheless, it is necessary to evaluate the effect of the presence of nonprofessional staff in such highly confidential and professional clinical interchanges. The child care worker must be made aware of the professional confidentiality of the conference. Some institutions find it wise to let only those child care workers who have proved their reliability and ability to remain with the institution participate in these clinical conferences. It is necessary to make sure that all participants can really participate, that materials are presented in a manner understandable to all, and that questions are encouraged and appropriately answered. The level of discussion may be affected by the heterogeneity of the staff. Some institutions have clinical conferences for the therapeutic staff only and other evaluation conferences for the complete team. The learning effect of these conferences will be enhanced if some of the findings on an individual case can be expressed so that their applicability to other cases becomes evident.

Staff training meetings. Clinical case conferences and group supervisory meetings are primarily operational structures in treatment centers. Their educational values are secondary gains. Thus, it is necessary to establish training meetings in which training is the primary goal. These training meetings are established for the sole purpose of educating the staff. They are necessary because they allow the staff to view individual cases in the light of a concept. Certain areas of knowledge in child care can be transmitted only in this form. What part of such knowledge can be best conveyed by intra-agency courses and what part by interagency courses remains somewhat of an open question. In general, it seems that every institution has to find ways to communicate to its staff the principal concepts by which it operates and on which its intake and program are based. The main questions to be considered by such intra-agency training courses are the following: What do we try to do here? Why are we doing what we do? What is your discipline's (in this case child care work) specific contribution to this goal? How does this relate to the work of other disciplines? Although the group discussion is not so limited to specific situations as the supervisory and case conference, it still views the material from the general point of view of the agency's practice.

The optimal use of these sessions can be made if the child care staff is able to participate in the selection of topics and presentation of some of the material. Nevertheless, the leader of these courses should be aware that many subjective considerations enter into the selection of topics, and he may have to guide the selection. There are certain topics that child care workers like to discuss again and again without necessarily incorporating the results of these discussion into their system of practice. The participation of the professional child care worker in the choice of topics is very helpful. He will be able to recognize the difference between the excitement of certain topics and their usefulness in learning. His presence is similarly advantageous for presentation of material, formulation of questions and recommendations, reports on literature, and participation and leadership in study subgroups.

The staff training meeting also presents an opportunity for the child care worker in search of a calling to get answers to questions arising in his work and to look at his work from a more objective point of view. Often his youth and eagerness to advance his opinions make him a somewhat belligerent participant in these discussions, and a good deal of patience and understanding on the part of the course leader is required. These courses can also help to evaluate to what degree the child care worker in search of a calling is on his way to becoming a professional child care worker.

The cottage parents are able to make valuable contributions to these courses, usually by giving examples of their own practice and by recognizing the degree to which this practice coincides with what they are taught. Their awareness that there is a lack of harmony between their practice and the underlying theory or between their own preinstitution practices and their present role may create a good deal of anxiety. This anxiety is expressed in different ways, such as nonparticipation, hostile participation, over-eagerness, overcompliance, and so on. It is necessary to handle this in supervisory discussions. Some cottage parents have a mature ability to look objectively at their practices without undue anxiety and to participate in these courses, which can be very helpful to them.

The question as to who teaches these intrainstitution inservice courses for child care workers must be answered differently for each institution. The group supervisory discussions and the case conferences are conducted by the people whose operational assignment it is to carry out these functions. The staff training meetings should be conducted by a person who is familiar with the material and who also can teach well and stimulate discussion and participation. This may be a psychiatrist, a teacher, a case worker, a group worker, or an administrator. If it is an administrator, he must make certain that his position does not stifle discussion and criticism, and that he does not become too defensive about the unavoidable discrepancy between theory and practice. If a person not connected with the administration gives these courses, care must be taken that the courses do not become mere gripe sessions against administrative practices. The person who gives these sessions should be identified with the general goals of the administration but should also be sufficiently detached from its practices in order to be able to look at them objectively.

Interagency Training Courses

The interagency courses can be taught on simple or more sophisticated levels, depending on the teacher and the staff members. The course can be conducted in an impersonal atmosphere if the child care worker is attending them only as part of his job obligation. It can also be a very personal experience where he not only accepts instruction but also is willing to undergo change, as Wasserman and Gitlin have described.[7]

The planned interaction between the agency and the classroom can be a very constructive aid to these courses. Wasserman and Gitlin have also reported on this from their experience in Cleveland.[8]

An increasing number of universities and schools of social work have developed such courses, often in conjunction with state departments of welfare or welfare federations. In 1960 the Child Welfare League of America reported on 15 such courses.[9] There are many more today. It was stated then that "instead of dealing with the cottage parent as an omnibus occupation in an undifferentiated way, encompassing all types of cottage parents operating in all kinds of institutions, we will have to become more specific and incisive."[10] These major handicaps still exist today.

The report suggests that possibly a differentiation should be made in the classification of cottage parents for the dependent, neglected child; the emotionally disturbed; the adolescent; the preadolescent; the neurotic; the psychotic; and others.[11] This statement points up the confusion in this area. Although there are certainly differences between what a child care worker working with preadolescents has to know and the knowledge required for one working with adolescents, the generic knowledge required by both is certainly greater than the specific differences. Even more questionable is whether the refinements in diagnostic classification of children would help in the training.

What is important is not the level of disturbances of the children, but the different levels of trainability of the child care workers. The cottage parents, as much as they may represent the hub of the wheel of the institution, probably get the least benefit from interagency courses. They may confuse rather than help the cottage parent unless supervision is immediately available for clarification of any conflicts.

By the same token, the people in search of a calling can

benefit greatly from such courses. The very fact that these courses are often connected with a university is a stimulus to learning. The people in search of a calling can see that the work they do is not just the incidental expediency of one institution but rather emanates from the scientific theory of academic teaching. This lends impetus to their work as well as to their search for identity.

These training courses are most beneficial for the professional child care workers. For them it is a step toward greater professionalization and the acquisition of an independent body of knowledge. Unfortunately, many of these courses are oriented toward those students whose interest and capacity for learning are limited. The teacher and the sponsoring organization often have a paternalistic attitude toward the "student" child care worker, and express this in the dispensation of easy praise and recognition rather than by setting realistic educational goals. This attitude seems to me not too dissimilar from that of the white missionary at the turn of the century. His attitude to the African native whom he taught was one of amazement, encouragement, and condescension. The attitude is perhaps understandable in the case of a 50-year-old cottage parent who, after many years of hard work with no stress on academics, decides to return to school. It is not a justifiable approach to the younger, more alert, and mobile child care worker who looks for a profession and a frame of reference. These courses should not be directed to the lowest common denominator, but rather to the highest learning potential in the group.

DIFFERENTIAL CONTENT OF LEARNING

Since we cannot teach the total process of group living in any inservice training, or any other training courses, some selection must be made. We have to select and focus on a few aspects of the total content of group living and omit many others. What are the most important aspects for the child care worker to know? I believe that everyone makes up his own list. Grossbard, in his monograph on cottage parents, states that all of this training has to be based on two simple assumptions: (1) "that the primary role of the cottage parent is that of a good parental figure" and (2) "that training . . . has to be oriented toward problem-solving" and anxiety relieving.[12] The content of the courses has to be determined by these goals.

On the other hand, Henry Maier struggles valiantly with the attempt to find a conceptual base for child care work and visualizes child care as "a social work method parallel to casework, groupwork, and community organization."[13] Although every child care worker must be ready to fill a parental role if the child's needs demand it,[14] I think that this function is only a part of the total task, and the one part that cannot be taught in courses.

Even though individual supervisory sessions have to be geared toward problem solving, the courses should be oriented mainly toward instruction. Certainly a personal contact should be established between the instructor and the child care worker, and the courses should touch the real problems of the children. Yet the very value of the courses is that they give an academic objectivity and an intellectual vision to the highly personal problem-laden material. It is for this reason that these courses should be oriented toward the professional child care worker and the worker in search of a calling.

The main areas that must be taught are: the meaning of separation, the growth proccess and its disturbances, group living, the meaning of therapy and education, recreation, daily life activities, concepts of discipline, the role of the natural parents, and the institution's relation to the outside world.

These basic areas can be further broken down according to the interests and abilities of the child care workers participating in the courses. Such concepts as the development of ego, of conscience, and of a value system can be further elaborated as the student's capacity grows through learning. One of the purposes of the course is to help the students to see the child as a total psychosocial entity, as well as the important part that the institution and the treatment play in the child's life.

SOME PROBLEMS IN TRAINING
CHILD CARE WORKERS

Of the many problems that have developed in this field, a few should be mentioned because they directly affect all attempts in the training of child care workers.

1. *The problem of availability.* Judging by our limited geographical experience, it seems that the parental type of child care worker is less available than years ago. The applicant of today, if a man, is often young, has a family, and wants to live with his family in relative privacy — usually outside the institution. He sees his value more readily in terms of economics and career advancement than did his predecessor. His dependency on the institution structure is not so great as his desire to use it as a stepping-stone. This is also true for some women who apply. On the other hand, among the women who do apply there are still some of the "matron group" from which we have formerly recruited all female child care workers.

2. *The confusion about handling dependency.* This confusion exists among many administrators and professionals. In general, one finds a great number of dependent people among child care workers. This dependency may express itself in different ways, including submissiveness, hostile dependency, rebelliousness against the power structure and the desire of the child care worker to achieve a personal quasi-treatment experience through his work. [15] The structure of the institution and the professional personnel may foster and encourage dependency. We know from the work of Stanton and Schwartz that this is undoubtedly the case in the mental hospital. [16] If organization, communication, and power structure at the institution foster the dependent submission of the child care worker to the professionals or administrative staff, it would be fallacious to expect training to undo his process.

3. *The absence of a science of social living.* The modern institution has three major functions: social living, special education and training, and psychotherapy. In the fields of psychotherapy and education there has developed over the

past decades a body of scientific information. It is taught through the official channels of academic structure, even though there are philosophical differences among various schools of thought within these professions. As far as institution social living is concerned, no such standardized body of knowledge has been developed. The child care worker is the instructor in the art of social living. He gets his knowledge not from a "professor" of social living, but rather from a therapist or educator. Often the two do not agree. Social living is a combination of therapeutic and educational principles, with one or the other predominating.

In spite of the noteworthy attempts by Konopka and her students,[17] the impact of group work has not yet been felt on this field to the extent that would be necessary to provide a reliable body of knowledge on group living. Unfortunately, Dr. Konopka's deep understanding of the group-living process is not yet scientifically established in the field. In case of conflict between the therapist and the educator, the child care worker, despite his educational limitations, has to make a decision as to whom to follow. Often the administration of the institution compounds this conflict rather than helps find the solution.

4. *The value system.* Everyone who stresses the parental role of the child care worker also implies that he becomes an ego ideal and a value setter. Whose values are being set? The cottage parents', the director's, the therapists', or the teachers'? Except for a few very basic practices, such as the permission of parents to visit, punishment, religious observances, and some others, there are and can be only few general directions. Although Grossbard's adage that "administrative and supervisory directives have to stop at the door of the cottage" is correct in many ways, it can become a confusing directive in regard to values.[18] In the modern treatment center the time has passed when one couple takes care of a dozen or so children. Three, four, or five may now have this responsibility. Each one will have a different value system. The modern treatment institution is necessarily occupied with treatment problems and has not yet come to grips with the value problems. Questions

about smoking, dating, and religious activities are often handled exclusively according to the needs of the child rather than also on the basis of some prevailing ethical value concept. Part of this is, of course, a general problem of our society. The task of teaching people how to be parents becomes more complicated through the avoidance of setting up a value system. The unsuspecting cottage parent is then asked to set values and may see himself holding a tiger by the tail.

These are some of the difficulties with which we are confronted in the training of the child care worker. We do not think that any of the problems are insurmountable if we can turn our efforts to the establishment of a force of workers who can deal with the child's problems of today without being bound by a nostalgia for yesterday's concepts of child care.

PLANS FOR A PROGRAM FOR THE DEVELOPMENT OF CHILD CARE WORK

The concept of professionalization of child care workers has been widely discussed in the past few years, and the hope has been expressed that there will evolve a professional child care worker.

In some quarters it was suggested that preprofessional training leading to a master's degree could be given to prospective child care workers. There is, at least, one university where a program had been established with this goal in mind. But, it soon became obvious that the person with graduate professional training would not want to remain a child care worker for very long. In a paper on differential training we included a category of the professional social worker doing child care work.[19] Our experience with this group indicated that the few professionally trained social workers in the field used the child care position as a stepping-stone to higher status professional positions in the institution. Although it is desirable to train social workers (or psychologists) as child care supervisors and administrators who have had, at least, an internship in direct child care work, it is obvious that such a program will train the supervisor rather than the practitioner. It will not substantially increase the number of available child care workers.

In recent years some universities have made attempts in the preprofessional undergraduate training of child care workers. These courses vary in length from a few weeks to a year. They are a combination of classroom and field work apprenticeship. This kind of program will be helpful to the extent that it will attract students who will later become child care workers. There seem to be two potential shortcomings: (1) there is a probability that it will appeal to young people, possibly new high school graduates who can be used only with the very youngest age groups and not with adolescents and preadolescents; and (2) although this preprofessional training represents a step forward, it will be used by a very small group of candidates and will not solve our major problems of child care shortage.

In order to promote the development of a professionalization of the child care worker, a great number of workers presently employed must be utilized. It was for this reason that we introduced the category of professional child care worker. We submit herewith a preliminary plan for nationwide training of these child care workers while they are in service. This plan will need more refinement and elaboration and is presented here only in its first and roughest form.

We believe *standardization and coordination* in training of this group are greatly needed. It is necessary for each organization that has good supervisory facilities and good child care staff to select those who qualify as potential professional child care workers. Standardized outlines for practice, supervision, and classroom instruction must be developed. A consciously planned effort must be made to provide these child care workers with comparable supervised experiences. The handling of homesickness by the child care worker, with or without the caseworker's assistance, would, for instance, be one such experience. The handling of mealtime supervision, certain forms of discipline, and recreational experiences all could offer standardized learning opportunities.

Particular attention should be given to the difference between planned and spontaneous handling of a situation and to the part it has in the total treatment plan. Superivsion would involve not only dealing with job tasks but also the relationship of the work experiences to the total field work plan. A national body, such as the Child Welfare League of America or the United States Children's Bureau, could develop such an outline for supervision and approve the supervisors in different parts of the country. Semiannual reports on the supervision of the child care worker would be submitted to such a central organization. Similarly, standardization outlines for training courses would be developed and used in classrooms at universities (containing, at least, the nine areas previously mentioned).

Child care workers selected to participate in such a course would qualify for our category of professional child care worker and would be intensely supervised for two years on the job. This would provide the basic training for the professional child care worker. These two years could be interrupted by a 6- to 10-week exchange apprenticeship. During this time the child care worker would work in a different institution approved by the central organization. The supervisor would submit the name of the child care worker for certification. At the end of the two years the child care worker may have to undergo some form of examination, consisting largely of an interview with a representative of the national organization to evaluate his general attitudes and experiences with children. Then the child care worker would receive certification as a "Professional Child Care Worker." This certification would be recognized by all institutions participating in the program. Salary scales and working conditions would be adjusted to attract the certified professional child care worker.

Although academic learning and classwork are necessary in such a program, the main emphasis of the plan would be on the systematic use of practice and supervision as a learning experience. Such a program would enable the child care worker to look at himself, not as an incidental product of one institution's training effort, dependent on this institution alone, but rather as a professional person with freedom to move from place to place in accordance with his training and with opportunities for advancement in a competitive job market.

Under such a plan, I believe a relatively large number of professional child care workers could be developed over a period of a few years. Together with professional staff they could become the binding force in institutions caring for children and help serve as standard setters for all child care workers.

This does not mean that we should (or would want to, or could afford to) eliminate the other categories of child care workers previously discussed. They are still needed and useful within the total spectrum of child care work. Yet, even their work and status would be enhanced by the development of a category of professional child care workers. Certainly with the establishment of such a category the modern institution will be better equipped to meet its growing challenge.

NOTES

1. Morris F. Mayer, "Differentials in Training Child Care Workers," in *Training for Child Care Staff* (New York: Child Welfare League of America, 1963), pp. 41-58.
2. See Susanne Schulze and Morris Fritz Mayer, "Training for Houseparents and Kindred Personnel in Institutions for Juvenile Delinquents," in *Training Personnel for Work with Juvenile Delinquents* (Washington, D.C.: U.S. Government Printing Office, 1954), pp. 44-69.
3. James F. Berwald, "Cottage Parents in a Treatment Institution," *Child Welfare* 39, no. 10 (1960): 7-10.
4. Hyman Grossbard, "Development of Self-Awareness of Child Care Staff," in *Training for Child Care Staff* (New York: Child Welfare League of America, 1963), pp. 14-26.
5. Mayer, op. cit., p. 46.
6. Grossbard, op. cit., p. 16.
7. Sidney Wasserman and Paul Gitlin, "Child Care Worker Training Experience: A Coordinated Effort between Classroom and Agency," *Child Welfare* 44 (1965): 35-40.
8. Sidney Wasserman and Paul Gitlin, "A Child Care Training Experience Revisited," *Child Welfare* 44 (1965): 35-40.
9. *Training Courses for Cottage Parents in Children's Institutions* (New York: Child Welfare League of America, 1960).
10. Ibid., p. 20.
11. Ibid.

12. Hyman Grossbard, *Cottage Parents: What They Have to Be, Know, and Do* (New York: Child Welfare League of America, 1960), p. 13.
13. Henry W. Maier, "Child Care as a Method of Social Work," in *Training for Child Care Staff* (New York: Child Welfare League of America, 1963), p. 81.
14. Morris F. Mayer, "The Parental Figures in Residential Treatment," *Social Service Review* 34 (1960): 273.
15. Jules Henry, "The Culture of Interpersonal Relations in a Therapeutic Institution for Emotionally Disturbed Children," *American Journal of Orthopsychiatry* 27 (1957): 724-34.
16. Alfred H. Stanton and Morris S. Schwartz, *The Mental Hospital* (New York: Basic Books, 1954), p. 193.
17. Gisela Konopka, *Social Group Work: A Helping Process* (Englewood Cliffs, N.J.: Prentice-Hall, 1963); idem, *Group Work in the Institution* (New York: Association Press, 1954).
18. Grossbard, *Cottage Parents*, op. cit., p. 11.
19. Mayer, "Differentials in Training Child Care Workers," op. cit.

18. Conflicts between Professional and Nonprofessional Personnel in Institutional Treatment

George H. Weber

In an effort to provide better diagnostic and treatment services for juvenile delinquents committed to their care, many institutions, in recent years, have added people from a number of professions to their staffs. These usually include social workers, teachers in special education, psychologists, psychiatrists, and recreational therapists. In institutions, these people are frequently known as the "professional staff." They are employed for the study and treatment[1] of delinquents, and the consultation with and guidance of other staff members.

In this latter function, the professionals may be asked by the administration to advise those workers who supervise and manage the everyday living experiences of the delinquents, such as getting up, going to bed, personal hygiene, eating, playing, and working. Within the institutions, these workers are commonly known as the "nonprofessional staff" (as differentiated from the

Reprinted from "Conflicts between Professional and Non-professional Personnel in Institutional Delinquency Treatment," *Journal of Criminal Law, Criminology, and Police Science*, vol. 48, no. 1 (June 1957), pp. 26-43, by permission of the author and the journal. The author wishes to thank Dr. Melville Dalton for his guidance and suggestions in the prosecution of the research on which this paper is based.

professional staff)[2] and usually include cottage parents, vocational and work supervisors, and maintenance workers.

This division of work, with its theoretical consistency and its apparent applicability, would seem to be acceptable to both groups as it is consistent with the currently accepted principles of delinquency treatment, personnel practice, and education. It is a plan that should allow the professionals an opportunity to increase their practical knowledge of delinquency and to apply the specific skills of their work to the delinquents and the institution. It is a plan that should also give the nonprofessionals an opportunity to increase their theoretical knowledge of delinquency and to receive some specialized help with some of their difficult problems.

In actual practice, however, this plan may encounter sharp difficulties in acceptance and functioning. Conflicts may emerge when professionals and nonprofessionals attempt to bring their specialties together. Value orientations, statuses and roles, and ideas of delinquency causation and treatment undoubtedly will differ in each group. Problems are likely to arise from the conceptions that the two groups have of themselves and each other in each of these different areas.

The material for this paper was secured from two private and three public institutions for delinquents and was gathered over a period of three years. The method of the study was that of participation and observation. The data were gathered by four people, including the writer, who worked in these institutions in either a professional or nonprofessional job. The institutions varied in the number of delinquents in residence from about 30 to nearly 400. The proportion of professionals to nonprofessionals varied from 2 percent to 37 percent. With the exception of two institutions, the nonprofessionals preceded the professionals in the setting.

In all institutions studied, conflicts were in evidence. In some, the conflicts were more intense, continuous, and dramatic than in others. In all the institutions, some cooperation transpired between the professionals and nonprofessionals, and the author does not wish to imply that all these conflicts occurred to the same degree in every institution or that they were continuous. However, conflicts were a significant aspect of the relationships existing between the professional and the nonprofessional in all the institutions studied.[3]

VALUE ORIENTATIONS

The professionals and nonprofessionals held different values regarding their own and the other's work. The professionals often stressed humanitarianism and service. They thought of themselves as primarily providing a service to the delinquents and believed that when they went into a particular case or group for study, they should assume full responsibility for it within their specialty. The professionals thought of themselves as cooperative, as sharing and exchanging information and ideas, as respecting the integrity of others and the right of others to express themselves. Keen observations and a reflective and critical approach to problems were held in high regard by them. Formal education and training, as such, were also respected by this group.

The professionals saw the nonprofessionals as holding two sets of values. One view regarded the nonprofessionals as being a hard-working, simple group of people, usually generous and kind to the delinquents in their care, and good-intentioned in their relationships and dealings with the other staff members. They saw them as valuing sincerity, friendliness, courage, simplicity, and industry. The other view regarded the nonprofessionals as strict disciplinarians who demanded hard work and obedience from the delinquents. They thought that they were rigid in their viewpoints, antagonistic toward professionals, and reluctant to take any suggestions concerning their work. Here they regarded the nonprofessionals as valuing formal and restrained behavior, compliance, and authoritarianism. In both of these conceptions, the professionals saw the nonprofessionals as having very little importance in working with problems concretely and had little regard for a theoretical approach to these problems. A psychiatrist alluded to several of these points when he was discussing a cottage mother's management of a boy:

> Mrs. S. wants Bobby punished for his stealing, immediately. She isn't interested in studying it more fully. She says that "if he did it, he should be punished and then he has paid his debt." If anyone expresses any other ideas on it, she feels her position is seriously threatened. If pressed on the matter, she'll take her feelings out on the boy.

On another occasion a psychologist, referring to the uncritical methods of the nonprofessional, said:

> It seems that many of the cottage parents have worked out rather simple schemes for dealing with behavior problems. It apparently makes them more comfortable, even though it may be harmful to the boys. It's difficult to approach them about these things because you are apt to break down whatever relationship you have.

The nonprofessionals emphasized kindness, firmness, the ability to get along with people, and hard work as necessary qualities for work with delinquents. They viewed the immediate, the concrete, the practical, and action — the "getting something done" — as important. Broad experience and intimacy with the problems of working with delinquents were considered indispensable by them. The nonprofessionals considered themselves responsible for the general development and welfare of all the boys.

The nonprofessionals regarded the professionals as generally pseudo-intellectual and theoretical. They also regarded the professionals as valuing material wealth and education. The nonprofessionals often pointed to the higher salaries given to the professionals for work they believed was "easier." They believed that the professionals valued leisure and comfort for themselves above that of the delinquents and that they tended to be authoritarian in their relationships with others. The apparent leisure and comfort of the professionals was referred to by a cottage parent when she said: "It's fine and easy for you people working up in the administration building to come at eight o'clock, leave at five, and have a half-day off on Saturday, but we cottage parents are with the boys all the time. If we aren't, one of our helpers is."

Another comment by a vocational supervisor illustrates this situation:

> We don't feel they [the professionals] understand or appreciate our job. It's easy enough for them to sit up in the main office in a nice soft chair and behind a fancy desk. They only have to deal with one boy at a time and he is putting his best foot forward most of the time when he is up seeing them. He knows they have a lot to do with the paroles.

The nonprofessionals charged the professionals with confusing "book learning" with workable knowledge, and of ranking such learning above the nonprofessional's practical experience. They contended this theoretical background and professional training, while important to the professional, actually hindered their grasp of the total situation at times.[4] This was being considered by a maintenance worker when he remarked:

> That guy who calls himself a psychologist is so busy studying what he calls psychopathology and working in therapy that he doesn't know the rest of the world the kid lives in. The way he is going about things, it doesn't look like he's going to have much chance to learn about it.

A psychologist, reflecting on this point, commented:

> The psychologist trained primarily in the psychology of the individual, the social worker trained mainly for casework, and the psychiatrist trained primarily in the diagnosis and treatment of the individual patient are not prepared to deal with the complex problems which the therapeutic management of groups presents. This is no reflection against them, unless they assume they are specialists in something they obviously are not.

Although many nonprofessionals saw the professional as emphasizing a theoretical background and professional training for work with delinquents in practice, the nonprofessionals viewed some as smooth operators without "real know-how," hiding their ineptness and, at times, some hostility behind good manners and the prestige conferred by schooling.[5] They also saw the professionals as placing power and status over democratic practices. A maintenance worker's comment illuminates the nonprofessional's view of some aspects of the professional's relations to others:

> These professional people talk about democratic practices and group processes, and that we have just as much to say about things as they do but I haven't seen it operate that way. Not only do they try to tell us what to do, but the caseworkers and the others are right next to the superintendent's office and they're telling him what to do. They have been off to school and while they haven't learned much, they have learned how to operate. When you give them a tough kid to deal with, they can't tell you what to do that's of much account — saying nothing about taking the kid on themselves.

Conflicts of values between professionals and nonprofessionals may be further illustrated by an episode in the parole planning for a delinquent. It shows that these conflicts can have a detrimental influence on the adjustment of the delinquents.

> Don was a 15-year-old boy who had been committed to the Boys' Training School for petty stealing. His father had died and his mother had deserted him. While he had been severely deprived of parental love and childhood friendships, his maladjustment was not extreme. His development at the school during his year of residence was excellent. His major activities included study in the academic school where he excelled in the sciences, and work in the school infirmary as an orderly.
>
> Don had been offered two placement plans. One placement was in the home of a dentist and his wife, who were interested in adopting the boy and giving him educational opportunities to the limit of his capacity and interest. The other placement was in the home of a farm family, who could offer him a good home but could not give him the education or the material advantages of the dentist's home.
>
> After discussing these possibilities with the social worker, Don also talked about it with his science teacher, cottage mother, and a nurse. The teacher encouraged him to accept placement with the dentist, emphasizing the educational opportunities. The nurse

encouraged him to do the same. She emphasized the possible material advantages of the dentist's home, the opportunity of making the right kind of friends, as well as the educational opportunities. The cottage mother, however, thought that he should choose the farm family because it was her opinion that they really wanted him and would love him more than the dentist and his wife. She also expressed the opinion that farm life was good and would present fewer temptations than life in the city.

When Don attempted to reconcile these different points of view with his own ambivalence about any type of placement, he became anxious, tense, and restless. He went to see the social worker about his confusion; she accepted his indecision and said it was unfortunate that he had been given so much advice.

After this conference Don talked with some boys who overheard a heated argument between the nurse and his cottage mother. They informed Don that the nurse had flatly informed the cottage mother that her own preference, as well as that of the science teacher, was for his placement in the dentist's home. The boys also told Don several other things: that the nurse insisted that the farm family only wanted to exploit him as a laborer; that the cottage mother had denied this, and pointed out that while he would have to do his share of the work, they had excellent farm machinery and some hired help and that the cottage mother had countered that the dentist only wanted the boy as a showpiece to follow in his footsteps.

Don became increasingly uneasy and confused. That night he ran away.

The teacher and nurse, as members of the professional group which valued education, social and economic status, favored the dentist's home for Don. The nonprofessional, in this case the cottage mother, attached the values of honesty and independence of rural life and favored the farm placement. This conflict in values, with Don caught in the middle, had damaging results for him.

CONCEPTIONS OF STATUS AND ROLE

The professionals thought of themselves as being primarily responsible for the study of delinquents for diagnostic and planning purposes. While they acknowledged the value of the nonprofessionals' diagnostic observations and opinions for institutional and postinstitutional planning, the professionals maintained that this area of responsibility was essentially theirs.

In addition to their diagnostic studies and planning duties, the professionals believed that they should devote a large portion of their time to treatment. For example, they gave suggestions for structuring the delinquent's environment to the nonprofessionals or offered some form of individual or group treatment to the delinquents. If they aided the delinquent by structuring his environment, the professionals usually worked with other professionals and nonprofessionals; if they offered some form of treatment, they worked immediately with the individual delinquent or group of delinquents.

The professionals' conception of their work also included assisting the delinquent to bridge the gap between the institution and the outside world by proper orientation upon entry, by communication with relatives and officials during his stay, and follow-up studies with parole agencies after he left.

The professionals thought of the nonprofessionals as primarily guiding and supervising the delinquents. They thought the nonprofessionals (1) were too restrictive with the delinquents, (2) did not try to understand the delinquents, and (3) resisted the professionals' ideas and recommendations. While the professionals recognized that the nonprofessionals had some duties in connection with diagnostic studies and program planning, they regarded such duties as minor. The idea that the nonprofessionals were too restrictive is exemplified by the remark of a social worker:

> That's what's the matter with these people, they are too hard on the kids. They want to make them follow a rigid and exact pattern which is their idea of being good. They don't want to hear what we have to say about management of the boys because so often it goes against their whole way of doing their job.

The rejection of the professionals' recommendations by the nonprofessionals was pinpointed by a psychiatrist when he said:

> I have been working with the D.'s [cottage parents] for approximately a year. I don't believe they have any intention of modifying their cottage management. I don't believe they ever will. We used to get open resistance from them; now it's passive resistance. For example, the strap was used openly, but now you never see a strap around; however, anyone who has anything to do with their cottage knows it's still being used.

A social worker commented further on this problem:

> I sincerely believe that we cannot move any faster in creating a good treatment program for the boys than some of the staff [nonprofessionals] are willing and able to move. I also believe in helping them to move forward but after awhile, it seems a little foolish to try to help some of these people become good rehabilitative workers.

On the other side of the picture, the nonprofessionals saw themselves as the backbone of the institution. Their constant intimate relationship with the delinquent was believed to be the major part of the delinquent's institutional program, and they felt responsible for the boy's total welfare while in the institution. They believed that their duties in this connection were performed in an interested, definite, firm, and consistent manner. A typical attitude was reflected by a cottage parent who said: "We ran this institution well for many years. I'm pretty sure that we did a better job with the boys than is done now with all this high-priced help. We are still doing a good job; if it weren't for us, this place couldn't run."

Whether a staff member is married and/or has reared a family seems to play a role in the staff conflict over the care and treatment of delinquents.[6] A nonprofessional's comment shows this: "I ought to know something about this. I raised five kids of my own and they are all doing all right. That is more than you can say for some of those young fellows up there in the office who are passing out the word."

On this same point a professional remarked:

> The trouble with our cottage parents and vocational supervisors is that they think they can treat these

> delinquents like they treated their own youngsters. They
> don't realize that these boys may be quite different. Nor
> do they recognize that, by thinking of these boys as they
> thought of their own children, they may get quite
> personally involved.

Occasionally some nonprofessionals saw themselves as having even broader duties, and they assumed responsibility for the delinquent's welfare outside the institution. This took the form of unofficial parole planning and, at times, unofficial parole supervision. In one institution, after a cottage mother had unofficially written to the relatives of a boy asking them to come and get him, as he was ready for placement, she said:

> Social work is fine, I guess, but there is too much red
> tape to it, or they make it that way. There's no reason to
> keep a boy waiting six weeks when he is ready to go and
> his relatives are ready to take him, just to make a lot of
> agency referrals. These referrals are for the purpose of
> studying the home to see whether it is alright or not, but
> what difference does it make? If it is alright, fine. If it
> isn't, they can seldom find another place for an
> "adolescent delinquent," as they say. So the boy is
> ready and waiting. If he doesn't get some satisfaction
> about placement, he soon will go downhill fast and all
> the good we have done for him will go, too.

There are some similarities in the way in which the professionals view their duties and the way in which nonprofessionals view them. For their part, the nonprofessionals considered the professional's duties as centering around: (1) the delinquent's admission into the institution; (2) initial diagnostic and planning activities; (3) communication with relatives and outside agencies; (4) considerable counseling on situational problems and limited special treatment work with delinquents; (5) some consultation work with staff members; (6) planning with the administration; (7) planning the parole of the boy; and (8) liaison work with the parole authorities after the delinquent leaves the institution.

The nonprofessionals formally conceded the diagnostic duties to the professionals, but they believed that diagnosis has only general implications in shaping a boy's program and probably very little significance for them in their areas of work. A cottage parent's statement makes this clear:

> I like to talk with others about the boys and plan for them because there is always a lot one person misses or fails to do. I do not appreciate having some person push an opinion of a boy's character and intelligence on me that they may have formed in a few hours' time. I've worked with some of these boys a long time and I think I know them, too. I've tried different ways with them [professionals]; now I just listen and then go ahead and do it my own way.

The necessity of having the professional's diagnosis was questioned by the nonprofessionals. The professionals' means of communication was criticized. A farmer of an institution had this to say:

> I work with boys all day long, every day. I know a boy, what he is like and what he's not like, what he can do and can't do. Just the other day, without me saying a thing, a boy told me all about his home and he cried. I can't put it in the language that those people in the administration building can — that is, put it up so that nobody but them can understand it — but I know this boy. That outfit up at the administration sees a boy for a few hours and they think they know the whole story and then want to tell us in language we can't understand. And besides, the kids come back to us all upset about these tests they give 'em.

The nonprofessionals were reluctant to concede the advisory or consultation role to the professionals. While there was some overt harmony, underlying negative feelings were strong. This underlying resentment was pointed out by a vocational supervisor who said: "I wouldn't mind this long-haired bunch up in the offices who have their education, but when they feel like they have been called on to give it to me too, I don't want it."

The superintendent of one of the institutions of this study who himself was a professional remarked:

> The ordinary run-of-the-mill professional clings to his theory too much, and unfortunately, theory is frequently too abstract to be directly applicable to

concrete problems. As a result, the cottage parents and others do not have too much confidence or respect for them.

In considering this problem, a social worker talked about professional workers without experience:

People with some professional education bring some valuable knowledge to their job, but they would be better off if they could appreciate themselves a little more realistically. You know, they haven't really learned what is needed to do their job, and all that it implies. Unfortunately, many of them feel compelled to give advice and suggestions. I guess they feel they have to justify their existence on the staff.

The work of the professionals that involved the delinquent's admission into the institution was generally accepted by the nonprofessionals; however, the cottage parents thought that considerable orientation and intake work needed to be done with the delinquents once they reached the cottage. They also accepted the role of the professionals in communicating with relatives and outside agencies, but some difficulties arose in this connection because the cottage parents would give different information to visiting parents than the social workers and other professionals did.

The nonprofessionals were troubled by the part professionals played in planning the institution's treatment program. They felt left out.[7]

The nonprofessionals also felt they were bypassed when it came to parole planning and actual placement. They thought their ideas did not receive adequate consideration. They also complained about delays in placing a boy once he was given parole.

Many conflicts occurred over these divergent ideas of statuses and roles.[8] Those stemming from the diagnosis and treatment of the boys were also found to be serious.

John had been in the Training School for approximately two weeks. During this period, his time had been largely taken up by his orientation program and diagnostic studies of him by the staff. The cottage parents had been orienting him to institutional and cottage life and had been observing him in a variety of situations. The psychologist had given him several tests. He had been seen by the psychiatrist, physician, dentist, and social worker.

At the end of these two weeks, a staff meeting was called and each member who had contact with John came with a report of his findings. A professional chaired the meetings, and the other professionals consumed the majority of the period with their discussion and recommendations. This was particularly so with the psychologist and psychiatrist, who became involved in a discussion about the nature and extent of the boy's anxiety and the defenses he had available for its control. The social worker raised the point of the historical development of this anxiety and its significance for programming.

After these lengthy discussions, the conference progressed to the point of concrete program planning. John was brought into the group at this time to participate in the planning. While he previously discussed his desires and wishes regarding his institutional program with his social worker, his inclusion here was an effort to have him share more directly in matters concerning his future. John expressed his interests and wishes to the staff. He said he wanted to be assigned to the tailor shop because he wanted to learn the trade.

John left the group, and his cottage mother questioned assigning him to Mrs. F. at the tailor shop because she did not believe John was especially interested in tailoring and she knew that the disciplinary control of the boys in the tailor shop was poor. She said she thought he had been attracted to tailoring by reports from the grapevine that this shop allowed more freedom than some others. She acknowledged John's anxiety but emphasized his aggressive behavior in the cottage and urged that he be considered for a work placement that offered more disciplinary control.

The professionals listened to her, respectfully, but no one responded to her ideas. Rather, they discussed other aspects of John's program.

John's case was summarized by the chairman, and his assignment to the tailor shop was included without comment. John's staff conference was finished; everyone returned to his place of work.

Several days later, the woman in charge of the tailor shop reported that John had not reported to the shop as assigned and she wondered what had happened. John's absence was investigated. It appeared that the complete rejection of the cottage mother's proposal and the lack of further discussion of it at the staff meeting had made her angry; she had deliberately sent John to another assignment.

When the cottage mother attempted to participate in the planning for John's program she indicated that she conceived of herself as having responsibilities for planning delinquents' programs. The professionals, reserving this role for themselves, rejected the cottage mother's participation. The cottage mother retaliated by ignoring the job assignment for John that the professionals arranged.

THE CONCEPTS OF DELINQUENCY AND DELINQUENCY TREATMENT

Generally, the professionals viewed delinquency as deviant behavior resulting from the interaction of etiological, predispositional factors with situational variants. They saw this behavior as emerging from the interplay of many elements in which the boy's conscious activity was only one of those involved. They believed that institutional treatment stemming from a constructive institutional milieu, as well as individual and group treatment, provides the boys with rehabilitative experiences and would help them modify their behavior.

The professionals were found to hold the delinquent responsible for his behavior, within a certain framework, but they did not morally evaluate it. Rather, they tried to understand the motivations for this behavior and if some appropriate therapeutic measures were available, they would recommend it. If the professionals thought it was indicated, they would participate in the treatment.

To the nonprofessionals, the professionals seemed inconsistent in their thinking about treatment. The professionals talked about many of the delinquents being activity and action oriented rather than thoughtful and verbal in their behavior, and thus the major way of treating them was to provide a variety of constructive everyday corrective environmental experiences for them. Yet the professionals continued to see boys in office interview situations. When this was explained to the nonprofessionals on the basis of diagnostic and special treatment work for selected cases, the nonprofessionals countered with: (1) Weren't the factors of comfort, easiness, and simplicity entering the professionals' decisions? (2) If their (the nonprofessionals') environmental treatment was the most effective approach to the delinquents, why the salary, status, and other differentials between themselves and the professionals?

Many nonprofessionals assumed that all similar surface behavior had the same dynamics or meaning. Thus they were confused when the professionals recommended dissimilar attitudes and activities for what the nonprofessional thought were like delinquents.

The criteria for selecting boys for individual or group therapy seemed confusing to the nonprofessionals, thus such questions as: "If good for some boys, why not for others? I've got a couple over in my shop that need something. I don't see why they weren't included." With little insight as to what the professionals were attempting to accomplish, the nonprofessionals were skeptical, suspicious, and, at times, opposed to therapy.

The majority of the nonprofessionals had not formalized their thinking about delinquency causation; however, many of them believed that delinquent behavior was historically and situationally determined. They believed that present situations and past experiences played an important part in bringing about delinquent behavior, but that once institutionalized, the delinquent would become penitent, see the error of his ways and of his own free will choose socially constructive goals despite his present obstacles and past experiences.

To the professionals, the nonprofessionals appeared inconsistent and ambiguous in their thinking about treatment. The nonprofessionals talked of past experiences and the current situation as factors in behavior but said that if only the delinquent "would make up his mind, he could do what is right, because after all, he knows right from wrong. If he doesn't know right from wrong, then punish him because a child always learns to leave a hot stove alone after he is burned often enough." At times they assumed that "if a boy has been mistreated, all you have to do is be nice to him and treat him right, and he will be O.K." In this instance, they viewed treatment as being synonymous with kindness. Some of these inconsistencies are apparent in the case of Jim.

> Jim was transferred to the Boys' Training School from the state orphanage because he was "incorrigible." Following the orientation and study period, the staff met to discuss the results of these findings and to plan for his stay at the school. The professionals generally agreed that the boy was suffering from an insidiously developing schizophrenic condition, that his controls over his intense anxiety and hostility were crumbling, and that his contact with reality was weak and intermittent. They viewed his judgment as severely impaired and anticipated bizarre hostile behavior from him. Their general recommendations included an environment of acceptance, security, and supportive psychotherapy.
>
> The cottage father listened to these analyses and proposals. He appeared to have difficulty with the terminology but understood it well enough to disagree in principle. He went on to describe several concrete episodes of Jim's behavior in which Jim had torn some plastic tile from the floor of the hall and had collected all the dirty socks he could find and put them in his locker. He further pointed out that when he had confronted Jim with this "nonsense" that he could stop it if he wanted to, especially if there was some penalty attached to such behavior, Jim agreed. The house-father commented that while the medical diagnosis might be "true" he still regarded Jim's behavior as rising from a wish to be "ornery" and that it could be changed "if people would put their foot down on him."

Some bizarre behavior borders on the normal. To the untrained observer, it is frequently difficult to determine where one stops and the other starts. Although Jim's cottage parent could understand the schizophrenic condition of Jim in theory, he could not recognize or accept it as it occurred in Jim's daily living. Perhaps he had known many boys who did some of the very things Jim had done, and they were relatively normal.

He was intimately aware of Jim's actions, but he did not have a diagnostic frame of reference that he could bring to bear on this behavior and thus was unable to understand Jim's condition as being anything else than simple orneriness.

SOME NEGATIVE EFFECTS OF THE CONFLICTS[9]

These conflicts had significant detrimental effects on the system of social relationships as a whole as well as on the groups and individual involved.[10]

In some of the institutions, conflicts between these groups resulted in the system of social relationships becoming so disorganized that constructive interaction among the staff was nearly impossible. For example, some of the institutions required all the professionals and nonprofessional people working with a particular delinquent to attend his staff meetings; however, many of the nonprofessionals could not "find time" to attend the meetings even though their work load or schedule of duties had not noticeably increased. In other institutions, the professionals and nonprofessionals avoided meeting each other informally, as in the cafeteria and the staff recreation rooms.

Both professional and nonprofessional groups were disturbed by internal frictions. At times, dissensions pitted the vocational teachers and maintenance workers against the cottage parents and the social workers against the psychologists and psychiatrists.

In all of the institutions, a varying number of staff members set up devices to protect themselves and withdrew from some of the normal and expected activities. This, of course, reduced constructive interaction. In one institution the professionals spent much of their time in research although this was not included in the duties of their job. At another institution, the professionals tended to ignore the organizational problems, and discussed instead the theory of their various fields. At several institutions, the professionals carried on exhaustive discussions regarding individual cases of delinquents and the institution's problems, but they rarely advanced beyond diagnosis of a delinquent or criticism of the administration and the nonprofessionals.

The nonprofessionals also had a variety of protective devices. Only one cottage parent would work when both were scheduled to work; the other would be upstairs resting. They would force particularly difficult boys into recreational activities outside the cottage rather than follow the professional's recommendations for providing activities for them at the cottage where the situation at the time was expected to be less complex.

Staff members, in their efforts to work in these situations and adapt to them, may become maladjusted. Anxiety, feelings of discouragement, aggressive and psychosomatic reactions were not uncommon responses among many of the workers in these institutions.

Situationally, these reactions appeared related to the staff conflicts as well as to the nature and intensity of the children's behavior.[11]

Some staff members sought "one-sided" solutions outside of the institution by feigning cooperation with the institution's efforts to achieve cooperation. For example, in one institution a group of dissatisfied nonprofessionals appealed directly to the commissioner of the institution's administration concerning their complaints. In several institutions, a powerful cadre of nonprofessionals worked undercover for a change of administration through special interest groups. They wanted to be rid of the present administration and many of the professionals. This group complained about the professionals "meddling with our discipline." In another institution, the professionals, thinking that the administration failed to support their ideas and recommendations, worked secretly to gain a change in the administration.

Further along this web of subterfuge, the acting out of certain staff members worked against the institutions' goals. For example, at several schools, the professionals left work early, commenting, "What's the use of staying? We can't get any cooperation anyway." Yet they always accepted full-time pay. In another institution, a few of the professionals appropriated books from the library rationalizing that "I might as well get something out of this job," and "You couldn't get anyone around here interested in learning about this."[12] A farmer at one institution was highly critical of administrative laxness concerning intergroup conflicts. He declared vehemently that people should be made to "toe the line or get out." Gradually his criticism waned and he would sarcastically remark, "I'm running my own little playhouse now, I expect others to run theirs. That's the only way a guy can get along here." A short time later he was caught stealing some livestock from the school.

As a result of these staff conflicts, the delinquent is frequently damaged rather than helped. Many delinquents came to these institutions from homes with extremely disturbed family situations where their needs for a secure and stable family life were ignored or where the parents were highly inconsistent. As a result, many delinquents developed devious means of satisfying their needs. They very shrewdly evaluated the social situations about them. They detected weaknesses, and they exploited and manipulated the situation for their personal ends. This behavior-attitude had played a strong role in their delinquency in the first place and was one of the behavioral tendencies that the institution tried to modify. Yet this was quite impossible if the delinquent was exposed to an institutional environment where the surroundings were similar to those that had contributed to his unhealthy condition.

> John, a delinquent at a Training School, was denied a holiday pass to his home by his cottage parent because he had persistently been intimidating younger boys and, whenever possible, beating them. Aware that there were differences of opinion regarding treatment methods between the social worker and the cottage parent, John went to see the social worker, complaining that he was restricted from his pass unfairly and that the cottage parent was "down on him" and that "he had just been playing with the other fellows." The social worker was sympathetic, and after the boy left she discussed it with the chief social worker. He took it to the superintendent who, in turn, asked to see the cottage parent. The cottage parent, threatened by this apparent display of power by the professionals, said that "he thought maybe a pass would be the thing to help him." Later, in talking with his associates, the cottage parent bitterly denounced the professionals.

Many delinquents are shrewd and devious in their actions. John was such a boy. By manipulating some staff members, who fell unwittingly into his trap, he got his pass. The conflict of status and role here between the professionals and nonprofessionals is evident again; a conflict over treatment methods is also indicated. Jim was aware of these conflicts and cleverly exploited them to his own advantage, and continued his delinquent way of dealing with the world.

SOME RECOMMENDATIONS TO RELIEVE THESE CONFLICTS

Education is obviously not a cure-all but the professionals might profit from training programs that provided them with a broader frame of reference and sensitized them to the practical functioning of an organization. If properly administered, such training should help them empathize with a greater variety of people. While the colleges do teach the professionals many things, there is a lot that the institution itself can do to add to this teaching process. Inservice training, internships, and residences at institutions for delinquents would be of considerable help.[13]

In order for the professional to understand the role of the nonprofessional, it might be well for him to work as a participant-observer in the various nonprofessional jobs during the early period of his employment. However, such a procedure would probably be difficult for many professionals to accept. In one of the institutions studied, the administration and the heads of professional departments agreed to provide this type of experience for the newly hired professionals. At first it was intimated to the professionals that one week's close sharing of cottage life would aid greatly in their orientation. Later they were told that such a period of observation and participation was expected, and that as soon as they were ready the process would begin.

Of the nine professionals to whom this opportunity was extended, three began it and only one completed the activity. When those who did not attempt it or failed to complete it were faced with their failure to participate, various excuses were made:

"I was too busy with other activities."

"After all, I'm not studying to be a cottage parent."

"Just how do you conceive of my role here?"

"My wife needed me at home at night."

"I can learn just as much by testing a boy as I can by watching him in a cottage."

This procedure and reasons for the expected participation had been previously explained to them.[14]

Concomitant with the experience of being a participant-observer in a variety of nonprofessional jobs the professional should meet with the nonprofessional of each job to learn of the activities and problems of the job from the standpoint of the nonprofessional. In such arrangements the professional would, of course, profit from constructive departmental and administrative leadership.

The total institution should be made aware of a new staff member's arrival in advance along with the position he is to fill and the role he is expected to play. Upon arrival he should be introduced to the other staff members, including nonprofessionals. Many times the new staff member needs some early reassurance, support, and friendly guidance in his efforts to work himself into the institution. In several of the organizations, efforts were made in this direction, but in the others, very little was done. Such procedures are as necessary for the nonprofessional as they are for the professional.[15]

The nonprofessionals need systematic frames of reference to use in shaping their experiences and firsthand familiarity with delinquents into an organized repertoire of knowledge and skills which provide them with new vantage points from which to view and work with the delinquents. This might be provided by inservice training.[16]

The nonprofessionals may need to take part in regularly scheduled classes in connection with their work. The classes should be small and carried on by conference and discussion, rather than by lecture. The subject matter of these classes should be focused on the personality of the delinquents and the behavior of groups in an institutional setting. Also, the nonprofessional worker should become familiar with some of the terminology and theoretical background that professional people use in approaching the problem of delinquency. This does not mean that the nonprofessional must be trained as a theorist but that he must have some understanding of this as it relates to his job.

The institutions need to refine and intensify their recruitment, selection, and orientation procedures for both the professionals and nonprofessionals. In many cases this means that in addition to sponsoring various programs to increase the efficiency of these procedures, the institutions must also raise wages and improve working conditions. [17]

Within the institutions, the administration as well as the professional and nonprofessional staff must always strive to keep the various channels of communication functioning. Administrative-department head conferences and departmental, along with interdepartmental, meetings can facilitate this. Various institutional service committees, such as staff recreation and library committees, might prove effective vehicles. An institutional planning board made up of equal numbers of professionals and nonprofessionals could help in planning the overall policies of the school and might have some value in decreasing the number and intensity of conflicts between the two groups.[18]

In addition to these attempts to structure situations that would be conducive to harmonious staff relationships, the institution must provide regular procedures through which conflicts can be managed. Different conflicts would require different types of action. Sometimes administrative action would be clearly indicated, as in the case of pay and hours, or unsatisfactory working conditions. In many cases, however, it would appear that the people with conflicts need an opportunity to meet, discuss, and try to "work through" their differences and problems, either individually or in groups, with an experienced, capable institutional worker who has a broad grasp of the situation.[19]

It should be remembered, however, that the routine employment of inservice training, conferences, or committee meetings will not insure the resolution or prevention of conflicts. None of these are a "package approach" to all situations. Rather, they provide several ways to work toward these ends. It takes a sympathetic and interested administration and some desire on the part of employees to improve staff relationships. Excellent leadership on the part of those working directly with the conflicts is required if any of these means are to be realized at their fullest potential.[20] Hostilities, anxieties, suspicions, resistances, and negativisms are involved in any of these approaches if they are employed intensively.[21]

> In one institution, a cottage mother expressed her hostility toward a teacher by criticizing her teaching methods. Actually, the teacher's methods were good, but the cottage mother was jealous of the friendly feelings and loyalty that the boys from her cottage were expressing to the teacher. This problem grew until each worker was openly criticizing the other. The psychologist was asked by the superintendent to work this out with them. In that institution, he assumed this role at times.[22]
>
> The psychologist talked with each individual for approximately an hour on two different occasions about these problems. After these talks, it appeared that a meeting including both workers could help in the resolution of this matter. Each agreed that such a meeting might be helpful. The meeting took place at a mutually convenient time and place. It progressed well until the schoolteacher pointed out one too many critical things about the cottage mother's attitude to her boys. In spite of the psychologist's efforts to help the cottage mother express her thoughts and feelings regarding this problem, she left the meeting in a defensive rage.

In retrospect, a number of critical considerations can be raised. Was the joint meeting premature? Had the psychologist moved too quickly in his effort to have the two people talk over their mutual problem? Should he have tempered the teacher's remarks? Instead of encouraging the cottage mother to express her feelings, should the psychologist have used different techniques in coping with the cottage mothers reaction? For example, should he have supported her in this crisis? Or should he have focused the discussion more on facts than on the thoughts and feelings of the cottage mother and teacher?

> The psychologist then saw the cottage mother the following morning. At first she was defensive and self-righteous. Following this, she began to express some guilt about her "walking out." The psychologist listened and accepted her expressions and then purposely focused the discussion on the more immediate problem. After another meeting with the cottage mother and the teacher individually in which each vented considerable hostility toward the other, a joint meeting was tried again. This meeting was a success in the sense that they were able to express their ideas and feelings and could accept those of the other in working out their mutual responsibilities and relationships to the boys.

The overt and readily apparent aspects of any institutional problems have their deeper counterparts in the personal problems of the staff members. Often the institutional problems of anxiety, jealousy, hostility, and competitive feelings stem in part from the personal and individual feelings of the staff members and are aggravated by them. The institutions for delinquents, because of their social structure and delinquent population, were fertile battlegrounds upon which the individuals brought their personal tendencies into play. Thus, this problem has both the individual as well as the institutional aspects.[23]

> A case in point is that of Mr. M., who was a rigid, caustic driving trades instructor. He was often officious about administrative unfairness. Also, he was ambivalent in his attitudes toward people in positions of leadership and authority. Mr. M. did his best work and seemed most comfortable when he was given encouragement and support by his supervisor. Under optimum institutional conditions, the approach was enough to offset his tendencies to be overly critical of people in superior positions.
>
> Shortly after Dr. H. joined the staff of this institution as a psychologist, he attended a meeting of department heads. Mr. M.'s supervisor was one of those in attendance. Techniques of supervision were considered by the group during this meeting. Mr. M.'s supervisor asked Dr. H. what caused people to be "hardheaded." Without questioning the supervisor further, Dr. H. replied, "Sometimes people do that to defend themselves against their real feelings." The supervisor

accepted this without question and then proceeded to discuss another subject. Several days after this department head meeting Mr. M. became irritable, critical, and uncompromising with his boys. His supervisor, in talking with Mr. M., commented that Mr. M.'s attitude must be caused by something else — perhaps anger toward the boys of this class.

This interpretation made Mr. M. angry, and he replied sarcastically that it sounded like a psychological idea. At lunch and after school that day he was very outspoken against all of the professionals as he talked with others. Some of what he had to say had its contagious effect and was carried to the school's administration. Following this, the superintendent talked with Dr. H. and the supervisor to learn more about the situation and how to correct it. Mr. M. learned of this meeting and suspicioned that plans were being made against him. As a result he became more defensive and exceedingly critical of others.

The general procedure used to attack these problems will influence the techniques used by the individuals who cope with a particular problem. However, the skill and knowledge of the person who works with the problems will probably be the dominant factors in determining the choice of procedures.

However, whatever the procedure or technique may be, the groups and individuals must be helped to recognize and face some of the more important conflicts. They must be shown how to explore those conflicts and learn about their causes, including their own contributions to them, and they must work these problems through to a better level of understanding and work relationships.

NOTES

1. "Treatment," as used in this paper, denotes all the systematic efforts that are carried on within an institutional setting to assist in the rehabilitation of the delinquent. This includes general environmental arrangements as well as individual and group treatment.
2. The titles "professional" and "nonprofessional" accentuate the differences between the two groups and appear to facilitate conflict rather than cooperation. It is an unfortunate differentiation. For an analysis of the difficulties in defining a profession, see M. L. Cogan, "Toward a Definition of Profession," *Harvard Educational Review* 23 (Winter 1953): 33-50.

3. Carl R. Doering describes some similar professional and nonprofessional conflicts in a penal system in the Foreword to *A Report on the Development of Penological Treatment at Norfolk Prison Colony in Massachusetts*, ed. Carl R. Doering (New York: Bureau of Social Hygiene, 1940). For conflicts between psychologists, psychometrists, and social workers on the one hand and the house officers on the other, see particularly pages xi and xii.

4. The specialist's limitations have been described by others: Harold J. Laski, "The Limitations of the Expert," *Harper's* 162 (December 1930): 102-6; Robert K. Menton, "The Machine, the Worker, and the Engineer," *Science* 105 (January 24, 1947): 79-81; and Wilbert E. Moore and Melvin M. Tumin, "Some Social Functions of Ignorance," *American Sociological Review* 14 (December 1949): 788-89.

5. This problem raises several questions: (1) Was the professional's education, on which he leaned for support in his work, relevant to and adequate for carrying out his assignments? (2) Was the web of conflicts so complex that the education could not be utilized?

6. In one institution where this was a point of conflict, 50 percent of the professionals were, or had been, married, while 97 percent of the nonprofessionals were or had been, married. In another institution it was 42 percent of the professionals and 84 percent of the nonprofessionals. The age differences also appeared to be important in the conflict between the two groups. In one institution the average age of the professionals was 30 years while that of the nonprofessionals was 41 years. In another institution the average age of the professionals was 34 and that of the nonprofessionals was 46. Statistically, these are highly significant differences. Together with the other data, they suggest that age differences and experiential disparities in family and parental roles were very important factors in the dissimilar orientations of the two groups toward the delinquents.

7. Status and role conflicts of the professionals are not limited to these institutional settings. Ruth Emerson says: "That there is too great a diversity of opinion among executives as to the nature of the return to the hospital, which should be expected from the activities of the social service department, seems indubitable. To some, the social worker is a glorified, and yet not altogether satisfactory, bill collector. She is sent on miscellaneous errands and asked to perform various institutional tasks for which there is no provision in the personnel of the hospital budget. Her position in some institutions is to be classed somewhat between that of the cash girl in a department store and the telephone clerk at the information desk" ("Standards in Medical Social Work," in *The Hospital in Modern Society*, symposium, ed. A. C. Bochmeyer [New York; Commonwealth Fund, 1943], p. 346). Further, in this regard, the professional-nonprofessional conflicts of this study bear many similarities to the staff-line conflicts of industrial organizations reported by Melville Dalton in "Conflicts between Staff and Line Managerial Officers," *American Sociological Review* 15 (June 1950):

342-51. In an unreported research by the author on 50 psychiatric aides, similar status and role conflicts were observed between the aides on the one hand and the physicians and particularly the nurses on the other.

8. One of the most important components of a healthy and vigorous staff morale is the opportunity the staff has to express their ideas and to contribute suggestions concerning the institutional program, particularly on those matters that involve them. For evidence of the motivational effects of group decision, see Kurt Lewin, "Group Decision and Social Change," in *Readings in Social Psychology*, eds. T. M. Newcomb and E. L. Hartley (New York: Henry Holt & Co., 1947), pp. 330-45; D. McGregor, "Conditions for Effective Leadership in the Industrial Situation," *Journal of Consulting Psychology* 8 (March-April 1945): 55-63; and Robert Tannenbaum and Fred Massark, "Participation by Subordinates in the Managerial Decision-making Process," *Canadian Journal of Economics and Political Science* (August 1950): 408-18.

9. This is not to imply that only negative and destructive phenomena are associated with conflict although this is the focus here. For a theoretical discussion of the positive as well as the negative aspects of conflict, see George Simmel, "The Sociology of Conflict," trans. Albion W. Small, *American Journal of Sociology* 9 (1903-1904): 490-525.

10. As in society, there were those who took difficulties and conflicts in their stride; however, frustration, anxiety, and other reactions were widespread. Some of these problems in society are characterized by Karen Horney, *The Neurotic Personality of Our Time* (New York: W. W. Norton & Co., 1937).

11. Information was given about these points by Ralph W. Coltharp and George H. Weber, "The Emotional Reactions of People Working with Emotionally Disturbed and Delinquent Children" (paper presented at the meeting of the Mid-Continent Psychiatric Association, Kansas City, Missouri, 1951).

12. For a discussion of this problem on a broader scale, see Lawrence S. Thompson, *Notes on Bibliokleptomanic* (New York: New York Public Library, 1944).

13. A program of the Training Branch, Juvenile Delinquency Service, United States Children's Bureau, is important in this respect. Under their leadership special training in the field of corrections was planned to assist various specialists working in the field of delinquency control. For example, a program was offered to university teachers and prospective teachers of social work at the University of California at Berkeley in the summer of 1956. See "Projects and Progress," *Children* 3, no. 1 (January-February 1956): 37.

14. The theoretical bases for the importance of being able to take the role of the other in interpersonal relations is set forth in George H. Mead, *Mind, Self, and Society* (Chicago: University of Chicago Press, 1934), pp. 360-76. For the practical application of this idea to training in industry see Alex Bavelas, "Role Playing and Management Training," *Society* 1, no. 2 (June 1947): 183-90. The work that has been done to improve the

relationships between supervisors and workers in industry, is suggestive in regard to improving the relationships between the professionals and nonprofessionals in institutions for delinquents. N. R. F. Maier, *Principle of Human Relations* (New York: John Wiley & Sons, 1952), describes how supervisors are taught to consider problems from the worker's point of view, to look at the various possible motives underlying the worker's behavior, to encourage the worker's self-expression, and to develop solutions to problems with the work group. The effects of employee participation in decision making on production in industry are presented by Lester Coch and J. R. P. French, Jr.) "Overcoming Resistance to Change," *Human Relations* 1 (1948): 512-32.

15. The importance of incorporating the new worker into an organization is described by Delbert C. Miller and William H. Form, *Industrial Sociology* (New York: Harper & Bros., 1951), pp. 676-97; Edwin E. Ghiselli and Clarence W. Brown, *Personnel and Industrial Psychology* (New York: McGraw-Hill, 1955), pp. 378-410; and Maragret L. Newcomb; Eleanor Gay, and Barry L. Levin, "A Training Program for Social Work Students in a Psychiatric Clinic," *Social Casework* 34, no. 5 (May 1953): 204-11.

16. In respect to the general problems of training nonprofessionals for training schools see Susanne Schulze and Morris Fritz Mayer, "Training for House-parents and Kindred Personnel in Institutions for Juvenile Delinquents," in *Training Personnel for Work with Juvenile Delinquents* (Children's Bureau Publication no. 348, 1954), pp. 44-71. The work of Bernard H. Hall et. al., *Psychiatric Aide Education* (New York: Grene & Stratton, 1952), is significant in a related field with similar problems.

17. This is particularly true for the nonprofessional. For the houseparent's problems in this connection see Morris F. Mayer, "The House-parents and the Group Living Process," in *Creative Group Living in a Children's Institution*, ed. Susanne Schulze (New York: Association Press, 1951), pp. 97-117.

18. The position of one side cannot possibly be clearly understood by those on the other side unless frequent communication occurs. For a vivid illustration of this truism see Alexander H. Leighton, *The Governing of Men* (Princeton: Princeton University Press, 1946). For the importance of communication for effective integration of any group see Fritz J. Roethlisberger, *Management and Morale* (Cambridge: Harvard University Press, 1941), pp. 62-63.

19. Should the spontaneous, informal day-to-day efforts of the staff to resolve their conflicts prove ineffective, administrators would undoubtedly find procedures of voluntary conciliation more acceptable to the members of the professional and nonprofessional groups than compulsory measures. In the area of labor and management it is interesting to note that most members of the Minnesota "fact-finding" commissions favored voluntary as opposed to compulsory arbitration in regard to labor relations problems. The "fact-finding" commissions are appointed under the Minnesota Law to place certain limitations on strike, See

Jack Stieber, "Minnesota Labor Relations Acts — An Opinion Survey," *Harvard Business Review* 27 (1949): 665-67.

20. For discussions of leadership see Chester I. Barnard, *The Functions of the Executive* (Cambridge: Harvard University. Press, 1938); George C. Homans, *The Human Group* (New York: Harcourt Brace & Co., 1950), pp. 415-40; and Leon H. Richman, "Sound Administration: The Key That Unlocks," in *Creative Group Living in a Children's Institution,* ed. Susanne Schulze (New York: Association Press, 1951), pp, 18-34.

21. Though outside of the framework of this discussion it should be recognized that many times the problem of conflict between professionals and nonprofessionals in institutions serving delinquents cannot be resolved by dealing only with the groups or individuals who experience the problems. In addition, determinants of conflict outside of the institution such as economic or political conditions must be included in this problem-solving process. Harold L. Sheppard, in "Approaches to Conflict in American Industrial Sociology" (paper presented at the Congress of the International Sociological Association, Liege, Belgium, 1953), stresses this point in respect to industrial conflict.

22. For the general rationale underlying this psychologist's approach to the workers, see Nathaniel Cantor, *Employee Counseling* (New York: McGraw-Hill, 1945), pp. 73-131; Carl R. Rogers, *Client-Centered Therapy* (New York: Houghton Mifflin Co., 1951), pp. 19-64; and Elliott Jaques, ed., "Social Therapy," *Journal of Social Issues* 3, no. 2 (1947).

23. See in this connection the special symposia. *American Journal of Sociology* 42 (May 1937) and 45 (November 1939); Sigmund Freud, *Group Psychology and the Analysis of the Ego* (London: Hogarth Press and the Institute of Psychoanalysis, 1948); and Fritz Redl, "Group Psychological Elements in Discipline Problems," *American Journal of Orthopsychiatry* 13 (1943): 77-81.

19. Observations on the Loss

of a Housemother

Jules Schrager

The person who is assigned the responsibility of giving the child day-by-day care in a children's institution is a key factor in his care and treatment. Whether he is called houseparent, child care worker, or counselor, his function is the same — to serve as parent surrogate. In the process of discharging his responsibility this person comes to represent in the child's mind all the attributes, both positive and negative, with which he has vested the concept "parent." It is within this relationship of the child with a parent or parent surrogate that his character develops.

The capacity of a child to develop physically, as well as emotionally, is connected with his ability to form these primary object relationships.[1] Although it is true that the younger child depends on these relationships to a greater degree than does the older one, all children continue to require mothering until a sufficient degree of autonomy has been attained so that each one can survive as a separate biological and social entity. The nature and quality of the nurturing influences in the child's daily life will determine in great part his social achievement, his adaptation to reality, his mastery over his instinctual impulses, and his ultimate independence.

Reprinted from *Social Casework*, vol. 37, no. 3 (March 1956), pp. 120-26, by permission of the author and the journal.

The purpose of this paper is to examine the effects, on both the children and the staff in a children's institution, of the termination of employment of a housemother. It is hoped that, through clarification of the by-products of such a routine incident, agencies will be encouraged to examine their own experiences in this connection in the hope that the number of such traumatic episodes may be reduced. Second, this paper has the equally important objective of pointing up the need for developing better methods of dealing with separation anxiety in the particular setting of the treatment institution.

THEORETICAL CONSIDERATIONS

The literature of child psychiatry is rich with information and observation concerning the effects on the child of the loss of primary object relationships. Children who have been variously described as "autistic" by Kanner,[2] "atypical" by Rank, and "schizophrenic" by Mahler are the products of distorted or emotionally empty relationships between parent and child. Whatever the nature of the particular distortion, it seems apparent that those attributes of mothering care so essential to the totally dependent child's survival and growth have been significantly reduced or totally absent. Where deprivation in the area of mothering has been part of the child's earliest experiences, his disturbance is greater. Cases such as those reported by Spitz reveal the devastating effects of such early traumata.[3] At all levels of the child's development, the absence or loss (permanently or temporarily) of significant parental figures creates disturbance in the child which, if left untreated, can permanently scar his developing personality and can cause him great difficulty subsequently in forming meaningful relationships.[4]

In observing children who come into placement, one is struck always by the number of times they have been exposed to separation experiences in connection with the parents' attempts at finding help for themselves and the children. Whether the experience is short and the anxiety transitory, as in the case of the child who leaves his mother to enter the strange playroom of the child guidance clinic, or more extensive, as in the parents' unsuccessful attempts at temporary private placement, the anxiety of the child is clear. He fears the loss of the person who has cared for him (however inadequate this care may have been), and dreads finding himself in a situation in which no one will fill the void caused by separation.

Whether the mother's difficulty in meeting the child's needs lies in an inhibition of motherliness which is a carry-over from her own disappointing childhood relationships, or whether the parents are extremely immature individuals, narcissistic and without capacity for deep emotional relationship, the child has already suffered intense feelings of deprivation. Placement away from his own home represents society's attempt to provide optimal conditions for the resumption of his physical and emotional growth.

Group placement is usually indicated when the problems have been of such a kind that they have produced in the child symptoms that are so disturbing to himself and others as to make it difficult for him to live in a family. Whatever the nature of the group, whether it is the highly organized and therapeutically conditioned residential treatment setting or whether it is the more typical (and more available) congregate setting of a children's institution, the specific needs of the individual child constitute the basis on which choice of a placement setting will be determined.

The group setting can offer a great deal to seriously deprived children. These positive values have been defined elsewhere.[5] The fact that the group offers a source of support for the fragile ego of the troubled child has been documented. It has also been noted that controls that are lacking in the child's character structure can be "built into" the institutional framework. That the total institution can be perceived by the child as an all-powerful symbolic parent, organized to meet his needs, has been reported. Much of the time of administrative and supervisory personnel goes into structuring the institution's characteristics in such a way that they may be exploited for the benefit of the child in care. It is perhaps easy to forget that these parental qualities are perceived by the child as available to him through *individual persons* who take on for him the significance of parent surrogates. When such identifications take place and are carefully nurtured, the institution has a most powerful tool available for the rehabilitation of the child.[6] When, however, these attachments are allowed to develop only to be interrupted precipitously, the institution is perpetuating the cycle of loss-restitution-loss which, as we have seen, is most detrimental to the growing child.

THE INSTITUTIONAL SETTING

The following material has been gathered from the records of staff members and from notes of staff meetings in a small institution for disturbed children. These excerpts illustrate how the children reacted to the loss of a "mothering" person, the housemother, and what the effects were on both professional and nonprofessional staff members. Although the situations described here are those of a specific setting, I believe that similar occurrences take place in most child care institutions.

In this particular setting, 13 children between the ages of 7 and 13 live together with 4 adults. They occupy an old residence that has been "done over" to meet the requirements of a children's institution. The circumstances surrounding the material to be discussed were as follows: A month before the actual date of separation, the children were told that the housemother was going to leave. This information was shared with the children by the unit supervisor at small group meetings. The children were told that the housemother was leaving because she was not satisfied with her present position. She wanted to be closer to her home, but had made no plans for taking another job. The housemother, however, had had difficulty in accepting supervision, had been unable to resolve her troubled feelings in this connection, and had discussed her dissatisfaction with the children. In the group meetings the children were given an opportunity to ask questions, to vent their feelings, and to express their concerns about future plans. They were assured that there would always be enough adults available to provide good care, and a plan for staff coverage was explained.

Although the general tenor of the meetings was somewhat depressed, the children were able to express some of their anxiety and seemed finally to accept the fact that they would be adequately provided for after the housemother's departure. The children who were more sophisticated about life in an institution and who had previously experienced the loss of a housemother dealt with the impending separation in more realistic terms than those who were new to the setting. For all, however, there was clearly a "choosing of sides." The children wanted to know the nature of the difficulty between the housemother and the supervisor, although this had not been mentioned in presenting her intention to leave. By reacting in this way the children recast the situation in terms that were comprehensible to them and that referred to the past and to earlier situations of a like nature. To them it appeared, "Mother and father cannot get along together any more; they are going to separate and as a consequence we are in danger of not being cared for." On another level, however, they took it to mean that *they* had been "terribly bad," and that it was their badness that had resulted in the rupture of the "parents'" relationship. They then became tremendously guilty and tried to cope with their intense feelings in characteristic ways as will be observed in the examples that follow.

FIRST OBSERVATIONS

Anna Freud has observed that "regression occurs while the child is passing through the no-man's-land of affection, that is, during the time that the old [love] object has been given up and before the new one has been found." The following excerpts from the institution's records offer some indication of the quality of disturbance that may occur when children experience a separation of this kind. First, how did the children express their troubled feelings in their relationships with child care staff?

out how safe they really are; whether anyone really cares about what happens to them; and whether anyone remains who is strong enough to protect them against external and internal influences with which they cannot cope alone.

REACTIONS OF CHILD CARE STAFF

The structure of a child care institution is often much like that of a family. To some extent this may be true because the unit has been designed in this fashion. Recognition is given to the fact that even in the institutional setting children need a spectrum of possible relationships available to them — relationships with siblings, with parent figures, and so on. Although it is possible for such roles to be *assigned*, one often observes that the characteristics of these roles are *taken on* by individuals because of their own character structures and are expressive of the needs they are satisfying by choosing employment in the institutional setting. Thus it happens that individuals who are assigned responsibilities that mark them as parent surrogates frequently operate as if they were older children in the "family" constellation, thereby acting out what they feel their position to be. In the context of the present problem of the loss of a parent figure, identifications may become blurred and roles may be reversed as each member of the staff attempts to sort out his own feelings and cope with them.

In the setting from which this material was drawn, the housemother is a figure of central importance in the living situation. Surrounding her and discharging the roles of "big brother" and "big sister" are young men and women who are called counselors. They have a basic responsibility as child care staff members which is colored by the fact that leisure-time supervision constitutes their specific function. Whenever the balance of their responsibilities is tipped toward "care" and away from "play," tensions arise that can be understood only in terms of their own identifications with parent figures projected onto the stage of the institutional group living experience. The following excerpts are taken from supervisory notes made during the period of crisis arising from the housemother's departure.

> (1) C, a young woman who has had long association with the program, had responsibility for coverage of the group from dinnertime through bedtime. She complained that the housemother often did not come on duty during the going-to-bed period, thus requiring C to remain for a longer time than her schedule called for, since this was a difficult time for the children. Her wish was that she could come on duty earlier and leave earlier.

> (2) Snack time is part of the daily routine. Customarily snacks are provided after school and again before bedtime. W, a young male worker, thought that the children "get too much food during the snacks." He felt that they should be limited in the amount they might take and was critical of the "lack of structure."

> (3) M discussed the fact that one of the children had asked her why the housemother was leaving. She had answered matter-of-factly that the housemother had "had difficulty in handling the job." Shortly afterward the same child had vomited. In a rather disgusted way, M complained that she had had to clean up his clothes and the mess.

A common plaint can be observed to run through all the excerpts above — one that can be roughly stated as follows: "Mother and father [housemother and supervisor] have decided to end their relationship; mother is leaving home and *we* are left to handle *her* responsibilities." In (1) the worker is saying she doesn't want to have to struggle with the children's problems when *she* [the housemother] should be on duty. That is *her* responsibility, and the worker wants to leave before it has to be faced. In (2) the worker criticizes the supervisor since basic policies, such as those governing the provision of snacks, are made by the clinical-supervisory-administrative personnel. Food giving, and especially the availability of sweets and snacks, requires careful planning if it is to fulfill the requirements of a therapeutic intent. Perhaps the worker is also saying that he cannot be comfortable in providing this kind of "tax-free love," a term used by Redl and Wineman to connote unconditional acceptance and love in its myriad forms.[7] The basic resentment, however, seems to be concerned with the fact that the worker has been placed *by the supervisor* in the position of being the giving, that is, the mothering, person. He resents this and protects himself against its implication by identifying with the housemother and criticizing the supervisor for "lack of structure." It is frequently observed that disturbed children respond somatically to a wide variety of upsetting stimuli. Differences in body posture, variations in skin color, and upsets of the gastrointestinal function are frequently connected with changes in the external environment and can be thought of as responses to these changes. In (3) the worker seems to be saying, first, that the housemother is not able to do a good job, that is, to be a good mother. On the other hand, placed in the position of the mothering person, the worker is angry that she has had to "clean up the mess" and to care for the child when he expressed his guilt, hostility, and anxiety by vomiting.

INVOLVEMENT OF THE THERAPIST

Thus far we have discussed the behavioral by-products of separation as they are expressed by the children and the child care staff. Within the pattern of life in a treatment milieu, another figure looms significantly — that of the therapist. Within the therapy hour and in the isolated setting of the office-playroom, he offers to the troubled child a corrective emotional experience with an adult. To the therapist, the child brings his own unique way of relating as this has been shaped by his life experience. The therapist points his effort toward helping the child to surrender those patterns of behavior that are archaic and self-defeating, while he helps also to develop newer, more satisfying ways of coping with life experiences. The raw material for the therapeutic process is drawn from the child's storehouse of past experiences, as well as from his present life.[8]

By definition, the therapist is a part of the total therapeutic influence that is being brought to bear on the child. Because he has to be free to deal with the

unconscious, irrational components of the child's personality, he is kept free of involvement in the daily life of the
child. To the extent that communication between child
care staff and therapist flows freely, the therapist will have
an adequate grasp of the experiences to which the child is
being exposed in the environment and will be prepared to
deal with this kind of material when it is brought to him
by the child. This communication can be planned and
organized in a variety of ways, some of which have been
dealt with elsewhere.[9] What cannot be planned or
predicted is the quality of the therapist's response to the
exigencies of life in the institutional environment. On this
level, the therapist relies on his objective appraisal of the
dynamics of the child's personality, and his intuitive
understanding of the ways in which the particular child
functions. Interacting with these are strong, unconscious
feelings and attitudes which stem from unresolved situations in his own life and which can be seen reflected in his
relationship with the child in treatment.

In terms of the subject matter of this paper, it will be
seen that the therapist cannot remain aloof from or
untouched by the psychosocial processes that are inherent
in the group living situation.

>(1) In a staff meeting, A, the therapist, said that he had
>observed his patient, F, running across the heavily
>traffic-laden street that separates the residence from the
>clinic, on the way to his therapy hour. F is an
>impulse-ridden child. The therapist asked, "Don't they
>[child care staff] know that he cannot be trusted to do
>this alone? Why isn't there anyone around to accompany
>him to the clinic?"

>(2) L wondered why her patient, C, was removed from
>the dining room. She stated that C had told her that he
>"had not done anything" but had been made to take his
>dinner alone in his room. She asked, "Are the staff
>having trouble controlling the children?"

>(3) D commented that his patients had been extremely
>upset during the last few treatment hours. He wondered
>"what was going on" in the residence and thought that if
>he knew more about it perhaps he's be able to be more
>helpful in the treatment hour.

It can be assumed that these situations were presented by the child and were handled by the therapist as any other productions of the patient would be, that is, as phenomena connected with the total process of therapy within the specific framework of the therapist-child relationship. What was brought to the staff meeting was the residual feeling that the therapist carried within himself. These feelings are less related to the desired course of therapy than they are to unconscious identification with the child and his feelings. In (1) the therapist was properly concerned with whether anyone could protect his patient from his own impulsivity. On the other hand, there was the tacit inference that no one was really interested in seeing that the child was protected. In (2) the therapist feared that in the absence of the housemother the children were at the mercy of punitive persons who treated them unjustly. Further, she feared that, with the housemother gone, the interests of the group would take precedence over those of her patient. She feared that arbitrary demands for conformity would be made of the child irrespective of clinically determined considerations. In (3) the therapist was implying that the disturbed behavior was primarily connected with the disruption of the institutional family. He displaced onto the group setting responsibility for pathology that had its genesis in the earlier experience of the child and which was reflected in the current situation.

CONCLUSIONS

In summary, then, this paper has been an attempt to point to some of the by-products of the separation of a key person from the child care staff of a children's institution. The attempts of children, child care staff, and professional personnel to deal with their own feelings and anxieties at separation have been explored. It has been possible to observe the enormous impact on the operation of the therapeutic milieu produced by a change in personnel.

Unfortunately, one of the significant facts about the

institutional employee is his employment mobility. There has been evidence of great fluidity in the staffs of institutions serving children. The structure of the institution appears as a relatively unstable amalgam, prone to disruption from influences within the group as well as within the individual.

In order to enlarge the effectiveness of the institutional setting, at least two things need urgent consideration. First, techniques need to be devised for handling the anxieties of the various staff groups, taking into account the intricate nature of the intrastaff and child-staff relationships.[10] Efforts at dealing with this problem in connection with similar situations in the maintenance of foster homes[11] and in relation to adoptive placement[12] have been in evidence for some time. Similar work needs to be done in connection with the problem of the children's institution.[13]

Second, the importance of the child care staff member needs to be affirmed. It is not sufficient to say that the child care worker represents an essential element in the treatment team. His real significance needs to be reflected in the conditions of employment to which he is exposed. It behooves each institution to examine its employment practices in an attempt to make the child care job more appealing to persons who are professionally trained. Moreover, the value of the child care staff becomes greater as the institution invests in increased inservice training and professional supervision. In short, efforts should be made to insure greater continuity of employment of those persons who function as significant parent surrogates in order that the recurrence of the damaging effects of separation may be prevented.

NOTES

1. Margaret S. Mahler, "On Child Psychosis and Schizophrenia; Autistic and Symbiotic Infantile Psychoses," in *The Psychoanalytic Study of the Child*, vol. 7 (New York: International Universities Press, 1952), pp. 286-305.
2. Leo Kanner, "Problems of Nosology and Psychodynamics of Early Infantile Autism," *American Journal of Orthopsychiatry* 19, no. 3 (1949): 416-26.

3. Rene A. Spitz and Katherine M. Wolf, "Anaclitic Depression," in *The Psychoanalytic Study of the Child*, vol. 2 (New York: International Universities Press, 1947), pp. 313-42.
4. John Bowlby, *Maternal Care and Mental Health*, monograph no. 2 (Geneva: World Health Organization, 1951).
5. Bruno Bettelheim, *Love Is Not Enough* (Glencoe, Ill.: Free Press, 1950); Herschel Alt and Hyman Grossbard, "Professional Issues in the Institutional Treatment of Delinquent Children," *American Journal of Orthopsychiatry* 19, no. 2 (1949): 279-91; Joseph H. Reid and Helen R. Hagan, *Residential Treatment of Emotionally Disturbed Children* (New York: Child Welfare League of America, 1952).
6. Norman Lourie and Rena Schulman, "Role of Residential Staff in Residential Treatment," *American Journal of Orthopsychiatry* 22 no. 4 (1952): 798-808.
7. Fritz Redl and David Wineman, *Controls from Within* (Glencoe, Ill.: Free Press, 1952).
8. Jules Schrager, "Child Care Staff Recording in a Treatment Institution," *Social Casework* 36, no. 2 (1955): 74-81.
9. Ibid.
10. Alfred H. Stanton and Morris S. Schwartz, *The Mental Hospital* (New York: Basic Books, 1954); Herschel Alt, "Responsibilities and Qualifications of the Child Care Worker," *American Journal of Orthopsychiatry* 23, no. 4 (1953): 670-75.
11. Draza Kline and Helen M. Overstreet, "Maintaining Foster Homes through Casework Skills," *Social Service Review* 22, no. 3 (1948): 324-33.
12. Margaret W. Gerard and Rita Dukette, "Techniques of Preventing Separation Trauma in Child Placement," *American Journal of Orthopsychiatry* 24, no. 1 (1954): 111-27.
13. Margaret W. Gerard and Helen Mary Overstreet, "Technical Modification in the Treatment of a Schizoid Boy within a Treatment Institution," *American Journal of Orthopsychiatry* 23, no. 1 (1953): 171-85.

20. Staff Development in a Treatment Institution

Bruno Bettelheim and Benjamin Wright

This paper is based on the work of the Sonia Shankman Orthogenic School of the University of Chicago, a residential treatment institution for severely disturbed children. It is a part of a study of how the institution's staff functions as part of a total therapeutic milieu. This school differs from other residential treatment institutions for children in relying mainly on its residential staff for the rehabilitation of very disturbed children. Staff psychiatrists have regular and frequent sessions with the children, but devote themselves primarily to consultation, staff training, and supervision. The psychological developments discussed here are in part due to this difference. Staff development cannot be the spontaneous and autonomous result of experience with the children where therapy is the responsibility of other persons.

At the Orthogenic School the main responsibility for therapy belongs to the residential staff. The psychoanalysts serve the resident workers as mentors and helpers. Without doubting the merits, for less disturbed children, of

Reprinted from the *American Journal of Orthopsychiatry*, vol. 25, no. 4 (October 1955), pp. 705-19, by permission of the authors and the journal. This investigation was supported in part by research grant M-476 from the National Institute of Mental Health of the National Institutes of Health, Public Health Service. The collection of data was greatly aided by facilities provided by the Abe Belsky Foundation of Chicago.

institutional settings relying on psychiatric or casework sessions for therapy, we have found that such a separation of function between houseparent or residential worker and therapist does not work well with extremely disturbed children. In our experience, residential staff members can accept and deal therapeutically with the threatening behavior of extremely regressed or violently acting-out children only if the workers also are responsible for all aspects of therapy. Without the rewards this implies, the workers' experiences with the children cause them to react in ways that are bad for both. Being repeatedly bitten, kicked, defecated upon, or otherwise abused results in defensive or punitive actions, cold indifference, emotional distance, or superior looking down on such "animallike" behavior. Though these may be rationalized as necessary interference, as the setting of healthy or socially required limitations, such attitudes interfere with rehabilitation. They can be avoided only if staff members know it is their responsibility, and only theirs, to help these children, if they receive all the narcissistic and interpersonal rewards that derive from being the children's main therapists.

The residential staff of the Orthogenic School is composed mostly of persons between the middle twenties and early thirties. Most of them are doing postgraduate work. When they start at the school they are, in comparison with psychoanalysts, relatively untrained for carrying on the difficult therapeutic work required of them, and this raises training problems. Our methods, however, are successful in rehabilitating children who did not improve under more traditional treatment methods in more traditional institutions.

These carefully chosen young adults are themselves experiencing a need for change, for intellectual and emotional growth. They believe that any change is possible, that there are limitations neither to their potentialities nor to their ability to achieve self-realization. Daily life with the children and our intensive training program of seven hours a week of staff meetings, in addition to individual conferences with the director and "bull sessions" among workers, meet these needs. All these experiences stimulate emotional and intellectual development as the workers learn to understand better the motivations, desires, and anxieties underlying the children's and their own behavior. In the "bull sessions" (facilitated by the residential staff's living together with the children in one large house) older staff members transmit the ethos of this therapeutic community to the younger staff members through teaching and advice as much as through personal friendships.

Still basically in opposition to (what to them appear to be) the oppressive mores of adult society, the young staff members, far from experiencing the children's antisocial behavior as a threat, tend to enjoy it. The children's defiance in the face of adult expectations touches feelings the workers still harbor in themselves. Though they have to curb the children when they go too far, their interference often is based on positive empathy with the underlying tendency and not on punitive rejection.

Such common feelings, unspoken and not acted upon by the workers but acted out by the children, permit the severely disturbed child to feel understood and appreciated in his rejection of the world. This can lead to the formation of personal relations for the first time. Equally important, the young adults' feeling that everything is still possible, their enthusiasm and belief in human potentialities, is contagious. It can give the child the hope that he, too, may fulfill his potentialities, contrary to the anxieties that previously have filled his life. Relations can b e established on such a basis, but they alone will not lead the child to higher integration. The severely disturbed child and the residential worker differ in one vitally important respect. The worker, whatever his feelings, has succeeded in society; the child has failed; exposed to the child's unintegrated emotions, observing them in their destructive consequences, the worker experiences an intensification of his own feelings. Consciously or unconsciously he may fear that he will never achieve his own adult independence, his own inner integration. The challenge to his integration presented by the children may be the push, both feared and welcomed, he needs to face his own problems.

Given the need and desire to achieve mature personal integration, dimly realizing that the nature of his work, the experiences it provides, will be a continuous challenge to higher integration, the worker experiences discomfort inflicted by the children as a relatively small price to pay for very considerable benefits. Some have remarked on the "dedication" of these young staff members. Dedicated they undoubtedly are, but not merely to the children under their care. They are dedicated also to achievement of their own integration, which they recognize as threatened by exposure to the primary processes in the child. Not wishing to put a barrier of emotional distance between themselves and the problems the children's behavior poses for them, or prevented from doing so by supervision, they have to find ways to integrate the emotions aroused by this experiencing of the primary processes. In doing that, at the same time they help the child to higher integration of his personality. It is his own need for achieving integration, his conviction that through his experiences at the school he will achieve it, that permits the worker to dedicate himself to the children under his care, to create that emotional closeness and unique empathy with the child that will set going again the process of development that broke down in the child's early years.

Similar, though by no means so severe, psychological mechanisms operate in staff member and child. Frustration of childhood desires led to a partial withdrawal from personal relations. Through his work the staff member enters into a relation with the child. This can lead to the direct or vicarious satisfaction of an old desire with a relationship and become the stepping-stone to higher integration. The worker's need forms the basis on which he sparks into action the child's previously frozen potentialities for relations and restitutive experiences.

Limitations of space permit us to present only a few examples illustrating this process.

The most vivid memory a worker had of his deceased father was their relation, or the absence thereof, around stamp collecting. When he was a child his father avowedly collected stamps for him but never gave him a real chance to do much with them. The boy was told not to touch the good stamps because he would not handle them properly. His father worked at the desk with the good stamps; the boy played on the floor with those of no value, feeling bored and deserted, cheated out of a relation he strongly desired, that seemed so near and yet unavailable. He lined up the stamps, hating them and his father for leaving him out, wondering what he could do to join in an activity that was supposedly joint. After the father died and the stamp collection really became the son's, he did not know what to do. Eventually he gave up stamp collecting and destroyed the album, retaining the stamps. Years later, he sold the stamps. But the moment he received the money he almost burst into tears and wanted to stop the sale.

This childhood experience had left a deep residue of unresolved emotions. Stamp collecting could have helped him sublimate primitive acquisitive tendencies within a personal relation. He could have learned not to collect objects aimlessly, not to line them up compulsively, but to order them sensibly according to higher principles. He could have become his father's helper, making a positive contribution in a way they could enjoy together. The father had teased the boy into believing a relationship would develop around the activity, while actually it further isolated father and son.

The worker encouraged stamp collecting by the boys under his care; and unlike his father, he tremendously enjoyed working with them on their collections. When these very disorganized boys, who never before had been able to stick to a task for any time, under his guidance began to take an interest in stamp collecting and to enjoy it, he was reminded of this activity with his father and suddenly began to want to collect stamps again himself; instead, though his decision was not arrived at consciously, he did it through the boys. He began to give the boys a great deal of help with their stamps, remaining, however, responsive to their wishes and leaving decisions up to them. Without being conscious of doing so, the worker made sure that in this relation he did not play his father's role, causing the boys to suffer as he had. He reenacted his own experience with his father and with stamps, but with a difference. It was as if he were compensating for his own early experience, as though the boys were himself and he was giving himself a happy experience to replace his old unhappy one. Also, in part, he wanted to master his old experience, about which he was still confused and puzzled. Why had he been inadequate at stamp collecting? Why had it been a joint activity with his father, and yet not? What did he want from his father, and what was wrong with him? His vested interest in justifying his anger at his father on the grounds that he could have helped, could have built up a meaningful personal relation, motivated him now to arrange it so that the boys could do well in stamp collecting and could enjoy it.

Stamp collecting and the relations formed around it thus became a corrective emotional experience for the worker and the child. It proved to the worker that not he but his father had been at fault. His fear that his father had been right and that he was inadequate to help, perhaps inadequate in every respect, turned out to be invalid; his anger at his father made sense. More important, his success in giving the boys a good time, in relating to them and in feeling them relate to him, demonstrated that while he could do nothing about the past experience, it no longer stood in his way in the present. An activity, and an emotional experience connected with it, which in the past had led to frustration and isolation, now led to satisfaction and interpersonal relations.

The preceding example illustrates restitutive experiences around an activity. A second example centers on a different psychological situation. A staff member in infancy had not received the babying care she desired, and the thwarting of this need remained in her as an as-yet-unresolved childhood residue. Because of the approval the school's ethos gives to the gratification of infantile desires, she was able to respond so enthusiastically to a little girl's repressed needs that with her the child, Jane, regressed, accepted and enjoyed infantile gratifications, and became cheerful through them. In prolonged treatment before Jane came to the school, a much more experienced therapist had not been able to get her to move out of her defiant and depressive pseudo-stupidity nor to give up her destructive acting out.

This staff member, at the time she became the child's counselor, was prevented from gaining true independence by an overstrong attachment to her mother, based largely on unfulfilled infantile wishes that she hoped, if she clung to her mother, the mother might satisfy someday. Because of this, she felt that giving and receiving infantile satisfactions was the most wonderful thing in the world, and this was exactly what she could offer to Jane. Since she projected all her negative feelings onto her mother, she concentrated only positive feelings on Jane, whom she experienced, reacted to, and spoke of as "such a wonderful baby." Jane's angry defiance and often wild acting out, far from detracting from the counselor's positive feelings for her — as they probably would have in a maturely integrated person, who would have suffered from Jane's obscenity, her continuous hitting, stepping on toes, her screaming, sticking her bottom in the face in reply to efforts at being nice to her — actually added to them. Jane did to her what she had wished to do and did not dare to do to her mother as a child, what she still wished she had done. Had she been able to behave toward her mother as Jane did toward her, the counselor felt, she would have lived a wonderful life.

Jane, like her worker, had had to repress early and totally her intense hostility toward her mother. Therefore, it was very meaningful to her to be confronted with a mother figure who had fullest empathy with her and approved of hostility toward a mother. This became the unconscious basis for a close relation between counselor and child. Because of it, and also because the worker could recognize and respond emotionally to the positive aspects of Jane's desire for infantile gratifications, the child for the first time was able to relax her defenses against permitting herself the satisfactions she craved so much. The counselor's response reassured Jane in regard to her destructive, cannibalistic wishes, which so far had caused her to hold her orality in check.

There were other common bonds between child and counselor. Jane, more than the counselor, suffered from guilt about her destructive wishes against her mother, and this had prevented her from accepting herself and from enjoying gratifications. The counselor, since she saw all mothers as frustrating, felt that all hostile wishes against them were justified, and her conviction provided reassurance for Jane in regard to her guilt feelings. That the counselor at this stage could see neither Jane's nor her own contribution to the bad relations between child and mother, while unrealistic, was helpful. In order to maintain the image of her mother as all bad, she had to prove that it was possible to give to a child unlimitedly,[1] despite the child's sullen resistance and active fighting back. By getting Jane to accept gratification the worker vicariously could enjoy gratifications she had missed in infancy. But this was of little importance when compared with the vital significance of proving that an all-giving mother could exist and that her anger at her own mother therefore was fully justified. At no moment could she allow herself to become a disinterested, disappointing, rejecting mother, as her mother had been. Thus she was strongly motivated to accept, even thoroughly enjoy, the child's regression to infancy, as well as her hostilities and destructiveness.

It probably would have become necessary through supervision to bring the worker to recognize, accept, and limit Jane's hostility and eventually help her to integrate it. But as often is the case an experience with the child at this point in their relation (and in the worker's emotional involvement with her mother) forced this recognition on the worker. The experience took place not in the privacy of a treatment room, but while Jane was interacting with other children.

Jane and another girl got into a scuffle, and the worker had to separate them by force. She was sorry because she feared she might have acted too severely toward Jane. But to her astonishment, the child, to quote the worker's report, "seemed rather relieved that I stopped her when I did in the way I did, rather than to hate me for what I did. Actually it disturbed me a great deal that her reaction was one of relief instead of anger." In terms of her old need to

separate herself from her mother, to become an independent person in her own right, she had to see that
interferences, particularly when she was a child, might
have been justified and might have been to her benefit,
might even have caused her to feel relief. Jane's reaction to
her active interference was confusing, since it suggested
that the worker's evaluation of her mother might not have
been valid. It started a process that led her to see her
mother, and herself and Jane also, not only in black and
white, as either angels or devils, but as real persons.

The development of Jane's counselor may further be
illustrated by means of some of the techniques we use for
gaining additional understanding of our workers and for
assessing their development. One of our evaluation
instruments is a drawing test. The worker's drawings are
analyzed by a method similar to that described by
Machover.[2] Drawings of a human figure (Figs. 1 and 2) —
most likely projections of herself[3] — were made by Jane's
counselor at the beginning of her relation to Jane and at

Fig. 1   Fig. 2

the time she began to recognize and to deal with Jane's hostility and to accept that mothers are not only and always bad.

The first drawing shows a young woman, curvaceous but nevertheless angular, standing firmly, perhaps stiffly, with one hand on her hip and one partially hidden by her skirt. She wears a grown-up dress, choker necklace, and low-heeled shoes; her hair is stringy and straight. She seems to look at the world in a questioning, interested, noncommittal way. Her facial expression is provocative.

The second drawing shows a gawky, knock-kneed girl, floating in mid-air, her long arms extended over her head holding a ball. She wears a skirt and blouse with round, childish collar; her hair is curly and tousled; her facial expression is bland, uncritical, smiling.

Following the suggestions for analysis of Machover, Levy, and Buck,[4] Figure 1 superficially suggests a relatively clear self-concept appropriate in age and appearance. The solid stance of the figure suggests an effective, well-set, although rigid and posed, adjustment. But the defenses are rather thin and precarious (narrow waist, zoning) and underlaid with conflict and anxiety (reinforced lines, shading). The contrast between the nice dress and necklace and the messy hair, low-heeled shoes, and smudgy outline suggests that infantile tendencies are inadequately controlled by efforts to appear mature. The drawing, despite its apparent solidness (firm stance, set at bottom of page), reveals a lack of confidence, an uncertainty about how much to participate in her environment (partially concealed and incompletely drawn hands, no reference to anything existing outside the figure).

Figure 2 is of a girl younger than the worker. When drawing this she commented, "I'm going to draw one of my children; I don't know who it'll be . . . might even be me." A figure drawn younger than the subject is often a sign of emotional fixation at the younger level with a wish to return to it.[5] Figure 2 suggests less security and self-esteem and increased feelings of general inadequacy (floating figure, greater space-to-figure ratio). But with this, there is greater freedom and participation in her environment (movement implied, long, straight arms reaching out). There is less aggressiveness and greater softness and femininity in areas representing social responsiveness and sensuality (rounder, freer line and form in head and hair). The decrease in zoning between head and torso suggests she has less anxiety about the relation between her "self" (head) and her body. The ball, a spontaneous addition, is childish. The theme has changed from mature femininity to childishness; but the ball implies another person with whom to play; so this second figure, though less mature, is experienced as being potentially related.

The differences in drawings reflect changes that have occurred in Jane's worker. Defenses that seemed set (if precarious) apparently began to unfreeze. The worker's body image seems to have regressed toward that of the children with whom she worked, suggesting increased acceptance of childishness. The worker, who before stood stiffly and anxiously watched, seems now to know what to do — to play. She has rejected her earlier, superficial composure, her forced identification with mature female sexuality, for what is a simpler, more forthright, honest self-image.

It might seem that such a disintegration of defenses as reflected in the less mature body image bodes ill for her work with children. But we found that it is beneficial for both worker and child if a precarious — though adequate-appearing — adjustment is exchanged for a franker, more realistic one, and if pretended higher integration is relinquished in favor of a lower but true-to-fact level of integration. (This sometimes creates difficulties in supervision). This second drawing shows greater self-acceptance and better relatedness to her environment. The contrast between the two drawings suggests she has become increasingly able to accept and gratify her own unfulfilled needs to receive and be like a child. Her identification with a childish image suggests greater emotional closeness between her and the children, a close relation to, if not identification with, the children under her care which is made explicit in her remark about whom she is going to draw. Such temporary diffusion of the boundary between their own and the children's personalities seems character- istic of workers who are able to relate to deeply withdrawn children (autistic, withdrawn, schizoprenic, pseudo-idiot), and through this relation to help them.

The second drawing shows her in a state of flux, but more accessible to emotional experiences. It suggests that there is growth in the direction of an easier, warmer, more expressive, and more natural emotional adjustment. These changes in personality were made possible by her gaining interpersonal gratifications through her work.

But what specific experiences in residential work with disturbed children produce such developments? We have more direct evidence from another counselor on how residential work helped her to develop the ability to enjoy personal relations and oral satisfactions. She had stated in her autobiography:[6]

> I feel like I never got enough of anything from my parents. This goes for food as well as less conspicuous necessities like a care for what I wanted. Mother had once mentioned to me that I was a good baby, never cried, ate well. I know that I was a very fat baby and for some reason when I was home this month I asked if I had gotten enough food. She said yes, but added that they were afraid that I was too fat and had put me on a diet. . . . This is very much in line with my feelings of deprivation. I can remember when I was seven or so saving food from parties I went to as if I never got enough candy. My mother had many ideas about the badness of candy, cokes, and so on, to teeth, and my teeth were always full of cavities. But after this summer [the first she worked with the children at the school and with them ate much candy and drank many cokes] of drinking cokes for almost the first time in my life, I had no cavities.

At approximately the same stage of professional development as that of Jane's counselor at the time of the incidents and tests reported here, this worker wrote in an autobiographical note:

> As anyone who looks at me can see I have, even in the short time I have been working here, undergone changes

> towards becoming a calmer, softer, more peaceful
> person. There are other areas which I am aware are
> changing. Just the fact that I can believe in the changes
> in me is something new to me.

This change was in part the result of her helping the
children become "calmer, softer, more peaceful" persons,
and her observations that such changes are possible in a
residential setting, of which she was then very much a part.

> I feel more settled; knowing that I will be some place for
> many years is very satisfying to me. It's as if I have
> found a place which I can keep if I try, which is stable
> and yet which I am sure will grow more satisfying as
> time passes. . . . I feel the comfort in many substantial
> ways, too. When I had a cold and took a whole big can
> of juice from the storeroom I offered to pay for it. I was
> told, no, that the counselors' wants were to be satisfied,
> as those of the children; only it was said in different
> words. This pleased me. So does being able to get food
> out of the storerooms or kitchen whenever I want it, at
> night if I want it. I sometimes stand in the storeroom;
> just looking at the amounts of food is wonderful. So was
> seeing the quantities of toys. I have been eating less, but
> I feel as if I can get what I want when and if I want it.
> This business of getting what I want has spread, for I
> now buy myself things, like a skirt or some chocolates,
> which I've wanted before but was unable to buy for
> myself. I guess this can be summed up by saying that I
> seem to be treating myself more in line with my needs,
> without employing any semiexternal criticism, such as
> that I shouldn't have too much when others are starving.

Staff members acquire a new personal dignity because
of their work for the children. Though they may continue
to doubt at moments that they are welcome or important
in the world, they soon become convinced that at least one
human relation, that to the child, is of great importance:

> Now, although I still feel that I may be not wanted, I am
> able to bring myself down to the [director's] office a
> few times and can reach him. . . . Now I feel surer that
> my problems with the children are of interest to him
> too, although I am still wary that because I am the one
> bringing the problems he may somehow lose interest. I
> know this is not realistic and perhaps after repeated
> good experiences it will abate.

Staff development as such, however desirable, is not the

goal of a children's institution, but only a step toward rehabilitating the children. How do changes such as those described above affect the workers in their work with and their view of their relations to the children? Drawings of a human figure may reflect personal development. The change in Jane's counselor in her work with the children may be illustrated by her drawing of a typical dormitory situation, at the same times as the drawings of a person.

In her first drawing of a dormitory situation (Fig. 3), she rendered two separate groups, drawn with uneven, reinforced lines in different perspectives, both floating in mid-air. In the center is a semiplan view of four figures seated around the end of a square table, the closest being Jane's counselor, "playing a game" with the next nearest figure and "telling the other two to stop fighting over the crayons although they probably won't." In the corner two figures sit on the floor, facing each other but looking at the dolls they are playing with. All figures are marked and underlaid with coarse, irregular, formless shading. The worker's facial expression seems to be worried, scared, and hopeless, quite different from the blank face of the single human figure she drew on the same day (Fig. 1). She is looking away from the child with whom she is playing and from the fight she is trying to stop. The facial expressions of the children seem to be angry, mean, or suspicious, with

Fig. 3

Fig. 4

the exception of one of the doll players who may be smiling as she looks at her doll.

Although the worker was performing conscientiously and with increasing skill at the time of this drawing, it suggests that beneath her efforts lay a painful state of rigidity (vertical arrangement, straight lines) covering up conflicts and anxiety (double perspective, reinforced lines, shading). There are suggestions of feelings of inadequacy and insecurity (whole constriction, floatingness, uneven lines) dealt with by a tendency to withdraw from emotional contact (constriction, profile faces, semiplan perspective) and perhaps a wish to reject the painful situation in which she found herself with the children.

The second dormitory drawing (Fig. 4), made at the same time as Figure 2, shows a more level view of the dormitory, drawn in firm, clear, even lines. Four figures are seated at a large table which, while still floating in mid-air, now is located in the center of things. The rest of the space is relatively well organized. One figure stands to the left, watching; one child to the right and above sits on the floor under a tent; and another child, still farther to the right and above, lies on a bed reading. According to the worker's explanation, the most disturbed child in the group is sitting on her lap. All children are mentioned by name and drawn in situations typical for them in reality, such as: A is "on her bed, she always withdraws"; B is in the tent — "That's her, all right"; and C, with her back to us, "is coloring as she does when left alone." The children in this drawing appear to have cheerful, if somewhat empty facial expressions; only the child on the bed looks sad.

Comparing the two drawings of dormitory scenes, the second appears livelier; it suggests a state of increased freedom, expansiveness, relaxation, and security (better use of space, grounded, full faces, firm line, increase in curves, less shading). Also there seems to be more awareness of the total working situation, suggested by the rendering of more dormitory details, of the posture and the varied activities of the children. The children are seen more as individuals. Perhaps even more important, there seems to be closer emotional contact with them (larger figures, more level perspective, full faces).

In the first drawing the worker is playing a game with one child while another pair of children fight and a third pair play with their dolls. The worker is too far from them to enter the play and is looking away, even from the child with whom she is playing. The only figures that are in direct contact are the two children who, we were told, are fighting over crayons. The only pleasure expressed in a face is to be found in the child who plays with a doll, far removed from the worker. In the second drawing the worker is holding a child on her lap, the contact of two or three other children centers around her, and she is in the middle of a group of four of the six children. While in the first drawing only one child looks at her while she looks at none or, at best, at one other child who is distant from her, in the second drawing the worker looks at the child next to her and possibly also at another child, while three and possibly four of the six children look toward her.

In the first set of drawings (Figs. 1 and 3) the single

human figure is set into space more securely than the worker in the dormitory setting. The single figure is large, straightforward, assertive, with a pretense of strength. In the dormitory drawing the figures are small, there is much empty space, the mood seems uncertain. In this first series the worker shows some security as a person when unrelated to others, but deep insecurity when functioning as a residential worker; that is, when close relation to others was required of her. In the second set (Figs. 2 and 4), made some six months later, the situation seems reversed. Now in the dormitory the figures are firmly set in space and drawn with relative security, straightforward and outspoken, while the single human figure is vague, floating, and inarticulate.

At the time the first set of drawings was made the worker maintained a superficial integration when by herself but was deeply insecure in her work. When she drew the second set a reversal had taken place; more secure in her relation to the children, her discovery of what emotional maturity required of her and made her less secure as a person. In regard to cause and effect, our experience with this worker and others suggests that as they become secure in interpersonal relations with the children, they are able to give up the pseudosecurity of a neurotically frozen personality; they can afford to become much less secure as persons because of their greater security within the residential setting, with their fellow workers, and, most of all, with the children. They are thus able to embark on a process of restructuring their personalities.

A further illustration of the development of Jane's counselor may be found in her reactions to a specially constructed Thematic Apperception Test. The standard pictures of the TAT provide little evidence as to what a person's reaction to an interaction with children might be. Therefore, we used a set of pictures whose content elicits statements on interactions between adults and children and among children. Only the stories told to one of these pictures will be discussed here.

This picture shows two young girls playing around a

lamppost in a street. They have tied a rope onto the lamppost. One is swinging on the rope far out over the street; the other is standing close by, watching. In the far background are buildings and persons. The first story was:

> These children are playing. . . a game where they've hitched the rope to the top of the lamppost and then tied the bottom of the rope around their waist. Then they wind it around the lamppost and jump very high. . . . They look like they're having a very good time though I should imagine the rope would hurt them. Not only in their waist, but holding on to it. The people around either don't give a damn or the game is perfectly all right because they're not concerned, and the children continue to play this way until they're tired of it. Then they'll find something else to do. That's it.

The second story, told about the time she made drawings 2 and 4, was:

> . . . These kids are playing a very dangerous game which looks like fun but which can, if they're not careful, bang their heads or strangle themselves. They're both doing this because they don't have anything better to do with themselves. Somebody should build them some swings and teach them how to be little girls. Or . . . if somebody helps them, they don't have to play games like that; they'll be okay then. If not they'll keep it up.

The main difference between the stories is the clearer recognition in the second of the potential dangers inherent in the game. The children play such dangerous games not, as in the first story, to have "a very good time," but out of desperation, only if "they don't have anything better to do with themselves." Thus a greater sensitivity to children's play seems to have developed in the interval. In the first story the surrounding world (of adults) remains disinterested, uninvolved ("The people around don't give a damn. . . . they're not concerned"). In the second, while again there is no adult involvement, she feels an adult ought to provide children with better, safer games. In the first story there is only a "getting tired" projected as the end of the activity, to be replaced by "something else" that is not viewed as basically different. The children do one undesirable thing, get tired of it, and move on to something else equally devoid of meaning. In the second story, if left alone, the children will "keep it up," but if a helping adult enters the situation they will not have to play empty and dangerous games, then "they'll be okay." In the first story the children are strictly by themselves, thrown onto their own resources with no hope for a development toward higher integration. In the second, while no such development is promised, it is stated out of what it must consist: a relatively unselfish interest on the part of an adult who is willing to provide the children with the means of enjoyable activities within a personal relation ("teach them"), a relation not based on the adult's preconceived notions of desirable activities. Instead, it must start with the children where they are (swinging) and move them within this, self-chosen activity, one step at a time toward greater safety and a socially more acceptable form of the activity ("build them swings"). Thus it must be a relation where the children and their desires are fully respected, where the adult provides children with better forms for the satisfaction of their own wishes. This relation with a mature adult, serving children out of his own free will, will "teach" them to be themselves, will guide them "to be little girls."

After about a year at the Orthogenic School this worker had acquired an understanding that permitted her to size up a situation, to recognize what type of personal relations were desirable and what the next step should be in their development. The step she suggests is a move from the dangerous, hurtful, and unsatisfying swinging around the lamppost to an organized game on a well-built swing — not a swing that simply happened to be around, but one that was built by the adult for these particular children. The change that made such a solution possible to her occurred in attitudes that had become so much part of herself that she expressed them without consciously knowing what she was saying or implying.

Still, there is no secure conviction that such favorable development will take place. All depends on a vague "somebody." While there exists the firm understanding that little girls should have safe swings and not be anything but little girls (not, for example, premature adults — see the two drawings of a person, Figs. 1 and 2), there is no certainty that this will be provided for them, nor that she is the one who can provide it. The development of Jane's worker as a staff member was not yet complete, but she was well on her way.

NOTES

1. Much as the worker in the preceding example derived satisfaction from demonstrating that it was possible for adults and children to collect stamps together with mutual enjoyment.
2. K. Machover, *Personality Projection in the Drawing of the Human Figure* (Springfield, Ill.: Charles C. Thomas, 1949).
3. Ibid., p. 11; K. Machover, "Drawing of the Human Figure," in *An Introduction to Projective Techniques*, eds. H.H. and G. L. Anderson (New York: Prentice-Hall, 1951), p. 350.
4. Machover, *Personality Projection*, op. cit.; Sidney Levy, "Figure Drawing as a Projective Test," in *Projective Psychology*, eds. L. E. Abt and L. Bellak (New York: Knopf, 1950), pp. 257 ff.; John N. Buck, "The H-T-P Techniques," *Journal of Clinical Psychology*, monograph supplement 5 (1948).
5. Machover, *Personality Projection*, op. cit., p. 85.
6. The workers participating in the staff's self-study write continual autobiographical notes, which are kept confidential unless they expressly permit us to use them.